The Irony of Victory

War is the health of the State.
—Randolph Bourne,
1918

The Irony of Victory

World War II and Lowell, Massachusetts

Marc Scott Miller

University of Illinois Press
Urbana and Chicago

This book is printed on acid-free paper.

Library of Congress Cataloging-in-Publication Data

Miller, Marc S.
    The irony of victory: World War II and Lowell, Massachusetts /
Marc Scott Miller.
        p. cm.
    Bibliography: p.
    ISBN 0-252-01505-3 (alk. paper)
        1. World war, 1939–1945—Massachusetts—Lowell. 2. Lowell
(Mass.)—Economic condition. 3. Lowell (Mass.)—Social conditions.
4. Oral history. I. Title.
    D769.85.M42L685 1988
    974.4′4—dc19   87-27212
                                                                                        CIP

Contents

Tables

Preface

From their physically safe vantage point thousands of miles from the battlefields, Americans felt their lives change forever under the impact of World War II. Those changes were complex, reflecting the past, contemporary events, the structure of the American political economy, and, on an individual basis, a person's role in that political economy. A working-class woman commuted to a new job and saw the world outside her hometown for the first time in her life. A middle-class woman whose brother threatened to disown her if she followed him into the armed services—instead of taking care of their parents—experienced the historical distinction of sex roles. The child who yelled "Kill a Jap" when crushing cans for wartime recycling learned about both war and racism. A labor organizer drafted unfairly didn't protest because for two decades some member of the family that owned the company he was organizing had been sitting in Congress. And economic laws and conditions that ignored the borders of any one community guided an industrial leader who, with regret, closed a hometown plant in 1946. Each of these stories happened in Lowell, Massachusetts.

By the time World War II began, Lowell had had a century-long history as a major industrial center and fifteen years of steady and severe decline. It shared the last of those years of depression with the rest of the nation, and with the rest of the nation, Lowell in the 1930s felt both the agonies of the Great Depression and the promises of the New Deal. World War II ended the pain, but also tempered the hope. Thus many historians view 1941 as a sharp break in American history, citing the prosperity of the war years and the abandonment of the most progressive and idealistic programs of the New Dealers.

An examination of the people in this one city—as individuals and as a community—suggests the opposite. World War II may have been traumatic and dramatic, but it did not change history. The essential aspect of the New Deal—active federal intervention in the nation's economy to protect industrial capitalism through political institutions—proceeded faster than during any other period in American history. For individuals—that is, for real people—memories of depression hardships continued to guide life during the relative boom years of the forties. For the community, war-induced prosperity, at best, did little to prepare Lowell for the postwar years. At worst, home-front developments—including prosperity, the draft, migrations, the educational system, the media—so distorted individual, community, and economic life that positive change was discouraged until after the war. War hastened, rather than halted, the declining ability of local power to induce prosperity or democracy—perceived and actual—that had been decried in the 1930s and long before.

Moreover, in a combination of continuity and change, some historians have said that World War II institutionalized the welfare aspects of New Dealism—its most revered legacy and the foundation of all Democratic party and most Republican politics for the past half century. But with the hindsight of fifty years, we can now see that this compassionate side is not an inevitable and immutable feature of American capitalism. Given a shifted balance of power, corporate leaders of the 1980s—with the aid of government—act with the same degree of unilateral freedom that their counterparts before 1932 enjoyed.

Lowell's unique history increases its significance as the subject of this book. At each step of the city's history, Lowell's citizens experienced the extremes of the advance of American society and its social and economic structures. Because Lowell's life as a city is so dramatic, changes in this archetypical community clarify trends that more moderated experiences in other communities might obscure.

Upon its founding in the early nineteenth century, Lowell symbolized what capitalism could achieve with the most rational, well-financed, and benevolent planning. Indeed, the first city in the United States to be created specifically as an industrial enterprise, Lowell could be considered the birthplace of modern industrial capitalism. Then, between the 1840s and the 1920s, Lowell became home to tens of thousands of immigrant workers. It developed into the quintessential multiethnic city of melting-pot mythology—including the conflicts and lack of melting that the mythology obscures. For more than a hundred years, Lowell suffered under the impact of a national and international economy driven by corporate profits, an economy unaware of any one community's well-being. When the economy changed, capital went to industries other than textiles, and when Southern states offered more hospitable locations for management's needs, Lowell's industrialists did not hesitate to abandon their grand experiment—and a hundred thousand people.

Lowell entered the Great Depression of the 1930s with more intensity than the nation as a whole and with less hope—in actuality and in the minds of its citizens. World War II presented one more opportunity for capitalism to prove its vitality and viability to the people whom it had brought to the "mile of mills on the Merrimack."

Many of the wartime transformations in Lowell can be documented with standard historical sources: government records, newspapers, corporate records. War, however, was a traumatic experience for Americans, and its effects can only in part be reduced to apparently objective facts and figures. World War II influenced life in the United States in subtle and personal ways that often are revealed only through the memories of those who lived those years. This book surveys the city's life during the war, in terms of what its citizens recall and report about their personal experiences.

Approximately seventy interviews with residents of Lowell—selected to represent a cross-section of economic, political, and social life—provide the foundation of the data for *The Irony of Victory.* So-called hard data—censuses, archives, newspapers, and town, state, and federal records—balance and place into perspective the picture of Lowell that resides in the subjective memories of Lowellians.

Relying on oral history data creates special problems. Memories tend to be generalized —and admittedly often defective and confused—with specific incidents uncovered almost randomly. On a trivial level, few Lowell citizens remember the exact dates of the war, placing American entry as early as 1939 and ending the war as late as 1948. Many older people confuse the two world wars, often remembering the first—the war of their youth—more vividly than the second. Less trivially, it proved impossible to use interviews alone in order to establish such a fact as whether General Electric arrived in Lowell during or after the war. The obvious resource for such inaccuracies and indeterminacies remains the written word. This book reflects the merger of the two sources, oral and written.

Much of oral history deals with judgment: the opinions and knowledge of researchers often conflict with reports by people who lived the experiences. One common basis for this conflict seems to be an interviewee's desire to create a positive image, both of self and of Lowell. For example, assertions that Lowell was free from ethnic prejudices contrast with the racial overtones of a clash involving white Lowellians and soldiers who were either black or Native Americans from Oklahoma, a contrast that must be examined in any comprehensive, honest look at the past.

Comparing the opinions of individuals from different classes reveals other judgmental inconsistencies. A school teacher's statement that the mills bled the city white contradicts the mill owners' self-image of local and responsible leadership. Similarly, a mill owner expressed love for his workers, yet he paid them the absolute minimum wage, and they bitterly recall his policies as an employer.

Oral data—just as written data—must be examined for its subjective biases. To omit or accept those biases uncritically—whether because of class, psychology, faulty memory, or any other cause—would create an inaccurate and incomplete picture of wartime Lowell, just as would reliance on written data alone.

Despite its limitations, oral history goes far toward overcoming the handicaps of traditional sources. It can be relatively free from the exclusively upper- and middle-class bias underlying most written documentary evidence. Written data, because only a small, special segment of the population produces and saves it, "lies" as often as does oral data. Oral histories reveal, as newspapers and statistics cannot, what most people valued, thus providing insight into how they made decisions.

Interviews also provide an excellent lead in determining what sorts of documentary evidence and which events to pursue. This becomes especially important when, as in the study of an entire city during World War II, enough documents exist to keep a careful historian occupied for decades, with only intermittent finds of useful data. And although oral data can be attacked for being "presentist," that factor does allow people to use years of experience to improve the reports of their own pasts. Oral data is based, in part, on a respect for the people being studied as valid historians of their own lives.

Oral history provides the color, personal view, and *humanity* that historians locked in libraries and archives find difficult to integrate with their documents. In this way, interviews serve a similar function to that of newspapers, except that oral history can come from many sources rather than being distilled by a select few.

Finally, a historian's role in collecting oral testimony results in an object that in a sense is new. An oral history has a value not only to historians; the person being interviewed recovers his or her own past. One woman, in the midst of a confidential story about receiving the news of the death of her cousin, interrupted herself with a realization: "It's funny, when you live something, you never forget. Like when you asked to interview me, I said, 'How will I remember those things?' But I'm telling you this now like it was yesterday because I lived this."

Using oral history in conjunction with traditional sources produces a portrait of an American city during World War II familiar not only to professional historians, but also to the people who lived through those years. And comprehending the changing patterns in a single city under the impact of war leads toward a fuller understanding of the process that created postwar America.

1

Lowell Before World War II

The Early History

When World War II startled Lowell out of its seemingly irreversible decline, the city still could look back with pride on 120 years of often glorious history, of once standing at the center stage of American industrial capitalism. In a very real sense, Lowell's factories provided part of the foundation for the greatness of that national economy. The million-dollar investments in founding the city were the first large-scale industrial ventures in the United States; the success of the experiment brought fortunes to the investors, the capital necessary for further expansions throughout the nation and the world, and ambiguous blessings to even the earliest workers, Lowell's famed "mill girls."

The industrial history of Lowell actually began in 1814 in Waltham, Massachusetts, with the founding of the Boston Manufacturing Company. By 1821, the Waltham success led its creators to search for a site suited to larger-scale factories. Ezra Worthen, a native of the Chelmsford area, suggested using the power of Pawtucket Falls on the Merrimack River. Paul Moody, master mechanic from the Waltham experiment, visited the falls and described them to the largest stockholder, Patrick Johnson, who then purchased for the company all the stock of the existing Locks and Canals Company, as well as the farms on the present site of the city of Lowell. In February of 1822, the purchasers incorporated as the Merrimack Manufacturing Company, ordered new canals to be dug, and commenced the erection of the Merrimack mills.[1]

The potential for water power quickly dictated a change in organization. Under a legislative amendment to its 1792 charter, the Proprietors of the Locks and Canals Company first separated from the Merrimack Company and then leased power to that company under the same conditions as power would be sold to the rapidly expanding number of establishments that followed.[2] Home to 200 people in 1820, the village of East Chelmsford had 2,500 inhabitants in 1826, with a machine shop, the Middlesex Mechanics Association, and two mills—construction had commenced by the Hamilton Company the previous year.[3] On March 1, 1826, the town of Lowell, named for Francis Cabot Lowell, who conceived of both the Waltham experiment and of the model industrial community of Lowell, was incorporated separately from East Chelmsford.[4]

In the next decade Lowell grew into a major city, an industrial experiment virtually unprecedented in scale and ambition. The Appleton Mills and the Lowell Manufacturing Company incorporated in 1828; the Middlesex, Suffolk, Tremont, and Lawrence Mills in 1830; the Lowell Bleachery in 1832; the Boott in 1835; the Massachusetts Cotton Mills in 1839. Each opened with a then astronomical value on the order of $1 million. In addition, smaller concerns dotted the city. The population was 18,000 when Lowell became a city in 1836, and 33,000 by 1848.[5]

Lowell's early fame rested not only on its scale of manufacturing and rapid growth, but also on its character as a planned city. The foundation of the planning rested on its labor system, necessitated by the need for tens of thousands of unskilled workers for the mills, yet inspired—at least in part—by the early socialist theories of Robert Owen.[6] Recruiters criss-crossed the New England countryside, encouraging young women, a largely untapped work force large enough to satisfy the needs in Lowell, to come to the city. In Lowell, the women lived in boarding houses seen as models of enlightenment. There the companies could protect—and control—the women's entire lives, not just their working hours. By 1848, the city was five-eighths female.

In the 1830s, distinguished visitors—including Andrew Jackson and Charles Dickens—relayed glowing reports of the working and "moral" conditions for the mills' employees. Until about 1840, textile workers received better wages than most workers in the nation.[7] An 1848 visitors' handbook to Lowell, complete with instructions for obtaining private visitor cards from Boston owners, glorified the new American industrial workers: "Girls from the country with a true Yankee spirit of independence, and confident in their own powers, pass a few years here, then return to get married, with a dower secured by their own exertions, with more enlarged ideas from their travels, and extended means of information, and their places are secured by younger relatives."[8]

In Lowell's early years, the women workers undoubtedly welcomed the opportunity to escape farms and receive unprecedented wages and independence; the average stay of only four and a half years helped them stay content in their temporary work. But the glowing words of the visitors' guide were out of date even before they were written.[9] During the decade of the 1840s, textile wages stagnated while wages for other industrial workers rose, and mill owners reduced labor costs by increasing the pace of work, although hours had already stretched from dawn until dusk. The resulting corporate profits in good years rose to as high as 22 percent, averaging 9.8 percent from 1836 through 1847.[10]

In defending their recruitment of New England's farm women to work in the mills, owners often cited the uplifting character of work and the Christian paternalism practiced in the city they had designed. But the motivation was clearly financial, and as conditions worsened for the workers, making New England recruiting increasingly difficult, the corporations shifted their hiring focus to immigrant men and women. The late forties witnessed the first influx of Irish workers replacing the Yankee women who left in droves, especially following a depression in 1847.

Mill owners continued to attempt recruiting in the United States but had to venture further afield. An agent for the Hamilton Manufacturing Company found forty workers in New York and Vermont in 1859, but thirteen left the mill before four months had passed.[11] The recourse was to recruit outside the United States, and agents prospected for workers in Ireland, England, and Canada. In 1830, almost all the Hamilton operatives came from Massachusetts; but in 1844–46, only half did. Even more dramatically, between 1844–46 and 1849–50, the proportion of workers from Ireland increased from a twentieth to a quarter, while the proportion from Massachusetts declined to a fifth.

Mill owners neither desired nor sought this change, but managers soon discovered that the Irish, accustomed to European conditions and tempered by the potato famine, accepted longer hours and harsher standards than the Yankees. Moreover, returning home for an immigrant was more difficult than for New England women (albeit not as difficult as for slaves in the South). Conversely, critics cared less about exploiting immigrants than New England farm women.

The high rate of labor turnover also necessitated, as Ray Ginger observes, "devis[ing] methods of production which would lower costs while utilizing a labor force composed of a 'succession of learners.' The rapid pace of technological advance in the United States derived in large measure from this set of circumstances."[12] The effort to apply mass-production techniques proved so successful that by the 1870s unskilled American weavers tended twice as many looms as their skilled counterparts in England.[13]

The city of Lowell, described as overcrowded by 1847, became the subject of an 1849 American Medical Association report that cited conditions worse than those in any prison. The mills were hot; the boardinghouses cold and overcrowded. Working conditions worsened as profits dropped to an average of 5.3 percent annually from 1848 through 1860.[14] By the Civil War, Lowell's experimental period was history, and the patterns for future deterioration completed. A rise in real wages after 1865 accompanied a declining standard of living; income that previously supported only single workers now had to support a family. As American capitalism in general flourished, real annual earnings per capita in Lowell (not per worker) fell 33.8 percent from 1844–46 to 1909.[15]

Meanwhile, physical connections tightened between Lowell and the wider political economy that was the city's reason for being. Railroad connections with Boston, begun in 1835, expanded and in 1874, they joined the major networks of the Northeast.[16] The construction of more canals earned Lowell the nickname "The Venice of the New World." Population rose more slowly than in the city's first two decades, reaching 41,000 by 1870 before jumping to 84,000 in 1895 and 112,000 in 1920.[17] The slow rise between 1848 and 1870 was due primarily to a severe depression during the Civil War, a downturn allegedly exacerbated by poor management policies and wasteful nepotism on the part of Boston stockholders; neither accusation was new.[18] On the other hand, Benjamin Butler opened the United States Bunting Corporation during this period so that the North would not have to import cloth for its flags. One of Lowell's most colorful capitalists, Butler gained notoriety for strongly supporting Jefferson Davis at the 1860 Democratic Convention, then becoming Lowell's foremost Union supporter as a Northern general.[19]

Following the Civil War, the mills attracted fresh waves of immigrants from new countries. French Canadians replaced the Irish on the lowest rungs of the ladder until Greeks and other Eastern Europeans began arriving in 1892.[20] The two decades after 1865 were years of pessimism and slow change. Many predicted the eventual death of the cotton industry in the North, while modern urban problems—deteriorating housing, indifference to urban planning, haphazard care for new immigrants—appeared as permanent features of Lowell's land-scape.[21] Once the second largest city in the Commonwealth of Massachusetts, Lowell fell to fifth place after the 1880s as other products and other cities replaced Lowell and textiles as centers of growth and investment.

By the time the United States entered the Great Depression—which actually began in 1925 for the Lowell cotton industry—the population had dipped to about a hundred thousand from its 1920 peak. The population steadied at this figure until after World War II.[22]

As cotton declined, Lowell attracted fame in the nineteenth century for a fresh product: the manufacture of patent medicines.[23] This diversification of the Lowell economy is more than a trivial event: other American cities, founded on the strength of sunrise industries, later found themselves hosting other even more marginal industries as their original source of riches fell out of favor in the investment marketplace. Jean Bellefeuille, a shoe worker from Lowell and also a labor organizer, described another example of diversification without development:

> With the exodus of the textile mills, the town fathers, who were the beneficiaries of the exploitation of working people, seeking a way out of their dilemma began trying to diversify industry. And they were successful in bringing in some shoe shops in that period beginning around 1929. I can give you some names of those shops: International Shoe set up a plant; Merrimack Shoe set up a plant; Becker Brothers set up a plant. By 1933 these plants had grown in size as far as production is concerned. Beckers, for instance, from 35 cases a day—35 cases a day was 35 lots of 36 pairs of shoes—had reached by 1933 a production of 500 cases a day. Merrimack Shoe was now producing a hundred or more; Continental Shoe had gone up to about 150 cases a day.
>
> The wage structure was constantly being depressed by these employers. They were using the excuse with the employees, for instance, that if they could become more competitive, they could reduce their cost, they could increase production, and that thereby the worker would gain. And it was that way that they were able to grow.[24]

Diversification, however, had limits, and they were not natural ones. Roger Kane was a city councilor at the outset of World War II, and he shared a widely held belief that Lowell's industrial leaders had long used their ownership of the Locks and Canals—in effect a monopoly over power generation—to work *against* broadening the choices of employment:

> In order to discourage these different industries that at that time [before World War II] were coming in—that wanted to come in, first they'd have to get power and the rates they'd charge them were excessive enough it

wouldn't be feasible for these people who weren't here. So that's how they remained a monopoly here, because the same people who owned the mills, they controlled . . . the Locks and Canals. . . . I don't remember any specific [examples]—it never got that far, because the people that were looking, they knew the set-up and they were discouraged before any kind of negotiations could take place. [Lowell] had that reputation. That goes way back to the 1800s.[25]

After the Panic of 1893 and until 1925, Lowell's economy stabilized, the plateau broken primarily by a minor decline in 1907. Lowell's most important strike occurred in 1903, when fifteen thousand cotton workers left their jobs, asking for a 10 percent wage increase. Eventually, a state commission upheld corporation claims that they could not afford to increase pay. The strike was broken, and only sporadic incidents arose over the next few decades.[26] The Massachusetts state government was notably more pro-labor than most, but the Cabots and the Lowells—the same families who owned much of the state's and Lowell's industry—still held the reins of power.

Responsibility for the early onset of the depression in Lowell lay in increasing competition from Southern mills that were closer to raw materials and able to pay lower wages. Moreover, attempts to keep Lowell's mills modern were minimal: capital invested in manufacturing in Lowell declined from more than $100 million in the early 1920s to under $50 million and steadily declining after 1930. The number of employed wage earners fell disastrously from thirty thousand to thirteen thousand.[27]

The City, 1940

The physical appearance and industrial condition of Lowell before the outbreak of World War II are described in Margaret Terrell Parker's *Lowell: A Study of Industrial Development,* published in 1940 and based on Lowell in the late 1930s. Briefly, the city consisted of three concentric circles in the total area of 14.1 square miles (see map).[28] In the center lay the downtown business district. It stretched from the "Acre," where City Hall and the library were located, west along Merrimack Street to Kearney Square where the newspaper occupied the city's skyscraper, then south along Central Street. Along these main streets and their tributaries were most of Lowell's department stores, movie theaters, banks, professional offices, the high school, and some dilapidated company-owned housing. Moody Street extended westward from City Hall between the river and Merrimack Street and then crossed the river to the Lowell Textile School. Home of bars and

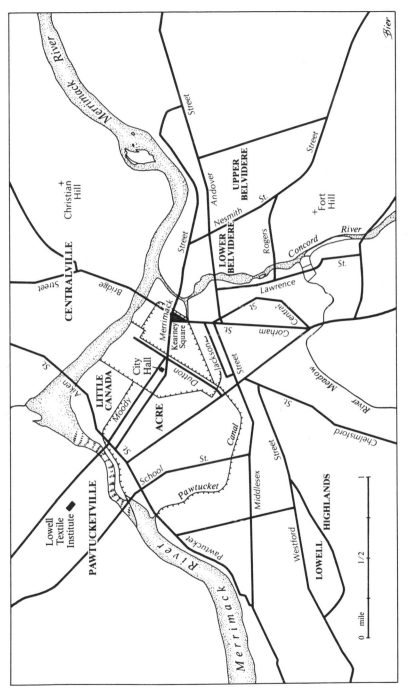

Lowell, Massachusetts, 1940.

nightclubs, Moody Street's fame and infamy reached throughout the world of American G.I.'s, and especially to nearby Fort Devens.

The mill buildings, many of which stood vacant by 1941, enclosed the central business district. To the north lay the "mile of mills along the Merrimack": the Lawrence Company, the Merrimack Mills, the Boott Mills, and the Massachusetts Company. South of Merrimack Street, the Appleton, the Lowell, the Hamilton, Lowell Machine Shop, and Foundry buildings had once used the Hamilton and Pawtucket canals paralleling Jackson Street. To the west, between Moody Street and the Lawrence Manufacturing Company on the Merrimack River, the Suffolk and Tremont mills had been powered by the waters of the Western Canal along Suffolk Street.[29]

The residential areas of Lowell surrounded the core of mills and retail shops. To a large extent this last ring was composed of neighborhoods, each with its own local shopping districts, its own churches, and its own ethnic homogeneity. From Dutton Street west to the river lay the district known as Little Canada. The Aiken and Moody Street bridges crossed the river to the north and west, connecting Little Canada with the two other French-Canadian concentrations. South of Merrimack Street near City Hall lived most of Lowell's large Greek population, while the Polish section lay north across the river from the Boott Mills.[30]

The highest quality neighborhoods were the Highlands to the southwest and Upper Belvidere to the east. Large, sometimes ostentatious houses for Lowell's wealthiest citizens lined Andover Street, dividing Upper Belvidere in half. Only a few blocks to the west, however, the Yankee concentration of Upper Belvidere gave way to the middle and working-class Irish stronghold of Lower Belvidere. Centralville, north of the river across Bridge Street, contained both good and bad housing. The best homes in the neighborhood occupied Christian Hill, but housing quality declined greatly, and the neighborhood's ethnic character changed from Irish to Polish down the slopes toward the river across from the mills on the Merrimack's south bank. In general, land values were highest and living conditions poorest in areas closest to the mills and the central core. The most desirable homes occupied hill tops further out.[31] At the borders of the city, a few families still raised their own chickens and lived without the benefits of city electricity.

Industrially, Lowell in 1940 retained its identity as a cotton city, although fifteen years of depression in that industry stimulated a move to wool as a crucial part of the local economy. The woolen industry, employing 2,419 workers, accounted for more than $18 million worth of goods in 1940. The cotton industry, employing six hundred workers more, produced goods valued at $9 million less. Knit goods, including both cotton and woolens, employed a thousand workers who produced $4.3 million worth. Other major industries, in order of decreasing value of product, were: rayon goods, boots and shoes, leather goods, printing and publishing, baking, and textile machinery and parts.[32]

Although the number of employees in cotton seems small, by far the largest segment of Lowell's workers found employment, if not directly in the mills, then in some enterprise serving or in other ways connected to Lowell's history as a cotton city. Most industrial establishments used the mill buildings and obtained their power from the Proprietors of Locks and Canals, some directly and some through the mill companies whose buildings they occupied. A few companies generated their own power at the falls on the Concord River, which divides south Lowell into east and west, and a few obtained power from the Lowell Electric Light Corporation.[33]

As late as 1940, Lowell had three English-language daily newspapers: the *Courier-Citizen,* the *Evening Leader,* and the *Sun.* A series of closings and mergers in 1941 left only the *Lowell Sun* and a weekly, the *Lowell Sunday Telegram.* Thereafter, the *Courier-Citizen* became strictly a publishing company. In addition to those in English, Lowell was served by several foreign-language papers, most notably *L'Etoile* in French.

On the eve of World War II, Lowell's housing was generally old. Of 26,000 units, more than 10,000 were constructed between 1890 and 1910; in all, 23,000 dated from before 1919. Indicative of the working-class nature of the city, only one-fourth of the units were owned by the people who lived in them. Almost all dwellings that tenants occupied rented at between $10 and $24, with an average monthly rent of $23.85. Of the 26,000 units, only 632 stood vacant in 1940.[34]

Family income in 1936 ranged from $500 to $1,500, with 40 percent of Lowell's families reporting in this bracket. Another 22 percent reported incomes of $1,500 to $2,500.[35] Two examples place these figures in perspective. The first is from Lucille Cordeau, the wife of a druggist:

> We were married in June 1941, and he was making $25 a week. We bought the house for $3,000 December 1941. We moved in in March 1942.
>   Due to the fact that wages were so low, of course, the food was low. I kept a budget the first year we were married and we'd eat—and we'd eat well—for $8 a week. And I tell you, we had steak and butter and everything we really needed for $8 a week.[36]

James Ellis, a textile worker who later became a professional labor organizer, went beyond the dollar figures to the difficulty of getting work:

In 1939 I was making $14.40 a week. I think there was a 37.5 cents minimum then. When I worked in the mill in 1939, it was really a slave shop. You have no idea what it was like. I worked in the dye house. If you're familiar with the shape-up system in New York with the long-shoremen, we used to report in the morning to the dye house, maybe forty, fifty young fellows. The boss would go around: "You're working today, you're working today." Three maybe out of forty would work. It was a daily routine. It was a very, very difficult way of life at the time. You've got to remember we were in the throes of the depression.[37]

Significantly, 45 percent of Lowell's workers earned less than $1,000 per year, with 16.7 percent of families reporting no income at all. Unemployment for women was about 10 percent below that for men in each age group. For the city as a whole, 3,627 men out of a working-age population of 37,722 and 1,984 women out of 41,760 sought work. The proportion of women listed as unemployed is so low primarily because only one-third of the women over fourteen are listed as in the labor force compared to three-fourths of the men. Only 61.5 percent of the heads of household had a job.[38]

Of Lowell's citizens who were employed, occupations broke down as follows: 13,000 operatives; 2,000 other laborers; 4,000 craftsmen and foremen; 6,000 clerical workers and salespeople; 1,000 in domestic service; 2,200 proprietors, managers, and officials; 2,800 in other services; and 2,327 professionals.[39] In 1940, about half worked a standard forty-hour work week and another 10 percent worked forty-eight hours.[40]

In 1940, a fifth of Lowell's population was born outside the United States. The most numerous ethnic group was the Irish, followed by the French Canadians, Yankees, Greeks, and Poles. Ethnic groups co-existed reasonably harmoniously, each in its own neighborhood. Out of a hundred thousand people in Lowell, the census listed only 137 as nonwhite.[41]

To a great extent, a person's ethnic background defined his or her opportunities, as textile worker Alice Swanton described:

In the Merrimack [textile mill], the Greeks could work in the dye house, the Irish could work in the yard, and the French could maybe work in the card room, but you never went any higher than that. You just didn't even think of—if you could go to night school and learn to better yourself, forget it. Not in the Merrimack Mill.

In fact, they did their hiring [for supervisors in] England. My in-laws, they were English people. My husband, as soon as he was out of school, he went right in there, it was just no question, he went in, he had a job as a runner, and from there he worked up to draftsman. But he had his choice, because he was of the right nationality and the right religion. And

I know all of his brothers and sisters, before they left England to come over here, they were secure, they knew they were going to have a job. Where the Americans, all nationalities, were outside in the morning, waiting outside for a job. The bosses come out, picked a few, and no more work. . . .

My husband and I were both different religions and different nationalities. He had a bad time when they heard he was marrying an Irish Catholic. . . . In fact, he had such a rough going, the times was so bad, that we just went out and got married quietly, got married and told them we were married, and just didn't blow any horns or have a great big wedding because it might have meant something to do with his job.[42]

A natural partner to high unemployment was exemplary school attendance, averaging around 98 percent. The high school even added an extra year to its curriculum, equivalent in all but name to a first year of college or trade school. The alternative for young people was to stay at home; school occupied their free moments and kept them out of an already crowded labor market.[43]

For all of its high unemployment and low wages, and possibly a cause for those conditions, Lowell had a reputation, dating from the nineteenth century, as a nonunion city, especially in comparison with its neighbor down the river, Lawrence. The Industrial Workers of the World (I.W.W.) had been mildly active in the years around World War I, but the pre-World War II textile industry in Lowell was basically unorganized. The textile mills' move south reinforced this: "After the first world war," said Thomas Ahearn, the president of the Lowell Central Labor Union, "when all the cotton mills moved out of the area, that scared the hell out of them [the workers]."[44] A few strikes of significant size occurred in the late 1930s at the Boott and the Merrimack, but none resulted in strong, nationally affiliated unions.[45]

The words "corrupt," "inefficient," and "conservative" were commonly applied to Lowell's political system during the years of the depression. "Irrelevant" could also be used, because who controlled political offices had little to do with the Yankee mill owners who, through economic power, controlled the city.

For the most part, the Irish plurality dominated the two major governmental departments, the city council and the school committee. Both bodies developed a strong reputation for graft and nepotism. The mayor in 1940, George T. Ashe, became involved in fights within his own party when he pushed a plan to eliminate city department heads. This was part of an efficiency effort meant to balance the city budget: in 1936, 1938, and 1939 the deficit stayed more than a half million dollars per year, climbing out of the red, as was the case in many

American cities, only after several years of war prosperity in 1943. Tax rates, however, were already among the state's highest, despite the large industrial base. Although Ashe's move did not succeed, it did enrage his own party and cut off many of his sources for campaign funds while making him popular among the voters. In order to run his 1941 campaign for mayor—Lowell's last campaign under a system based on a strong, elected mayor—Ashe raised his own money and won, only to face major scandals in the city water and purchasing departments. Eventually, during the war years, these scandals sent Mayor Ashe to jail and resulted in the city's disillusionment with the strong mayoral system of government.[46]

In sum, Lowell before the onset of World War II had all the makings of a dying city. The government, inefficient at best and corrupt at worst, served few of the needs of a depression-ridden city. Lowell's ethnic groups kept pretty much to themselves in their own neighborhoods and organizations. Housing was old, and few Lowellians could afford to own the homes in which they lived. Wages were infamously low, even after federal actions had raised them considerably to a legalized minimum. Unemployment much higher than the national average accompanied the low wages. Few unions existed with any influence except among skilled workers. Those unions that did operate, and a few came in after 1937 and 1938, had little power to increase wages or improve conditions when the tendency was for industry to leave the city and move south. Decades of minimal investment in renovating and modernizing Lowell mills made the migration seem that much more unavoidable. The cotton industry, Lowell's lifeblood and birthright, was simply closing down.

Victor Luz, a student at the time and later a teacher, sums up the history with bitterness:

> Actually, the money people in Lowell, who controlled the mills really, I don't think had any interest in Lowell, per se. Probably some of them were idealistic when they built the city, but I think, just from my experiences in the textile industry and from living in Lowell, that I'd say for the most part people wanted to get as much as they could out of the people of Lowell, the actual workers. And, sad to say, they bled the city white. When they couldn't get any more, they pulled out.[47]

From a different point of view, Edward Larter in 1975 told how his father bought a textile mill in 1929; it survived the depression and operated until 1980. Although his story is one of triumphing over the odds, it reinforces the picture of a dying city: "This company has been run by sweat and blood ever since it started. And the only damn reason that the company's still alive today is my father put his heart and soul into it, and I guess I have, too. And if you stopped to gasp for one minute for fresh air, it'd take three days to catch up again."[48]

Margaret Parker concluded in 1940, with no consideration of the war to follow, that survival for Lowell depended on major changes in the city's industrial structure which, in turn, depended on conditions in the nation as a whole. Competition from the South could not be met without unionization in those mills or federal laws equalizing wage scales throughout the country. Diversification of Lowell's narrow industrial base required new business, but that remained impossible as long as the entire United States suffered economic depression. Only a major event could have saved Lowell or even delayed its death.[49]

War was that event, but its impact was felt differently in each class, each neighborhood, each house. For a pregnant mother, the war meant the difficulty of finding a doctor who wouldn't be drafted; for a pipe fitter, the war meant assured and high-paid work; for a grocer, it meant the paperwork of ration coupons; for a child, it meant growing up without a father around—and inspiration for new games.

United in their support for the war effort, the people of Lowell nevertheless had individual reasons to fight against fascism. Each person benefited or suffered—in the short and long run—based on many things, including class, race, age, neighborhood, familial relationships, and ethnicity. To the rich, and to corporations not tied to a hometown, the war often brought unprecedented wealth and power. For the people who called Lowell home, the legacy of victory, and even of the escape from the depression, was more ambiguous.

NOTES

1. John Coolidge, *Mills and Mansions* (1942, repr., New York: Russell and Russell, 1967), 18; *Handbook for the Visitor to Lowell* (Lowell: D. Bixby, 1848), 34–35.

2. Henry Adolphus Miles, *Lowell, As It Was, and As It Is* (1846, repr., New York: Arno Press, 1972), 30–31.

3. Charles Cowley, *Illustrated History of Lowell* (Boston: Lee and Shepard, 1868), 72; Miles, *Lowell, As It Was,* 40.

4. Cowley, *Illustrated History of Lowell,* 73.

5. *Handbook for the Visitor to Lowell,* 11–16, 30.

6. Coolidge, *Mills and Mansions,* 22.

7. Robert G. Layer, *Earnings of Cotton Mill Operatives, 1825–1914* (Cambridge, Mass.: Committee on Research in Economic History, 1955), 45.

8. *Handbook for the Visitor to Lowell,* 32.

9. Louis T. Merrill, "Mill Town on the Merrimack," *New England Quarterly* 19 (March 1946): 22.

10. Paul F. McGouldrick, *New England Textiles in the Nineteenth Century* (Cambridge, Mass.: Harvard University Press, 1968), 38, 108, 147.

11. Ray Ginger, "Labor in a Massachusetts Cotton Mill, 1853–1860," *Business History Review* 28 (March 1954): 87–88.

12. Ginger, "Labor in a Massachusetts Cotton Mill," 90.

13. McGouldrick, *New England Textiles,* 39–40.

14. Merrill, "Mill Town on the Merrimack," 25.

15. Layer, *Earnings of Cotton Mill Operatives,* 51.

16. Margaret Terrell Parker, *Lowell: A Study of Industrial Development* (1940; repr., Port Washington, N.Y.: Kennikat Press, 1970), 80–82.

17. Parker, *Lowell,* 89.

18. Frederick W. Coburn, *History of Lowell and Its People* (New York: Lewis Historical Publishing, 1920), 305, 308.

19. Interview with Edward Stevens, 26 November 1974.

20. George F. Kenngott, *The Record of a City* (New York: Macmillan, 1912), 30.

21. Coburn, *History of Lowell,* 341.

22. Parker, *Lowell,* 5, 18.

23. Coburn, *History of Lowell,* 56.

24. Interview with Jean Bellefeuille, 15 July 1975.

25. Interview with Roger Kane, 16 September 1975.

26. Coburn, *History of Lowell,* 407–13.

27. Commonwealth of Massachusetts, Depart of Labor and Industries, *Statistics of Manufactures in Massachusetts, 1920–1938,* Public Document no. 36 (n.p., n.d.), 25.

28. United States Department of Commerce, Bureau of the Census, *Areas of the United States,* 1940 (Washington: GPO, 1943), 129.

29. *Handbook for the Visitor to Lowell,* frontispiece.

30. Parker, *Lowell,* 14.

31. Ibid., 93–95.

32. Commonwealth of Massachusetts, Department of Labor and Industries, Division of Statistics, "Census of Manufactures—1950—Lowell, Mass.," mimeographed (n.p.: 1950), 2–3.

33. Parker, *Lowell,* 124–25; see 32–55 for a detailed description of Lowell industry just before the effects of World War II could be felt.

34. United States Department of Commerce, Bureau of the Census, *Sixteenth Census of the United States, 1940, Housing, Third Series, Characteristics by Monthly Rent or Value, Massachusetts* (Washington: GPO, 1943), 44–46; *Sixteenth Census of the United States, 1940, Housing,* vol. 2: *General Characteristics* (Washington: GPO, 1942), 519.

35. United States Department of Commerce, Bureau of the Census, *Population and Housing, Families: General Characteristics, 1940* (Washington: GPO, 1943), 273.

36. Interview with Lucille Cordeau, 2 April 1975.

37. Interview with James Ellis, 16 June 1975.

38. United States Department of Commerce, Bureau of the Census, *Population,* vol. 3: *The Labor Force,* pt. 3, *Iowa-Montana* (Washington: GPO, 1943), 449; *Population and Housing, 1940,* 260.

39. Bureau of the Census, *Population, Second Series,* 1940, 116.

40. United States Department of Commerce, Bureau of the Census, *Sixteenth Census of the United States, 1940, Population, Third Series, The Labor Force: Occupation, Industry, Employment, and Income: Massachusetts* (Washington: GPO, 1943), 143.

41. United States Department of Commerce, Bureau of the Census, *Population: Characteristics of the Nonwhite Population by Race, 1940* (Washington: GPO, 1943), 6; *Population, Second Series, Characteristics of the Population, Massachusetts, 1940* (Washington: GPO, 1943), 111.

42. Interview with Alice Swanton, 4 June 1975.

43. United States Department of Commerce, Bureau of the Census, *Population, Fourth Series, Characteristics by Age, Marital Status, Relationship, Education and Citizenship: Massachusetts* (Washington: GPO, 1943), 31.

44. Interview with Thomas Ahearn, 8 March 1976.

45. Interview with Andrew Jenkins, 31 January 1975.

46. Mary H. Blewett, "The Mills and the Multitudes: A Political History," in *Cotton Was King: A History of Lowell, Massachusetts,* ed. Arthur L. Eno, Jr. (n.p.: New Hampshire Publishing Company in collaboration with the Lowell Historical Society, 1976), 182–83.

47. Interview with Victor Luz, 23 April 1975.

48. Interview with Edward Larter, 22 March 1975.

49. Parker, *Lowell,* 211–16.

2

Blue-collar Men

Before the war all the good jobs in the mills, the high paying jobs—all the loom fixers were French, barring none.
The dye house was pretty much Greek. The spinning room
was pretty much Greek, Syrian. The cutting room, which
was the velvet cutting and the corduroy cutting—which
were high-priced jobs at the time, they were making maybe
$25—that was mostly Irish.
 During the war years, the shortage of labor . . . forced
management to take others. The foremen were Irish; the
French were the foremen in the loom-fixing department.
When they couldn't get enough of those, they brought in
the others—the Poles and the Greeks and everybody else.
But it was economic necessity that brought about this inte-
gration, not the war at all. Had it not been for the war,
we'd have wallowed in the Depression.[1]

Work provides the means to purchase necessities. It is also a primary
means through which people define themselves. To work is to participate in and contribute to the life of a community. When a society fails
to provide meaningful work—or even any work—it fails to make use
of its members; the unemployed, in turn, fail to feel a stake in the
community, a feeling in which they may very well be justified. The
longer unemployment lasts and the greater its extent, the greater will
be tensions within individuals and within society, and the greater will
be pressure on that society to change.

As World War II approached, Americans felt this alienation strongly.
Lowell and the rest of the United States still stagnated in the Great
Depression. As late as June 1940, nine million Americans—17 percent
of the labor force—were unemployed. The census for Lowell showed
that 3,000 experienced men sought work compared to 22,000 who were
employed. In addition to the 3,000 officially unemployed, 630 "unexperienced" men were out of work, and 3,322 had government emergency work—in other words, they would have been unemployed without New Deal jobs programs. Marginally employed men and those

who had given up seeking work were not even listed. In Lowell, only about 75 percent of the men in the labor force had other than government-emergency work. Nor could the bulk of jobs be called ideal. Out of the total employed in Lowell, almost a third were operatives, that is, low-skilled factory workers. All but 14 percent fell into blue-collar categories, including operative, laborer, craftsman, foreman, and clerical worker. Despite the image of the United States as a three-class society, Lowell was thus almost totally working class.[2]

Insufficient wages accompanied the limited job opportunities. Average wages for a year of labor in a Lowell manufacturing establishment ranged from a low of $735 for workers who made knitted outerwear to a high of only $1,500 for those in commercial printing. The average manufacturing wage for the whole city—less than $1,000 per year—compared poorly to the national average—$1,250. Employers spent three times as much on manufacturing materials as they paid in wages.[3] Contributing to low annual wages was the fact that a worker could rarely expect to work a full twelve months each year.

Symptomatic of the omnipresence of economic hardship into the early war years was the importance in Lowell of the federal relief agency, the Works Progress Administration (WPA). The city council in mid-1941 wrote to the WPA director asking the agency to reinstate 1,200 people who had been laid off because of budget cuts. "We find practically no defense industries here" to take up the slack left by WPA cutbacks.[4] Even as the war boom reached Lowell, some layoffs at the textile mills continued into spring 1942. In mid-1943, three thousand people in Lowell still collected unemployment checks. As late as March 1943—three months after Roosevelt ordered WPA liquidated—city councilor Bart Callery pushed to have a WPA sewing project continued because the women it employed did not expect to find jobs in war industries.[5]

The Varieties of Work

War prosperity, of course, did eventually come to Lowell, and the first local effect of the approach of World War II was renewed activity in languishing industries. Employment in the nation's cotton mills rose from under 400,000 to more than 500,000 in the initial years of the war, and from 5,500 to 7,000 in Lowell. For the first time in twenty years, in June 1941, a Lowell mill appealed for workers. Other local industries similarly were reborn. The shoe industry, Lowell's second largest employer, increased its work force by 50 percent in one year, reaching 1,800 in 1941.[6]

Like mills in Lowell and factories in almost every American town, shoe factories converted to war work whenever possible. John Pilling Shoe Company, the only major company in Lowell that produced men's shoes, easily switched to producing shoes for soldiers. Other companies, however, found conversion technologically more difficult; faced with a loss of workers to war industries, many closed. Shoe worker Jean Bellefeuille remembered:

> The workers were not going to remain in these sweat shops when defense industries were coming in, so there was an exodus of shoe workers out of the shoe shops. The only shoe shop that had any war contracts was the John Pilling Shoe Company. . . .
>   You see, a shop couldn't convert from women's shoes to men's shoes. . . . The process for manufacturing women's shoes and men's shoes would be different. Most men's shoes were welt shoes. Women's shoes is a cement process, or a different type of stitch process. They're stitched through an inner sole into the inside and then cement the outside sole to it. To convert from one to the other meant a change in machinery, a change in lasts, a change in patterns, a change in everything. People who worked in men's shoes were more highly skilled usually than those who worked on women's shoes, because they seemed to put more quality usually in the men's shoes.[7]

Women's shoes were the exception. To most established industries, war seemed, at least at first, a godsend. In the case of Lowell's third major industry, commercial printing, the mushrooming demand for forms and reports was a rewarding sidelight of wartime bureaucracy.[8]

The most dramatic employment possibilities came with the arrival in Lowell of new, war-based companies. No textile mill in Lowell during this period employed anywhere near the five thousand men and women Remington Arms had at its peak. By spring of 1945, almost half of the manufacturing establishments in Lowell had war work. But the percentage of Lowell workers employed in these companies was even higher (55 percent), indicating that the larger companies had the contracts for war work. However, the extremes of war prosperity bypassed Lowell, because major war industries simply did not come there. The proportion of workers employed on war work in Lowell was significantly less than the proportion for the entire state (66 percent). Remington lasted only a year, and even Remington was small potatoes compared to major war industries across the country.[9]

Even if the city didn't lead the recovery, to the people in Lowell the economy was clearly moving again. Even before Pearl Harbor, war production began to provide employment for a few, mostly skilled, Lowell workers. For example, Paul Santilli, a pipe fitter, was employed only irregularly during the depression, but he found steady work at the Boston Navy Yard beginning in 1939.

Because the pool of unemployed, available labor in Lowell was so large, Washington decided to locate an ordnance center there: the government-owned Remington Arms plant provided the first real opportunities for masses of Lowell's skilled workers when $5 million worth of construction—an investment harkening back to Lowell's glory years in the early nineteenth century—began in 1942 on its two Lowell plants. Everett Harris, a plumber's union leader, described the result: "It was very common to see in the morning when I was at those plants when we were hiring, as far as laborers, a hundred, two hundred young fellows all ages trying to get on." When Remington closed at the end of 1943, General Electric occupied part of its buildings and employed some of its workers. Lowell's modest version of prosperity continued.[10]

The city council actively tried to encourage the development of war industries in Lowell, although the effectiveness of its actions cannot be determined, and its power in the context of national and international events was limited. The city set up an industrial commission that periodically asked federal officials and corporations to establish businesses in the city. Congresswoman Edith Nourse Rogers—with her Washington base, power, and contacts—seems to have been more directly successful: she received much of the credit for Remington's decision to build in Lowell.[11]

As a result of the war boom, men found themselves with a novel option: a choice of jobs. Previously unemployed textile workers could now earn pay from Remington, General Electric, or United States Rubber in Lowell, at Fort Devens a few miles away, or at the Boston Navy Yard thirty-five miles south. Lowell workers willing to relocate were welcomed in areas where labor shortages were "acute": Hartford and Bridgeport, Connecticut; Springfield, Massachusetts; and Portland, Maine. Jean Bellefeuille, blacklisted as a radical in Lowell, took this route in his new career as a carpenter:

> I worked in Lowell, I worked in Hartford, I worked in Lawrence, I worked in Manchester.
> I started working as a carpenter in the campsite, Camp Devens, which was the place to get used to carpentry and to develop a skill because there was a great demand for construction workers and there weren't very many of them who were skilled.... And when I got through there I went to work in Grinnear Field in Manchester. And from there, I worked in Bedford.... By November of '42 I got a job in Hingham Shipyard as a maintenance carpenter.
> By the summer of 1943, I had enough of getting up at five o'clock in the morning and driving to work through the city of Boston every day

... and not getting home until 7:30 or 8:00 at night. [My wife and I] determined finally that the proper thing to do would be to move nearer to my work. This was to be only a temporary move, but it proved to be the proper thing to do for us, because I was able to further my skill and find that also from an economic point-of-view that there was a better opportunity for me to earn a living in the south shore of Massachusetts than there was to go back to Lowell. . . . Most of the construction workers in the city of Lowell work out of town, and out of the jurisdiction of their local.[12]

Thus the textile and shoe industries, with average annual prewar wages of under $800, soon faced an exodus of previously "loyal" employees. By 1944, only 5,600 workers remained in the mills and 1,300 in Lowell's shoe factories, approximately the 1940 level even though war business had increased the demand for workers by these industries. Bellefeuille cited the wartime loss of workers as a major cause of the death of the shoe industry in Lowell.[13] By comparison, the printing industry—with a prewar average annual income of $1,500—suffered far less.

The demand for workers naturally shifted the balance of power between management and labor toward the latter. As James Ellis observed, after a century of blatant discrimination, employers were forced to accept a changing and varied work force as a way of life. Increased civilian migration, such as Bellefeuille's, was another aspect of workers' new freedom. Just as in the 1920s—and in contrast to the 1930s—the search for a good job induced migration. In the last five desperate years of the depression, 2,800,000 Americans moved each year; from 1940 to 1945, 4,700,000 Americans migrated each year in the search for a better place to earn a living.[14]

Money: Getting and Spending

The changed workplace balance of power was most obvious in the most important arena: money. Throughout the nation, wage rates rose 24 percent during the war while weekly earnings rose 70 percent. Weekly pay for male workers rose from $30.77 in 1939 to $57.70 in 1944 (although the value of the 1939 dollar decreased to 75 cents by 1945). In textiles, which started from a much lower base than the standard for manufacturing, hourly wages rose 60 percent from 1939 to 1945, and weekly earnings rose 84 percent.[15] These figures represent average wages for employed workers; the gradual disappearance of unemployment and the increased weekly pay combined to dramatically improved workers' economic security.

As in the rest of the nation, earnings in Lowell rose significantly, but as a town based on marginal, labor-intensive industries, Lowell's wages rested at the low end of national figures. In 1943, average Lowell weekly wages in manufacturing reached $31.88—approximately the prewar level for the country as a whole.[16] Even war-based industries followed the low-wage pattern. U.S. Rubber had a great deal of trouble getting enough workers with its starting pay of 53 cents per hour for women and 58 cents per hour for men. Just as did the mills, "a house-to-house canvas [was] inaugurated by the company in an attempt to interest housewives in employment. . . . Results have been negligible," according to a confidential War Manpower Commission (WMC) survey.[17]

Lowell's low wages derived primarily from its established industrial base. The WMC survey showed that entry-level pay in the U.S. textile industry was still below 60 cents per hour in mid-1944. Table 1 gives annual income for workers in those industries traditionally important in Lowell. Each is low-wage: in 1940, the average U.S. manufacturing wage was $1,432, and rose 76 percent to $2,517 by 1945.

Wages might have risen even more, but a nationwide freeze kept them relatively stable. On the other hand, some raises could be won by applying through official channels. When Remington needed more steamfitters, Everett Harris, the head of the local union, first "had to send out telegrams from Maine to Florida, New York, Cincinatti, and a few other cities to get them in here." When that didn't do the trick, "we had to put through a letter to the Wage Adjustment Board in Washington, D.C., to bring the scale up so it would entice the plumbers and the fitters to come into this area. So that came through after two months, and it brought the wages up to somewhere near the Boston

Table 1. Average Annual Earnings, Lowell and U.S.

	Lowell			U.S.		
	1940	1945	percent increase	1940	1945	percent increase
All manufacturing	$946	$1,775	88	$1,432	$2,517	76
Woolen & worsted goods	$956	$1,776	86			
Cotton goods	$853	$1,601	88			
Boots & shoes	$841	$1,601	90			

Sources: Department of Labor and Industries, "Census of Manufactures—1950—Lowell," 2–3; United States Department of Commerce, Bureau of the Census, *Historical Statistics of the United States from Colonial Times to 1970,* Pt. 1 (Washington: GPO, 1975), 166.

scale. So in that way, we were successful in getting men in from all around, that is, pipe fitters and plumbers. Of course, laborers were no problem on that."[18]

In other cases, the government—in an effort to appease labor while controlling inflation—granted limited increases to offset increased living costs. It used the formula known nationally as "Little Steel," first negotiated in 1942 to cover workers at Bethlehem, Republic, Youngstown, and Inland steel companies. Any increases beyond the 15 percent cost-of-living raise in the Little Steel agreement meant waiting through long delays for approval from Washington. Lowell locals apparently respected these guidelines for several years, except for engaging in a few short wildcat strikes.[19]

Discussions in the city council indicate, however, that Little Steel was not popular. Several councilors, naming no names, reported that employers had said they would gladly raise pay, but could not due to Little Steel. Perhaps the need to hold employees would have led employers to raise pay during this wartime prosperity. Another possibility is that employers found federal edict a convenient excuse to continue old habits. In any event, the city council in 1944 passed a resolution against the Little Steel formula and for "the small wage earners."[20]

It was possible for take-home pay to rise more than 15 percent— both within the Little Steel guidelines and by bending the rules. According to John Mullen, then a union steward in the woolen and worsted industry, "One of the things that I think helped to take the pressure off abiding by the 15 percent was that we were able to persuade the board to give consideration on vacation pay, upgrading of classifications for increased wages per hour, and that kind of thing. Overtime pay was increased—time-and-a-half for overtime, that kind of thing— made a difference at that time to help keep a lid on that kind of situation."[21]

Working more hours to earn more money was not only acceptable to the government, but was also encouraged. Weekend and overtime work shot up, and bonus overtime pay became a regular feature after Remington introduced the policy to the city. For the first time, Merrimack workers got paid holidays and time-and-a-half for Saturday and overtime work. Offered their first one-week paid vacation early in the war (after a strike), Merrimack workers demanded a second week of vacation with pay in 1944. Nationally, only 12 percent of textile workers received vacations with pay in 1937; by 1943, one week's vacation was the rule, and two weeks common.[22]

Concessions were often meant to discourage union activism, just as welfare capitalism in the 1920s had been intended to do. Many companies preferred to improve fringe benefits rather than raise hourly wages, and the government supported this choice. The War Labor Board (WLB) readily accepted—and sometimes ordered—paid holidays and increased vacation time. In 1944, the WLB approved a liberalized vacation plan for Boott workers, negotiated through the Textile Workers Union of America (TWUA). Near the end of and after the war, the Wage Stabilization Board allowed the Merrimack to make retroactive pay increases. Similarly, in November of 1944, "General Electric workers," reported the *Lowell Daily Sun,* "members of the International Ladies Garment Workers Union, held their first jubilee dance . . . in the Knights of Columbus Hall in celebration of the payment of retroactive pay from June 12." On the other hand, the Wage Labor Board fined four smaller Lowell companies in 1945 for not getting permission before raising wages.[23]

Having more money to spend gave rise to a question of how to spend it. As war advanced, savings (to a greater extent) and direct taxes (to a lesser extent) absorbed a significant amount of money, whereas before the war they were almost negligible. Personal expenses fell from approximately 80 percent of income to 65 percent, while taxes took approximately triple their fraction of a worker's income. Beginning in 1943, income taxes were deducted compulsorily from weekly paychecks. An Office of War Information pamphlet put this in terms of a move by Roosevelt, saying "The President has urged that all taxes should be on a pay-as-you-go basis."[24]

The government did, of course, do more than urge. The Revenue Act of 1943 introduced withholding taxes for most workers. The Victory Tax, which began January 1, 1943, imposed a 5 percent withholding tax on all incomes over $624 per year.[25] A man with a wife and two children and earning under $2,000 paid no tax either before 1943 or after 1945. In 1943, he missed $35 from his packet; in 1944 and 1945, $39. Savings took under 10 percent of income in 1939 and more than 20 percent by 1945. In all, Americans saved $35.3 billion in 1945 compared to $6 billion in 1939.[26]

In Lowell, too, people saved rather than spent. Few of the working men interviewed thought that increased income changed their lives much during the war. As the most obvious cause, many consumer items were unavailable during the war, especially "luxuries" such as appliances and automobiles.

The result of shortages and wartime savings was a rash of major purchases after the war, ranging from coats to down payments on houses. After 1944, Lowell's savings banks steadily increased the number of real estate loans they made.[27] Perhaps because people were buying homes, demand for apartments dropped: between 1940 and 1950, median rent in Lowell stayed almost constant in the $20 to $24 per month range and, therefore, took a proportionately smaller portion of a paycheck.[28]

However, the unavailability of luxury items is not the whole explanation of increased wartime saving. People who wanted to spend money found ways, as is shown by the boom in the nation's entertainment industry. Moreover, the petty, but omnipresent, black market could absorb large amounts of cash. Even the price of legally purchased food rose approximately one-third over 1935–39 levels.[29] Instead of indulging themselves, people in Lowell found the memory of the 1930s and the possibility of postwar depression major incentives to bank their pay. The postwar trend of home buying fit the same pattern: families saw some continuing prosperity and tried to secure their future with a permanent home. Claire Contardo remembered:

> Towards the end of World War II [my parents] purchased a house. They lost a house during the depression, and then they had been renting. Then it was shortly before my husband came home from overseas that they bought a house. That house they had paid $4,300. . . . It was not just that [the children] were in the service, it was finally that we were growing up and most of us were able to work and help. Because my parents had had it kind of tough, like everybody else, during the depression years, my father had been kind of leery about buying another home.[30]

Bond purchases represented a great portion of workers' wartime savings, and the purchase of savings bonds rose significantly. By late 1942, 28 million workers (76 percent of those in companies with purchase plans) purchased bonds through their employer, spending 8 percent of their incomes. According to a 1943 estimate, textile workers bought $35 million worth of bonds each year. The fraction spent on bonds stayed almost constant as income increased; 1944 E-bond sales took 7.1 percent of personal income after taxes. At one point, the Merrimack Manufacturing Company held $50,000 on account collected from its Lowell employees for war bonds.[31]

Bond sales were even more significant than numbers indicate: most people in Lowell remember bond drives in the city and factories better than any other facet of wartime social life. Everyone bought at least a few, and many people cite these purchases as the prime example of patriotism in Lowell. The *Lowell Daily Sun*, when it gave each of its employees a $25 Christmas bonus, also purchased bonds for its sixty-four former employees in the services. Paul Santilli purchased bonds despite the fact he considered their low interest rate a swindle; he bought bonds to help his country.[32]

Besides taxes and bonds, a third item could be deducted from pay, and this one carried direct potential benefit for workers. In *The Home Front* (1943) David Hinshaw indicated that War Labor Board policy made the check-off for union dues almost universal.[33] Although Hinshaw may have exaggerated somewhat, the check-off did reach into Lowell eventually. A dispute mediated by the NWLB between U.S. Rubber and a Lowell union local centered on the check-off. James Ellis, the principal union organizer at the Merrimack Mill, reported that dues were collected in cash until almost the end of the war or just after. He had to personally approach each worker to collect dues. With the new policy, the Merrimack union's finances finally stabilized. Although the check-off lessened the daily requirement that unions respond to the rank and file, union members did on the whole benefit— the check-off is almost a prerequisite for a strong union. The Textile Workers Union of America's national finances went into the black for the first time in 1940; by 1946, 86 percent of TWUA contracts had check-off provisions.[34]

Speed-Ups and Productivity

In the absence of a pool of unemployed workers to drive wages down, employers stressed productivity. For the nation as a whole, the Department of Commerce in 1943 estimated that output per worker was one-third greater than in 1939. However, the cotton industry did not follow the national trend toward efficiency: output per worker-hour steadily declined during the war after a slight rise in the last years of the depression. In comparison, the woolen industry—less important to Lowell—improved.[35]

Despite difficulties in the cotton industry, Lowell's industrial companies did increase their efficiency as measured by value added in manufacturing, rather than by quantity of goods. Comparing 1939 and 1947, the value added rose from about $2,000 to almost $5,000 per worker. Similarly, Massachusetts showed a rise from $2,600 to $5,600.[36] Profitability improved markedly for the whole textile industry (Table 2).

Of several factors tending to increase production per worker, the most important was probably the increased hours that each person worked. A 1943 presidential decree established a minimum forty-eight-hour week in munitions, with the added incentive of overtime for Sunday and holiday work.[37] The cotton textile industry initiated a standard forty-eight-hour week on May 14, 1944, by order of WMC commissioner Paul McNutt. A WMC press release said "a continuing decline in production particularly in fabrics essential to the war" made

Table 2. Textile Mill Products Industry, U.S.

	1940	1941	1942	1943	1944	1945	1946
Profits per dollar of wages ($)	.232	.481	.479	.514	.507	.498	.707
Profits per production worker ($)	199	490	704	706	738	774	1,277
Profits per worker hour ($)	.107	.244	.337	.327	.339	.362	.611

Source: TWUA, *Nation's Most Prosperous Industry,* 18–19.

the step necessary. A meeting of New England textile executives, including J. R. Flather of the Boott, a notoriously anti-union employer, proposed a alternative to overtime wages for increasing production: "It was suggested that if the W.P.B. could change the Union's attitude toward workload, production could be stepped up immediately."[38]

For all manufacturing industries, the average work week nationally increased from thirty-eight hours in 1939 to forty-five hours in 1944.[39] As war production declined, so did the average length of the work week, reaching about forty-one hours per week in the second half of 1945.

In almost every case, Lowell workers took on extra tasks during wartime. Joseph Nawrocki, a foreman at Ames Worsted, had his basic wage frozen at $40 per week, but did up to twenty hours of overtime each week. John Zawodny, working in the Wannalancit shipping department, put in sixty hours per week. He had an extra night-time job elsewhere until his wife, who also worked, threatened to leave him unless he gave it up. The twelve-hour average wartime shift at Ames Worsted made overtime discussions between labor and management quite important.[40]

Some companies circumvented the Little Steel wage freeze by exaggerating overtime hours, as is indicated by this statement from a foundry owner:

> It was difficult to hold onto workers. You couldn't give them bonuses, so what you did was . . . you give them some overtime. . . . [You'd] say, "Come back at six and work till ten." They'd actually work till eight o'clock and then take off. So, you know, they'd work two hours, [for] which you'd have to pay them at time and a half under the wage-hour law. So you pay them four hours for two hours, which actually we'd be paying them like six for two. But then you're a little touch and go doing it, because you're afraid that one of them would get a little vocal, and you'd be in the ragbag with the government.[41]

Although overtime, whether real or just on paper, gave the biggest boost to production, other factors contributed. Seventeen Lowell companies participated in the WMC Training-Within-Industry (TWI) program; more than a thousand workers received TWI certificates, eventually earning more money based on their newly acquired skills.

More important, some speed-up occurred in Lowell, such as one reported by Andrew Jenkins, manager of the Newmarket Manufacturing Company. Newmarket, which produced nylon tents and balloon cloth, conducted time studies and sent an academic study group into the plant to gain the good will and cooperation of workers. Following the studies, it doubled the speed of work, no doubt contributing to the TWUA's success in finally organizing Newmarket and in a dispute sent to the NWLB.[42] (When interviewed, Jenkins insisted little labor organizing existed in the company despite the speed-up, citing IWW activities in 1915 as the last organized resistance.)[43]

But overtime, speed-ups, and increased efficiency did not keep pace with increased production demands and the loss of millions of men to the services. To compensate, young and elderly men and women of all ages entered and expanded the labor force. In April 1944, 800,000 more men over 55 worked than would have been expected in "normal" times. Abbott Worsted, several miles away in Andover, sent special busses into Lowell to get workers. Abbott advertised in the *Lowell Sun* for war workers' wives, high school boys and girls, servicemen's wives, housewives, schoolteachers, laborers, and store clerks. They "used anybody and everybody that could lift a bobbin," said Frederick Burtt, Abbott's superintendent. An eighty-year-old watchman was put to work making sure spindles were straight. "Dear old ladies could put up bobbins on rails." Burtt believes that "if it hadn't been for the old people . . . those mills wouldn't have opened."[44]

Increased overtime and inexperienced workers cut into productivity in some cases. Abbott found that untrained older people contributed to accidents. Such accidents threatened not only new workers, but also experienced people working alongside them. The accident rate was especially high during night shifts. Total accidents nationally in manufacturing rose from 286,000 in 1939 to a peak of 802,500 in 1943 and 786,900 in 1944. Accidents declined somewhat thereafter until 1950. In all industries, 1,603,500 accidents were reported in 1939; 2,414,000 in 1943; and over 2,000,000 per year from 1944 to 1948.[45]

With many Lowell people working two jobs, absenteeism rose, according to the *Lowell Sun*. The more hours a person worked, the less efficient he or she could be. In an extreme example, the late shift at the Navy Yard was notable for people sleeping at work. Given the demands of work and the shortage of workers, this problem tended to get handled laxly, with employees getting many warnings. Employers relied on the draft and wartime migrations to get rid of bad workers.[46] According to Richard Polenberg, for the nation as a whole, "absenteeism and a high rate of job turnover affected production more seriously than did work stoppages."[47]

Another reason may have existed for absenteeism. Although war jobs paid more than most workers had received previously, the work often tended to be extremely boring. Money and patriotism only partially compensated for dreary assembly-line routines.

Controlling Dissent

The atmosphere of world conflict offered management the possibility of extending control over U.S. workers to an extent that would have been impossible in peacetime. In the postwar reconversion, many of these innovations persisted.

The draft was the primary instrument that controlled working men. No single institution affected their lives more. The millions of men entering the service pressed upon work and social life of all, draftable or exempt.

The Selective Service System's most immediate impact fell, naturally, on those eligible for the draft. Many Americans believed the rich got passed over, while working-class men got "selected." In contrast to this contention, sociologist W. Lloyd Warner, in his study of Jonesville, showed that percentages of a social group in the service matched almost exactly the percentage that each group represented in the town. Warner neglected to note, however, the rank with which people entered the service. Interviews in Lowell suggest that wealthier men received commissions as officers—based in many cases on a college background—but workers usually entered as privates. Moreover, overwhelmingly working-class Lowell had a high enough casualty rate to be recognized by *Life* magazine.[48] Warner did observe that the upper class preferred the navy, thought to be the more elite of the services, while workers tended to enter the army.[49]

For employers, the draft was extremely effective for holding good workers and eliminating poor ones. Two foremen, Joseph Nawrocki and Paul Santilli, received exemptions based on their skills and dedication. These exemptions—granted at the request of Ames Worsted and the Boston Navy Yard—effectively tied the men to those employers. Ted Larter, whose father owned the Wannalancit Mill believed work quality improved "because a lot of guys wanted deferments. . . . They were willing to do whatever you wanted them to do in a pretty nice manner, or they were ousted."[50]

The draft was not an omnipotent control lever, however. Because it removed millions of experienced workers from the labor force for up to four years, the remaining men and women had tremendously increased power when they bargained with management. The draft as a management weapon could be wielded most effectively when used selectively, as it was against labor organizers and radicals.

Louis Vergados and James Ellis played key roles in a successful drive to organize the Merrimack Manufacturing Company, a drive that finally succeeded immediately after Pearl Harbor. Both men then moved on to organize the Boott Mill. Louis Vergados was drafted to stop the organizing:

> My objective was to bring [the Boott workers] into the CIO, but the CIO was charging 25 cents for dues at the time. And the loom fixers, who had been an independent organization for years (exclusively French—it was just a French drinking club) they had 10 cents dues. When we brought the weavers in with the loom fixers, to tell them [their dues would be] 25 cents would be to wreck the boat completely. So we had to move them in slowly. And I was getting to that, but [the draft] dragged me [in].
>
> They didn't care about [national Selective Service director] Louis B. Hershey's orders at all that the leaders should be given serious consideration for deferment. But because I was organizing the Boott Mill—and of course, Mrs. Rogers was closely associated [with the Boott Mill]—what deferment? They dragged me in right off the bat. . . . There was never any indication on their part that they were willing to accept the union. All their moves were designed for the purpose of destroying the union.[51]

James Ellis remembered:

> My dad had died in December of 1940 and under the Selective Service Act I would have been entitled to a 3-A classification. I had three younger brothers with my mother, . . . but at the time I was trying to organize the Boott Mills, which was at that time controlled by the Edith Nourse Rogers interests. She was congresswoman at the time. And they made sure that I was drafted. . . . And that ended my organizing days in Lowell. It was all part of a scheme. They felt that one troublemaker at least was out of the way.
>
> I didn't appeal it. As a matter of fact, I was in Washington on a war labor case or something at the time and I called my mother. She said, "You got a draft notice. You're to report Monday morning." I wasn't even afforded the fourteen-day furlough that was normally offered to draftees to settle their affairs before going."[52]

The ramifications of drafting two key organizers cannot be over-emphasized. Both men considered the Boott and the Merrimack as the important mills in the city; if these mills were organized, the rest of Lowell would be simple. The new Merrimack union ran into trouble soon after Ellis and Vergados left Lowell. The man who was hurriedly found to replace the organizers was also drafted, and key rank-and-filers moved to war industries. Other potential leaders now feared the draft more than ever. By the end of the war, the company co-opted the Merrimack union. The Boott Mill was only successfully organized later in the war, ironically, under pressure from the navy.

Even in the service, the freedom of dissenters was curtailed. Officers harassed Louis Vergados for two years, during which, because of his record as a labor leader, he was continually transferred to undesirable jobs despite special training; he eventually received a special court martial. A dossier of his activities during the 1930s followed the second organizer, James Ellis, through the service. His Officer Candidate School examination consisted entirely of questions about his political beliefs and activities.[53]

Social pressure proved as effective as legal pressure to coerce organizers to enter the service. Thomas Ahearn, president of the Lowell Central Labor Union, also worked for the International Ladies Garment Workers Union (ILGWU) as an organizer, and had a wife and three children ages five, seven, and eight. He didn't get drafted, but soon after he began organizing at the local G.E. plant, he volunteered for the armed services: "You get sick of people looking at you walking down the street." The stigma of avoiding the draft was especially effective at neutralizing organizers who had to maintain a positive personal image. John Zawodny, a worker loyal to his employers at Wannalancit, faced the same hostility toward his 4-F status: "I got a few digs. As a matter of fact I had a fight up here by the city hall one time. Guy called me a draft dodger. I got a good rap in the mouth. I'll never forget it. . . . I felt like an outcast."[54]

Such pressure on men not in the services existed throughout the country. In Jonesville, "the young man not in uniform was constantly the recipient of blunt questions regarding his draft status." Warner found two cases in Jonesville of overt action against young men not in the service.[55]

All men, not just working-class men, felt the eyes of their neighbors upon them. The wife of a Lowell mayor recalled a man who committed suicide in part because of his 4-F status.[56] William Doherty—who recalled "one instance [in the metal industry] where a guy began to raise a little labor problem and he was drafted three days later"—ran a business, and enlisted because of the stigma he felt for not being in the services:

I went in the service because we had guys in our plant that were married with kids that were getting drafted. It got to a point where, though I didn't have to go because I was exempt, I went because I said, "the hell. . . ."

But the war was a strange mix of things. For instance, they said I was in an essential industry. Now this [other] guy has six kids . . . I said, "Holy Mother of God, if I'm going to live in this town, how can I walk down the street? . . ." I went down to the draft board and said, "I want to go." Said, "No way." I had to . . . get this guy from the newspaper who had some clout . . . to get ahold of the head of the draft board, Judge Eno, who is now dead. He went to Eno and he said to Eno, "He wants to go, now give him a release."[57]

Alice Swanton summed up the force with which community opinion hit the men who remained in Lowell:

Any male civilian that was around got a rough time, a very rough time. They were questioned—what were they doing here, why weren't they there, what was their excuse for not being in the service? But if they could walk and talk, everybody figured they should be in the service. No question about it, *they had a rough time.* In fact, so many of them got a rough time that they . . . if they had been deferred, unless they were actually *physically* so badly handicapped they couldn't possibly get in, *they went* because they couldn't stand it here if they didn't go. They couldn't take the riding they got and the abuse.[58]

Federal intervention in individual lives was also imposed through official agencies. Mayor Sweeney identified one to the *Lowell Sun* in 1943: "No single board has ever influenced the daily habits of people to the edicts of Washington Big Whigs as has the War Labor Board."[59] Although Sweeney may have exaggerated, the War Labor Board did control to some extent every major aspect of labor-management relations.

All labor-management disputes went to the three-person WLB panel in Boston (one labor representative, one business representative, and one public representative). The WLB had to approve all negotiated raises, and no strikes were allowed in war industries without thirty days prior notice to the board. When 130 Lowell cab drivers—certainly not essential workers—struck in 1943, the WLB ordered them back to work after 36 hours and gave the case to the National Labor Relations Board (NLRB) to settle. After their contract expired, 1,500 Merrimack workers struck in 1944. At the WLB hearing in Boston, even the labor members of the board lectured the Merrimack workers on interfering with war production; the strikers nevertheless defied a WLB order to return to their jobs. The strike ended when the company agreed to negotiate under WLB arbitration. A strike at American Hide and

Leather company ended in one day after the intervention of a federal conciliator.[60]

Thomas Ahearn, who served on a WLB dispute panel until he entered the services, described the board's operation:

> All increases had to go through the War Labor Board in the regional office in Boston. When there were problems they had a dispute panel. . . . The labor representative would meet with the union involved and their representatives, and management would meet with management separately. And then we'd get together as a committee with the representatives of both management and labor in the dispute to present the cases and answer questions. Then the dispute panel would make a recommendation, which was followed in most cases.
>
> The only case I served on involved the taxicab drivers of Lowell. The truck drivers union was representing them at the time. If I recall correctly we recommended a vacation depending on length of service and also an adjustment in their wages based on their percentage and an increase in their guaranteed wage.[61]

In each case, the WLB achieved peace by making workers forego possible immediate achievement of goals in return for a promise of government support for arbitration and a future settlement. Until completion of arbitration, the old contract or conditions remained in effect. As during the New Deal, government recognition of a dispute could deflate organized and heated drives. Lowell's heavy-duty truck drivers, among others, considered government intervention a delaying tactic and took a one-day "vacation" to express their dissatisfaction with the long time (two months) the WLB had been taking to settle their dispute.[62] Nor were managers ignorant of WLB's potential to control workers. The Newmarket asked the WLB to handle a dispute "to stabilize conditions," citing almost a dozen stoppages and slowdowns.

Conflict at the Boott before the war led to two strikes in 1940 and an arbitrated decision that the courts threw out in 1942. Eventually, with a union, a Boott dispute made it to the NWLB in June 1944. The NWLB did not settle the dispute, however; after a lengthy board process, the parties finally came to an agreement among themselves in November 1945.[63] The chronology of events after the NWLB received the case highlights the slow pace of its deliberations:

June 14, 1944	Case certified to NWLB
November 20, 1944	NWLB panel report submitted
December 18, 1944	NWLB Directive Order issued (an NWLB decision on the dispute)
December 23, 1944	Union's petition for review received (appeals process begins)

December 30, 1944   Company's petition for review received
January 13, 1945   Union's answer to company petition received
April 28, 1945   Supplemental Directive Order issued
September 13, 1945   Union gives thirty-day strike notice, charging company with not bargaining in good faith
September 26, 1945   Modified thirty-day strike notice, charging company with not bargaining in good faith
October 2, 1945   Company reinstates appeal
October 25, 1945   Case received in National Industries section
November 4, 1945   Parties come to an agreement
November 26, 1945   All appeals withdrawn.[64]

Paralleling the WLB's operation was the War Manpower Commission, created in the spring of 1942. Historian George Flynn concluded, "With the exception of the Selective Service System, no other agency offended as many people as [did] the War Manpower Commission." The WMC, through 1,500 local United States Employment Service offices and the local Labor Stabilization programs operating under its authority, severely limited the theoretical range of a worker's ability to change jobs.[65]

Everett Harris, president of the Lowell Building Trades Council, was labor's representative on the Lowell WMC. He recalled how it operated:

> We had one or two meetings a week on this War Manpower Committee. We had people working in plants that weren't on defense and they were trying to leave them and go into defense plants, which were a little more money for them. We had to interview them and see what job they were leaving. Was it necessary to keep them on that job or was it necessary to take them off to help the war effort? . . . So they'd have to come before this board here, the War Manpower Committee, and then we'd go through all phases of it and we either did move them or we'd tell them, "No, you stay where you are. . . ."[66]

Under Lowell's stabilization plan, approved in May 1943, workers needed a statement of availability from the WMC before they could be hired away from "essential employers." The WMC would grant this statement only for limited reasons that stressed the failure of a company "to employ a worker at his highest skill." All advertising for workers in essential industries was done through the United States Employment Service. Companies that violated the plan were punished by being denied referrals from the U.S.E.S. In addition, the WMC supervised training and placement of workers—often in cooperation with unions—and oversaw draft deferments. (Printed at the bottom of the Boston WMC's stationery were the words "Mobilize," "Stabilize," and "Utilize" and a reminder to buy war bonds.)

The WMC's Area Manpower Priorities Committee and the WPB's Production Urgency Committee met together regularly to decide on employment ceilings for individual companies, priority categories for hiring workers, construction, and staffing progress. Its decisions could be enforced by denying companies permission to hire workers. Both Parker Bobbin and John Pilling Shoe Company suffered this penalty because their standard week was only forty hours.[67]

The operation of the WLB and the WMC in Lowell support Staughton Lynd's conclusions twenty years later on the ultimate significance of World War II for national labor-management relations: "Despite wildcat strikes in unprecedented volume, the modern pattern of labor relations was firmly established during the war years. When a problem arose under the contract the aggrieved worker was told not to take direct action, but to 'write it up.' The problem then disappeared into a paper blizzard. Months or years later, a government board (after the war, an arbitrator) would make a binding decision."[68]

At Remington, the government maintained the final voice of control. Although Remington Arms operated the plant, the federal government owned it.[69] This was true not only in Lowell, but also at almost all ammunition plants across the country. Only in a third of such plants did private companies even share ownership with the government. Through the Defense Plant Corporation (a subsidiary of the depression agency, the Reconstruction Finance Corporation), the government invested nearly $7 billion in 2,300 war plants nationwide, following the model of the World War I agency, the War Finance Corporation.[70]

Finally, several informal methods functioned with indeterminate effectiveness to keep labor in line. Mill companies, sometimes with government encouragement, relied a great deal on human relations and traditions of considering a mill as a family. Fringe benefits, personnel offices, and visiting WACS and WAVES during inspections all contributed to maintaining morale . . . and a peaceful workplace.

More important, in contrast to their tarnished depression image, employers freely identified their financial interests with those of the war effort, the nation, and the community. References to patriotism and espionage statutes pervaded the atmosphere of most establishments. And the red, white, and blue army-navy E-Pennant awarded to many companies was intended as an incentive to workers: each employee received a tiny *E* pin to wear on his or her clothes.

When the Boott stayed open on New Year's Day in 1942, the company offered the national interest as an excuse, as the *American Wool and Cotton Reporter* told other manufacturers: "A notice posted by the management state[d] that the Secretary of the Navy has asked them to comply in vigorous prosecution of the contract, and their answer to the Navy Department gives assurance of the patriotism of everyone in the mill."[71] A similar appeal, invoking family and nation, greeted Remington workers:

> Today this industrial family is called upon to repeat what it has done many times before, to heed the call of our Government; to use their knowledge and resources and managing experience unstintingly to locate sites and build new facilities, to employ and train unbelievably large numbers of new people and to insure the United States Government all commitments will be met and the standard of quality, which meant so much to the success of our Company over the years, will be unfailingly maintained.[72]

Transformation of the Union

Throughout the 1930s, union drives to organize American workers challenged the status quo. In stark contrast, as World War II ended, writes Geoffrey Perrett, "The AFL, the CIO and the U.S. Chamber of Commerce acknowledged that the days of open warfare were over by signing a peace treaty in the spring of 1945 pledging each to cooperate in the postwar era."[73]

In part, union co-optation occurred both by conscious policies—government and business—and by the simple fact that increased power gave unions an interest in maintaining the security that a new status quo provided. Changes such as the dues check-off stabilized union finances, but also made the organizations less immediately responsive to grievances. A great deal of this transformation is rooted in events occurring and precedents set during World War II, especially the developing cooperation among powerful labor groups, corporations, and the government.

Ironically, postwar union conciliation followed a superbly successful five-year period of organizing workers during World War II. Based on New Deal labor laws, full employment, and the wartime federal policies—especially as expressed through the WLB and the WMC—trade union membership rose from 8,900,000 in 1940 to 14,800,000 in 1945. In fact, WMC director Paul McNutt ordered local U.S.E.S. offices not to help—directly or indirectly—employers seeking scab workers during

a labor dispute. The TWUA signed 844 contracts with previously unorganized plants between 1941 and 1946.[74]

In Lowell, decades of frustrating struggle to organize the textile mills
suddenly reached a successful conclusion. By 1943, the Merrimack and
the Boott, the two largest mills in Lowell, were unionized as companies
chose to avoid conflicts while government orders poured in. According
to organizer James Ellis, the Merrimack "management didn't try as
hard as they might . . . to destroy the union." After Pearl Harbor, a
state representative came from Boston to settle a Merrimack strike.
The Boott succumbed to navy and TWUA pressure and, according to
manager John Flather, an election "demanded" by the NLRB. At Ames
Worsted, the personal approach to handling grievances fell apart while
Ames Stevens served in Washington; the company, says his son Edward Stevens, "acquired a union, the only one we ever had." The
Ames settled with the TWUA in the spring of 1945; so did Newmarket.
Several smaller companies signed contracts with the TWUA, the Amal-
gamated Clothing Workers of America, and the United Textile Work-
ers-AFL.[75]

Everett Harris, a union steward, found organizing easy simply because so many more people worked both in previously organized plants
and newly organized plants. "There were people asking for organization. . . . It was an easy time to organize." The *Lowell Sun* reported
that membership in the Lowell Central Labor Union rose from 5,000
to 13,000 in 1943 out of a potential 18,000. (Official state figures,
however, show the rise in Lowell to be from 6,477 in 1941 to 10,592
in 1945, and only slightly above a 1937–38 peak of about 9,000.)[76]

The improved labor market, ironically, posed special wartime problems for unions. John Mullen, later Lowell Central Labor Union president and then a union steward, believed that

> such large numbers of women entering the work force was a confusing
> thing for most people to accept, especially some of the older AF of L
> people. CIO people were conditioned more or less for it where the trades
> people were not. And to have them involved in central council discussions
> of conditions, overall conditions, they weren't used to having women in
> the room where they could say [things] pretty much the way they wanted
> to express themselves. So there was, I think, an adjustment that the labor
> movement [went] through because of the large numbers of women en-
> tering the work force.
>   Strengthwise, why of course they were just adding numbers to their
> roster, but I'm talking now on the effectiveness of what each member
> knew the organization was about. With the large numbers of women
> coming into the work force, there was a tremendous amount of education

that had to be done at the same time to have them understand why certain things were done and why certain positions were taken in the work force.[77]

Of course, women posed no problems to those Lowell unions, such as the plumbers, which continued to be all-male.[78]

The most important hindrance to unions was the reverse side of government intervention. Although the government supported union-ization when it would stabilize production, regulations restricted or-ganized labor from winning major advances in most disputes. In-creased minor victories—or even the major advance of the right to organize—meant postponing or eliminating many major successes at a time when employers were vulnerable.

Nationally, the fast growth of unions, coupled with the loss of key organizers and many experienced rank-and-file union activists, neces-sitated increased bureaucratization and centralization of the organi-zations.[79] But beyond this, during the war years unions developed into a powerful tool for actually controlling workers. Union leaders from Lowell proudly reported that organized labor cooperated fully with the war effort, usually voluntarily, at times under government pressure. (The Merrimack strike in December 1941 ended when the navy pres-sured *both* sides to settle.) Ellis noted that the unions were "very lenient with the companies. We knew there was a war on . . . . We relented some, but not much . . . . [The navy] just didn't want any upheaval." AFL or CIO affiliates in Lowell called no major strikes for most of the war except, recalled Mullen, for a few short stoppages "to keep man-agement in order." At least through the spring of 1943, the anti-union *Lowell Sun* could say that "Not a single war plant has been affected by any strikes." That the Central Labor Union neither called nor threatened any work stoppages in this period led local conservative boosters to renew Lowell's nickname as "the strike-free city."[80] Thus, along with respectability came a new union conservatism.

Unions also played a role in weeding out dissident and "poor" work-ers. When the Remington plant was under construction, Everett Harris recalled, the workers wanted double-time on holidays: "But the gov-ernment wouldn't allow double-time, so the men walked off. And those men that did walk off, well, they were done. They didn't get back on the job when it was straightened out. We had to replace them. The majority of the men were from Boston. Then we had one of our own from Lowell that was in that group, but he had to go to Boston to work due to the fact that they took it on their own, not through the sanction of the union, to walk off on that holiday."[81]

When Remington fired workers who refused to operate more than one machine, unions again said nothing. At the Merrimack Mill, the union helped get rid of one man whom "they called a Trotskyite at the time" and who had a long history as a radical.[82]

The national no-strike pledge of major unions effectively prevented many disputes from interrupting production. The result was that most strikes were wildcats and officially opposed by the unions (although extensive unofficial support of wildcatters probably existed).[83] Wildcat strikes in Lowell followed the national pattern described by Joshua Freeman: "The typical wartime strike . . . was initiated without union involvement, might include the use of picketing, would last at most a few days, and generally ended as a result of union mediation. . . . It was the blatant, almost arrogant refusal of the business corporate producers to make even a gesture towards equal sacrifice that set the psychological background for the stoppages that did occur."[84]

Despite the national no-strike pledge, World War II was, however, far from free of labor-management conflict. In the course of the war, the NWLB handled 17,650 disputes involving 12 million workers.[85] The number of strikes stayed at prewar levels, dropping slightly in 1942 and 1943, but peaking in 1941 and 1944 and after. In the textile and labor industries, work stoppages in all war years were higher than in 1938, 1939, or 1946 to 1950, but lower than in 1937, the CIO's peak organizing year. By the spring of 1945, 30 to 40 strikes occurred daily.[86] The amount of time lost during strikes did drop from 16 million person-hours per year from 1935 to 1941 to 4,180,000 in 1942, but rose again to 8,600,000 per year from 1942 to 1944.[87] The major issues in strikes shifted from union recognition to wages, hours, and miscellaneous causes, showing the effect of government pressures on employers to at least accept unions' right to exist.[88]

No long-term strikes occurred in Lowell between Pearl Harbor and 1943. However, as already indicated, several short strikes and many slowdowns both with and without union sanction did occur, despite Mullen's assertion that "the labor movement in the Greater Lowell area didn't have any man-hours lost through strikes during the war years."[89] Continuous agitation plagued the Boott and the Newmarket, and the Lowell Building Trades Council called a few minor strikes during the war over "differences of opinion," as Everett Harris termed them:

> Some might have been [over] wages, some might have been conditions where the firing was unreasonable. Little things that were cleaned up pretty quick. Sometimes a steward put on the job by the union, why if the foreman in that construction firm might not like them or didn't like his attitude, why he'd turn around and probably lay him off. Well, the

union clause there was that the steward put on the job is the last man on the job, and he takes care of the interests of the union. So that would create a problem if he was laid off for no justifiable reason.[90]

The Merrimack had several strikes in the early months of 1942 before the no-strike pledge when management attempted to renege on several petty promises. In 1944, the city council had to appoint a committee of three to "meet with those involved in the strike at the Merrimack Manufacturing Company to see if something cannot be done to assist in settling the matter." The 1944 Merrimack strike was Lowell's first large-scale wartime stoppage, and the company initially refused to negotiate. The workers demanded a closed shop, a second week of paid vacation or a $25 Christmas bonus, and life insurance for all workers paid by the company.[91]

Despite sustained agitation, and in part due to its success, the war marked unions' entry into the mainstream of the American establishment, a fact recognized by their participation in government and social service agencies. Labor representatives sat on the WMC and the WLB both in Washington and in Lowell. The Lowell Central Labor Union (CLU), the AFL, and the CIO selected Sidney LeBow, Everett Harris, James McLaughlin, Daniel Coakley, and Alton Hodgman to serve on local agencies such as the draft and rationing boards. Everett Harris, Lawrence McLaughlin, and Edward LaBelle were appointed to the local Advisory Stabilization Committee of the WMC. As Thomas Ahearn recalled, "I was deputy controller in Northern Middlesex on civilian defense. I was on the rationing board. I wasn't on the War Manpower Commission because other delegates were assigned to that. You can't be on everything." In almost every case, labor appointees were the business agents or the presidents of an established union local.[92]

Unions also participated formally in bond drives, civil defense, and blood collections in Lowell. In one case, the CLU initially refused to help a Red Cross fund drive. In a letter to the Lowell Red Cross, CLU secretary Sidney LeBow referred to a national agreement stipulating that "representatives of Labor would be appointed to the local Chapter's Governing Bodies. This has never been done in Lowell." The CLU took part in the fund drive after labor representatives were appointed the next month.[93] It took continued pressure like this from Lowell's labor groups to gain their acceptance into the middle-class institutions. Ironically, the successes of labor in this respect detracted from the potential of working people to present a critical challenge to the patterns of life and economics in the coming years.

The End of the War and After

"It takes a war to put us to work."[94]

World War II's conclusion disrupted Lowell's life and economy almost as much as had its onset. Most new industries had been built specifically for the war and could not be expected to operate very long after hostilities ceased. Yvonne Hoar recalled, "They didn't last and people didn't expect it to last either—figured it was just a wartime effort." The Remington building in South Lowell had been constructed to stand only five or, at most, ten years. Knowing it would locate in Lowell only temporarily, Remington Arms Company had refused to build its own filtration system for its factories in the city.[95]

A major city council concern after V-J Day was to determine the future plans of the various war industries and to encourage them to stay. The council notified the local congresspeople "that when the War ends, that the employees of the various plants should not be turned out on the streets . . . and that they do all in their powers to have all the war plant [*sic*] to continue in some business."[96]

Efforts to keep the local economy strong had little success. U.S. Rubber, which had moved into the vacated Remington building, shut down on January 1, 1946. In the week after V-J Day, 2,750 people were laid off in Lowell.[97] In the first month of peace, employment in 66 Lowell concerns surveyed dropped more than one thousand, but the total in Lowell doing war work dropped five thousand. While 31 of the 66 establishments had war work on August 15, 1945, only 19 still had war work on December 15.[98]

The major factor contributing to the success that did occur in transferring workers to peacetime work was a large postwar demand for civilian goods. When the 2,750 people noted above were laid off, the U.S.E.S. office listed 1,200 job openings, chiefly in textiles. This demand, coupled with large numbers of women leaving work, allowed companies to keep from laying off extreme numbers of war workers, yet to follow their obligation to rehire returning servicemen. (Louis Vergados, the business agent and organizer of the Merrimack union, could not get his job back in the now company union. He went to work for the CIO at the Boott Mill instead.)[99] By 1947, Lowell still remained better off than it had been in 1939, with 25 more manufacturing establishments in operation and 2,300 more production workers employed. Total 1950 employment stood at 38,000 compared to 33,000 in 1939.[100]

The war and postwar boom improved Lowell's occupational balance slightly. Census classifications showed a slight trend toward more employment in the higher status categories. Those listed as seeking work had dropped from 4,437 in 1940 to 2,963 in 1950 (Table 3).[101]

The war then seems to have advanced the lives of working men just as it did for their employers. Jobs improved, income rose, unemployment dropped. Morale and self-image improved to some degree as workers could see a reason for the fighting abroad and some reason, outside of earning a living, for their labor power at home. This emotional security augmented the financial security of a steady job with plenty of overtime. As had been advertised, the American system could benefit capital and labor together.

The fact remains, however, that the depression ended for Lowell only when the nation went to war. The postwar prosperity, small by the wartime standard, was artificial and could only last until civilian desires for luxuries unavailable between 1941 and 1945 were filled. The employment statistics just quoted do show improvement, but they also reflect the contribution to prosperity of the cold war and the Korean War. Take away spending for war and wartime personal savings, and Lowell's economy came out essentially where it had begun: in a final crisis of decay. The rise of wages, adjusted for inflation, ended as early as winter 1944–45; real wages fell one-sixth from 1944 to July 1946.[102] When James Ellis returned to Lowell from the service, he found little change in the city: "The textile manufacturers controlled the city, controlled everybody, and they weren't anxious to bring in higher-paying industries. So the Lowell I found after the war was pretty much the same. It was heading in the same direction, and they failed to diversify the city when they had the opportunity to do it. And when the mills, when the textile industry started to migrate to the South, then Lowell and Lawrence and the whole Merrimack Valley found itself in a very depressed situation."[103]

It became clear that short-term victory in war did not mean long-term prosperity for Lowell's working men. Lowell's return to depression was sealed in the early 1950s when both the Boott and the Merrimack closed and war industries moved closer to Boston. The war could not alter Lowell's position as a nineteenth-century anachronism in the twentieth century. On the contrary, it had postponed tackling necessary transformations of the city. Further, as the disillusioning cap to the twenty years of essential stagnation that began in 1925, war solidified the almost unanimous opinion that peacetime progress was impossible.

Meanwhile, victory in a war for freedom internationally helped transform homefront institutions in a manner that made fundamental change even more necessary. Even the power of unions to fight for

Table 3: Employment in Lowell

	1940				1950			
	Men	Women	Total	% of total work force	Men	Women	Total	% of full-time work force
Professional & semi-pro.	1,084	1,515	2,599	8	1,392	1,826	3,218	9
Managers, officials, proprietors	2,008	225	2,233	7	2,341	383	2,724	7
Clerical & kindred	1,306	1,910	3,216	10	1,545	2,775	4,320	11
Sales	1,685	897	2,582	8	1,483	978	2,461	7
Craftsmen foremen & kindred	4,048	134	4,182	13	5,011	250	5,261	14
Service (except household)	1,794	945	2,739	9	2,150	1,096	3,246	9
Laborers (except farm & mine)	1,664	105	1,769	5	1,936	109	2,045	5
Operatives & kindred	7,903	4,967	12,870	40	8,075	6,236	14,311	38

Sources: Bureau of the Census, *Population, 1940, Third Series, Massachusetts,* 31–33; *Population, 1950, Massachusetts,* 21–78.

their workers was lessened: the success of organizing in Lowell and New England was a double-edged sword. While it strengthened worker power in one region, it hastened the movement of the textile industry to regions where state power had combined with corporate power to secure a union-free environment. Victory at home, therefore, like victory in war, proved a passing glory.

NOTES

1. Interview with James Ellis, 16 June 1975.
2. United States Bureau of the Budget, Committee on Records of War Administration, War Records Section, *The United States at War* (1946; repr., New York: Da Capo Press, 1972), 173; United States Department of Commerce, Bureau of the Census, *Population, The Labor Force,* pt. 3 (Washington: GPO, 1943), 31, 449; *Population,* vol. 2: *Characteristics of the Population,* pt. 1, *U.S. Summary* (Washington: GPO, 1943), 49, 97, 98, 173, 174; *Historical Statistics of the United States from Colonial Times to the Present* (Washington: GPO, 1976), 127; Alan Clive, *State of War: Michigan in World War II* (Ann Arbor: University of Michigan Press, 1979), 30.
3. United States Department of Commerce, Bureau of the Census, *Sixteenth Census of the United States: 1940, Census of Manufactures, 1939,* vol. 3 (Washington: GPO, 1942), 421, 457; United States Department of Labor, Bureau of Labor Statistics, *Employment and Payrolls, January 1937* (Washington: GPO, 1939), 8.
4. City of Lowell, "Journal of the City Council," typescript, 15 July 1941; U.S.E.S., *Monthly Labor Market Report,* 16 March 1942–15 April 1942, 12; U.S.E.S., *Joint Quarterly Statistical Bulletin,* April 1942–June 1942, 17.
5. Lowell, "City Council Journal," 16 March 1943; David Hinshaw, *The Home Front* (New York: G. P. Putnam's Sons, 1943), 149–50.
6. Department of Labor and Industries, "Census of Manufactures—1950—Lowell," 2–3; *Boston Herald Traveller,* 12 January 1941.
7. Interview with Jean Bellefeuille, 15 July 1975.
8. Interview with Thomas Ahearn, 8 March 1976; National Archives, Record Group 211, "WMC Records."
9. Massachusetts Department of Labor and Industries, Division of Statistics, "Employment in War Work in Leading Manufacturing Industries and Municipalities in April 1945," mimeographed (n.p.: 1945), 3.
10. *Newsweek,* 5 February 1944; interview with Paul Santilli, 21 January 1976; interview with Everett Harris, 17 September 1975; *Boston Herald Traveller,* 5 April 1975; *Lowell Daily Sun,* 28 January 1944, 1.
11. Confidential interview; Lowell, "City Council Journal," passim.
12. Interview with Jean Bellefeuille.
13. Bureau of the Census, *Census of Manufactures, 1939,* 457; interview with Jean Bellefeuille; Department of Labor and Industries, "Census of Manufactures—1950—Lowell," 2–3; *American Wool and Cotton Reporter* 57, no.

40 (1943): 34; records of the Merrimack Manufacturing Company, Baker Library, Harvard Business School, Cambridge, Mass.; George Q. Flynn, *The Mess in Washington: Manpower Mobilization in World War II* (Westport, Conn.: Greenwood Press, 1979), 39.

14. Frances E. Merrill, *Social Problems on the Home Front: A Study of Wartime Influences* (New York: Harper and Row, 1948), 15–16.

15. Richard Polenberg, *War and Society: The United States 1941–1945* (Philadelphia: J. B. Lippincott, 1972), 27; Joan Ellen Trey, "Women in the War Economy," *Review of Radical Political Economics* 4, no. 3 (1972):45; Richard R. Lingeman, *Don't You Know There's a War On: The American Home Front, 1941–1945* (New York: G. P. Putnam's Sons, 1970), 126; Textile Workers Union of America, Research Department, *The Nation's Most Prosperous Industry: An Accounting of the Postwar Financial Experience of the American Textile Manufacturers* (New York: TWUA, 1948), 20.

16. Interview with Andrew Notini and Barbara Notini, 27 January 1975; *Lowell Daily Sun*, 22 June 1943, 1.

17. Record Group 211, "WMC Records: Manpower Situation in the Cotton Textile Industry," July 1944.

18. Interview with Everett Harris.

19. Interview with John Mullen, 16 June 1975.

20. Lowell, "City Council Journal," 2 October 1944.

21. Interview with John Mullen.

22. Interview with Thomas Ahearn; interview with Hazel Fiske and Frank Fiske, 3 December 1974; interview with James Ellis; *Lowell Daily Sun*, 6 November 1944, 1; Textile Workers Union of America, CIO, *Executive Council Report, 1939–1941 to the Second Biennial Convention* (n.p.: 1941), 63; TWUA, *Fourth Executive Council Report*, 68.

23. National Archives, Record Group 202, "NWLB Records"; *Lowell Daily Sun*, 3 November 1944, 1; 6 November 1944, 10.

24. United States Office of War Information, *Battle Stations for All: The Story of the Fight to Control Living Costs* (Washington: February, 1943), 33.

25. Polenberg, *War and Society*, 29; OWI, *Battle Stations for All*, 32.

26. Committee on Records of War Administration, *United States at War*, 260; United States Department of Labor, Bureau of Labor Statistics, *Handbook of Labor Statistics* (Washington: GPO, 1950), 237; Lingeman, *Don't You Know There's a War On*, 126.

27. Commonwealth of Massachusetts, Department of Banking and Insurance, Division of Banks and Loan Agencies, *Annual Report of the Commissioner of Banks*, pt. 1, *Savings Banks and Institutions of Savings* (n.p.: 1943, 1944, . . . 1950); United States Department of Commerce, Bureau of the Census, *Sixteenth Census of the United States, 1940, Housing, Fourth Series, Mortgages on Owner-Occupied Nonfarm Homes, Massachusetts* (Washington: GPO, 1943), 37; United States Department of Commerce, Bureau of the Census, *Census of Housing: 1950*, vol. 2: *Non-Farm Housing Characteristics*, pt. 3, *Detroit-Memphis SMA* (Washington: GPO, 1953), 86–88.

28. Bureau of the Census, *Sixteenth Census, Housing, Third Series,* 44; United States Department of Commerce, Bureau of the Census, *Census of Housing, 1950,* vol. 1: *General Characteristics,* pt. 3, *Idaho-Massachusetts* (Washington: GPO, 1953), 21–18.

29. Department of Labor, *Handbook of Labor Statistics,* 111; figures for more than twenty-two major cities show retail prices for food 28.3 percent to 50 percent above prewar prices.

30. Interview with Claire Contardo, 16 September, 1975.

31. OWI, *Battle Stations for All,* 41; Polenberg, *War and Society,* 30; TWUA, *Executive Council Report, Third Biennial Convention* (n.p.: 1943), 103; Auditor's Report, 2 January 1943, Merrimack Papers, Baker Library, Harvard Business School, Cambridge, Mass.

32. Interview with Paul Santilli; *Lowell Daily Sun,* 13 November 1944, 1.

33. Hinshaw, *The Home Front,* 197–200.

34. Record Group 202, "NWLB Records"; TWUA, *Second Executive Council Report,* 14; TWUA, *Fourth Executive Council Report,* 68; interview with James Ellis.

35. Lingeman, *Don't You Know There's a War On,* 136; United States War Production Board, Program and Statistics Bureau, General Economic and Planning Staff, *American Industry in War and Transition, 1940–1950,* pt. 2: *The Effect of the War on the Industrial Economy,* Document no. 27 (Washington: 20 July 1945), 40.

36. United States Department of Commerce, Bureau of the Census, *Census of Manufactures: 1947,* vol. 3 (Washington: GPO, 1950), 279.

37. Lingeman, *Don't You Know There's a War On,* 136.

38. *American Wool and Cotton Reporter* 58, no. 6 (1944): 178; WMC press release, 11 April 1944, Northern Textile Association Papers, Merrimack Valley Textile Museum, North Andover, Mass.; Fisher memo, 11 December 1944, NTA Papers.

39. WPB, *American Industry in War and Transition,* 8; Committee on Records of War Administration, *United States at War,* 435.

40. Interview with Joseph Nawrocki, 31 January 1975; interview with John Zawodny, 22 March 1976; interview with John Mullen.

41. Confidential interview.

42. Interview with Andrew Jenkins, 31 January 1975; Record Group 211, "WMC Records"; Record Group 202, "NWLB Records"; TWUA, *Fourth Executive Council Report,* 47.

43. Interview with Andrew Jenkins.

44. Merrill, *Social Problems on the Home Front,* 14; interview with Frederick Burtt, 3 November 1974; *Lowell Daily Sun,* 21 December 1945, 15.

45. Interview with Frederick Burtt; Department of Labor, *Handbook of Labor Statistics,* 178.

46. *Lowell Daily Sun,* 24 March 1943, 4; interview with Frederick Burtt; interview with Paul Santilli.

47. Richard Polenberg, *America at War: The Home Front, 1941–1945* (Englewood Cliffs, N.J.: Prentice-Hall, 1968), 42.

48. W. Lloyd Warner, et al., *Democracy in Jonesville: A Study in Quality and Inequality* (New York: Harper and Brothers, 1949), 273–74; *Lowell Daily Sun*, 27 January 1944, 1.

49. Warner, *Democracy in Jonesville*, 273–74.

50. Interview with Joseph Nawrocki; interview with Paul Santilli; interview with Edward Larter, 22 March 1975.

51. Interview with Louis Vergados, 18 September 1975.

52. Interview with James Ellis.

53. Interview with Louis Vergados; interview with James Ellis.

54. Interview with Thomas Ahearn; interview with John Zawodny.

55. Warner, *Democracy in Jonesville*, 274.

56. Interview with Lydia Howard, 18 March 1975.

57. Interview with William Doherty.

58. Interview with Alice Swanton.

59. *Lowell Daily Sun*, 10 February 1943, 7.

60. Interview with Thomas Ahearn; *Lowell Daily Sun*, 12 May 1943, 1; 6 September 1944, 1, 12; 9 November 1944, 1; Record Group 202, "NWLB Records."

61. Interview with Thomas Ahearn.

62. *Lowell Daily Sun*, 30 October 1943, 1, 3; 10 November 1944, 10.

63. *Massachusetts Reports* 311 (1942), 223–27; Record Group 202, "NWLB Records."

64. Record Group 202, "NWLB Records."

65. Flynn, *The Mess in Washington*, 18, 107.

66. Interview with Everett Harris.

67. Committee on Records of War Administration, *United States at War*, 184; *Lowell Daily Sun*, 15 May 1944, 6; Record Group 211, "WMC Records."

68. Staughton Lynd, "Workers Control in a Time of Diminished Workers' Rights," *Radical America* 10, no. 5 (1976):7.

69. Remington Arms Co., Lowell Ordnance Plant, *Information for Employees* (n.p., n.d.):1.

70. Gerald T. White, *Billions for Defense: Government Financing by the Defense Plant Corporation During World War II* (University: University of Alabama Press, 1980), vii, 10.

71. *American Wool and Cotton Reporter* 56, no. 1 (1942):39; *Lowell Daily Sun*, 19 December 1944, 11; *L'Etoile*, 7 September 1945, 5.

72. Remington, *Information for Employees*, 4.

73. Geoffrey Perrett, *Days of Sadness, Years of Triumph: The American People, 1939–1945* (New York: Coward, McCann and Geoghegan, 1973), 403.

74. Perrett, *Days of Sadness*, 403; Polenberg, *America at War*, 42; Lingeman, *Don't You Know There's a War On*, 161; TWUA, *Third Executive Council Report*, 35; TWUA, Fourth Executive Council Report, 41; Flynn, *The Mess in Washington*, 118.

75. Interview with Hazel Fiske and Frank Fiske; interview with John Flather, 9 December 1974; interview with James Ellis; interview with Edward Stevens; *Textile Challenger*, passim; *Textile Labor*, passim; *The Advance*, passim.

76. Interview with Everett Harris; interview with John Mullen; *Lowell Daily Sun*, 2 March 1943, 9; Commonwealth of Massachusetts, Department of Labor and Industries, Division of Statistics, *Fortieth Annual Directory of Labor Organizations in Massachusetts, 1940,* Public Document no. 15 (n.p.: 1940), 92; *Forty-Fourth Annual Directory, 1946,* 116.

77. Interview with John Mullen.

78. Interview with Everett Harris.

79. Joshua Freeman, "Delivering the Goods: Industrial Unionism During World War II," *Labor History* 19 (Fall 1978):588.

80. Interview with James Ellis; interview with John Mullen; interview with Thomas Ahearn; *Lowell Daily Sun*, 1 April 1943, 14; 2 March 1943, 9.

81. Interview with Everett Harris.

82. Interview with James Ellis; *Lowell Daily Sun*, 18 July 1943, 1.

83. Rosa Lee Swafford, *Wartime Record of Strikes and Lockouts 1940–1945,* Senate Document no. 136 (Washington: GPO, 1946), 16.

84. Freeman, "Delivering the Goods," 583, 592; see also Ed Jennings, "Wildcat: The Wartime Strike Wave in Auto, *Radical America* 9 (July-October 1975).

85. Polenberg, *War and Society,* 157.

86. Perrett, *Days of Sadness,* 405.

87. Lingeman, *Don't You Know There's a War On,* 137; Department of Labor, *Handbook of Labor Statistics,* 145.

88. Swafford, *Wartime Record of Strikes,* 4, 9; Karl Drew Hartzell, *The Empire State at War: World War II* (Albany: State of New York: 1949), 74; interview with Everett Harris.

89. Interview with Thomas Ahearn.

90. Interview with Everett Harris.

91. Interview with Louis Vergados; Lowell, "City Council Journal," 6 November 1944; *Lowell Daily Sun*, 21 July 1943, 1; 16 August 1944, 1; Massachusetts Department of Labor and Industries, Division of Statistics, "Strikes of Long Duration in Massachusetts, 1935–46," carbon (n.p.: 1946); *Lowell Daily Sun*, 3 November 1944, 1; 5 January 1944, 1; Record Group 202, "NWLB Records."

92. Memorandum from John Mullen to Marc Miller, 16 June 1975; interview with Thomas Ahearn; *Lowell Daily Sun*, 16 August 1944, 6; Record Group 202, "NWLB Records."

93. Sidney Lebow to Theodore Reed, 6 February 1944, Lowell Red Cross Files, Lowell, Mass.

94. Interview with James Ellis.

95. Interview with Yvonne Hoar, 6 May 1975; *Lowell Daily Sun*, 4 March 1943, 1, 4; Lowell, "City Council Journal," 8 October 1942.

96. Lowell, "City Council Journal," 13 August 1945; 20 August 1945.

97. *Lowell Daily Sun*, 10 October 1946, 1; U.S.E.S., *Joint Quarterly Statistical Bulletin*, April 1945–June, 1945, 3.

98. Massachusetts Department of Labor and Industries, Division of Statistics, "Employment of Wage-Earners on War Work in Manufacturing Estab-

lishments in Massachusetts: By Leading Industries and Municipalities, August and September, 1945," mimeographed (n.p.: 1945), 4–5.

99. Interview with Louis Vergados.

100. Bureau of the Census, *Census of Manufactures, 1947,* 26; *Population, 1940, Third Series, Massachusetts,* 113; *Population, 1950, Massachusetts,* 21–78.

101. Bureau of the Census, *Population, 1950, Third Series, Massachusetts,* 113; *Population, 1950, Massachusetts,* 21–78.

103. Joel Seidman, *American Labor from Defense to Reconversion* (Chicago: University of Chicago Press, 1953), 240–41.

103. Interview with James Ellis.

3

Women at Work

From its origins to the present, Lowell has contradicted the myth
that American society frowns on women working outside the home.
In the minds of the men who conceived and planned the city, the work
force for this great industrial project would be almost entirely female.
Even the design of early housing for workers reflected this idea: the
city fathers built boarding houses for single women and their house-
mother-supervisors, rather than family homes that assumed a father
as breadwinner.

Although women were the labor force for Lowell's mill industry
when it commenced production in the 1820s, both men and women
took jobs in the mills as immigration increased. The balance between
the sexes equalized, but women continued to provide a significant
proportion of the labor force for Lowell's mills. As late as 1940, women
filled almost half the textile jobs, excluding skilled positions, although
women comprised only a third of the city's labor force. Only the most
basic mill positions were open to women, however: in 1940, women
held only 134 of the more than 4,000 supervisory and skilled jobs in
Lowell. At the low end of the scale, 46 percent of Lowell's employed

women were operatives on the eve of World War II, compared to 37 percent of men. Textile mills were, by far, the largest employer of women.[2]

The women who would staff war-related industries came from a variety of prewar backgrounds. Nationally, 49 percent of the women in war industries and 39 percent in essential supply industries had previously been listed outside the labor force. Of women workers new to the labor market, 55.8 percent had been housewives and 34.3 percent had been students.[3] The number of women working jumped from 10.8 million in March 1941 to more than 18 million in August 1944, reversing a downward depression trend that pushed women out of the labor market.[4] Many American women, however, had considerable prior work experience. Twenty-nine percent of women workers in 1944–45 had more than ten years' experience; another 19 percent had worked for over five years.[5]

Statistics specifically for Lowell are unavailable, but interviews and indirect data indicate that the idea of working was not a novelty to the city's twentieth-century women. The 1940 census counted 13,000 of Lowell's 35,000 women over age 20 in the labor force—double the national proportion.[6] A survey of women workers in the Springfield-Holyoke district, another Massachusetts textile area, showed significantly more women than the national average working before the war, fewer who were solely housewives, and more with over ten years' prior work experience. The *Lowell Sun* reported that "working wives have been the rule rather than the exception in Lowell for a long time."[7] Yvonne Hoar, who got her first job in the 1920s, followed a family path: "I worked in the Merrimack. My father was in there for years, so when we [his children] got of age he got us all in there."[8]

More Lowell women entered the work force after 1941 and in new jobs, but that doesn't mean they hadn't wanted to work previously. They simply had no choice with few jobs available. Significantly, only two people interviewed—both middle-class men—cited World War II as the period when wives began working.[9]

The creation of new jobs under war prosperity made the biggest difference for women workers, just as it did for men. In the 1930s, when Doris Poisson "was in school, there was nothing." During the war, those seeking work found that, in the words of *Redbook* magazine, "Women are needed almost as much as men, in modern war, to serve their countries." The female proportion of Lowell workers, 35 percent in 1940, was more than 50 percent by 1943.[10]

Until Pearl Harbor, the change came slowly. But when the transformation came, it was dramatic, as Alice Swanton related: "At first

. . . we were sending bundles to Britain. It was all over there. It was only when they started hitting home, when the boys were starting to be drafted that I think people realized we were in the war. And then the defense factories started opening up and Lowell was full of them."[11]

From Lowell's Mills to Boston's Navy Yard

During World War II, the same companies that employed Lowell's men employed its women. As always, textile mills—principally the Merrimack, Boott, Ames, and Wannalancit—were one major source of income. The other type of employer was new: war-based industries—within Lowell, principally Atlantic Rayon Company's Parachute Division, Remington Arms, General Electric, and United States Rubber, plus employers in the greater Boston area such as the Boston Navy Yard.

Mill work differed little from what women had known their whole lives. Old mills reopened, but companies invested only minimally in modern machinery; instead, they repaired antiquated machines to last "for the duration." Lowell's products changed from domestic to military uses, but mill tasks rarely changed, and workers learned no fresh skills they could take to other occupations. A spinner's task remained essentially the same whether the product was civilian cloth or army khaki.

What differed was the availability of steady work after first the Boott and then other mills converted to war production. In one twelve-month period beginning July 1942, women's employment in Lowell rose 53 percent; men's, 19 percent. This reflected the national rise in employment in cotton mills from 396,000 in 1939 to 510,000 in 1942.[12]

For Lowell's larger mills—notably the Merrimack—increased need for workers meant hiring proportionately more women. The draft and better work elsewhere monopolized the pool of working-class men. Before the war, 40 percent of workers at both the Boott Mill and Newmarket Manufacturing Company were women; by 1943, 60 percent of the employees were women, with the proportion still rising.[13] Atlantic Parachute Company hired women as power stitchers in early 1942, assembling a force of three hundred within a few months and one thousand by year's end.[14] At General Electric in South Lowell, where Dorothy Ahearn was an assembler, "It was all women in this room where I worked because it was small parts. We sat down at benches, with a table, and that's where we worked."[15]

As demand for workers escalated, Jesse Clark, wife of the Lawrence mill manager, went door to door asking women to work. This was despite the Lawrence's relatively small turnover.[16] The severity of the shortage of workers was clear in the women's page of the *Lowell Daily Sun* in 1944. All ellipses for this excerpt appeared in the newspaper, and the column's format made it impossible to know if U.S. Rubber had paid for the advertising:

> Honey, stop that grease from growing under your feet. If you're sweet eighteen or over ... if you have the use of your eyes, hands, feet and brain ... if you want to do something to help some guy trounce the enemy ... if you have any spare time at all and if you care whether or not this country says PEACE in 1944–45 ... then it's your turn to do the talking ... right up at the interview desk of the U.S. RUBBER COMPANY. The exchange of a few questions they ask you will run like clockwork ... you'll find yourself playing up your abilities without even a blush ... and the next thing you know ... they'll be offering you a JOB ... in fact, they're offering you that right now, before the interview even starts.[17]

Women disliked textile work at least as much as did men, and they showed it: although demand for cotton products continued, textile employment dropped by almost one hundred thousand nationally by V-E Day from the mid-war peak. In Lowell, many textile companies operated at half-strength. The primary cause of the drop after 1943 was not the draft, but alternatives—for men and women. Merrimack's velvet cutting department employed highly skilled women, but they quickly abandoned textiles for higher paying work at Remington and other war industries.[18] At Remington, ex-Merrimack worker Yvonne Hoar "worked with a couple of school teachers. They were elderly and I believe they had given up school, retired, and they were working there. People from all walks of life were coming to it."[19]

New, war-based occupations provided fresh routines, albeit still routines, for Lowell's working women. The biggest employer, Remington, created headaches for mill owners who lost their low-paid workers first to Remington, which closed on December 31, 1943, and then to its successors: General Electric, U.S. Rubber, and others. Remington's payroll reached 5,000, of whom 70 percent were women and 90 percent from the Lowell area.[20] A Textile Workers Union of America postwar report summed up the causes of the mass exodus from traditional industry: "Decades of mismanagement had resulted in a disinclination to work in textile mills. Wages were low, so the workers sought other industries. Mills were physically unattractive and management continued ancient practices; accordingly, they could not attract enough workers to their mills."[21]

Remington produced .50 caliber armor piercing cartridges and, in the opinion of the *Lowell Sun,* was "the biggest thing that has happened to this city since the Cartridge Shop was going full blast during the last war."[22] The tasks Remington women performed ranged from grease monkey for the machines to "floor ladies." Most women worked on the assembly line. With "skilled key workers . . . transferred from the parent company" in Connecticut,[23] Yvonne Hoar's tasks proved fully as tedious as had her mill jobs:

> We'd sit there with a big box of bullets, and we'd have to inspect the bullets to see if they were all smooth and the tips were right and everything, and pack them in a box. I believe there was a dozen to a box. And we'd have to put them on a conveyor belt, and there was a girl at the end of the conveyor belt that would seal them and count them. Then they'd be packed into cartons and shipped from there. . . .
>
> There must have been a dozen or more girls on just one short belt. I would say it was [about fifty feet]. And, of course, when the belt broke down, well then, we'd have to keep packing the bullets and pile them on a table aside and then, when the belt started again, we'd have to keep putting them on. [The workers] didn't like it [when the belt broke down] because it doubled their work. We'd have to keep packing them, and then taking them off when the belt broke down, and when the belt started we'd have to put them back on again. And people were kind of resentful of that.[24]

Textile tasks, although they paid less, almost always involved some skill and experience. The U.S. Department of Labor describes the detailed demands on a weaver:

> Operates battery of looms to weave yarn into cloth: Observes cloth being woven to detect weaving defects. Removes defects in cloth by cutting and pulling out filling. Adjusts pattern chain to resume weaving. Examines looms to determine cause of loom stoppage, such as warp, filling, harness breaks, or mechanical defects. Repairs warp break by tying piece of yarn to broken end and threading yarn through wires, heddle eyes, and reed dents, using hook. Repairs filling breaks by pulling out broken filling and pushing shuttle through shed to insert new pick. Notifies LOOM FIXER . . . of mechanical defects. Marks or cuts cloth when sufficient yardage has been woven and notifies CLOTH DOFFER . . . . May place quills or bobbins in battery or magazine of loom . . . . May replace empty bobbins in shuttle with full ones on nonautomatic looms . . . . May tend winding units attached to looms that wind filling onto quills.[25]

Textile mills were once famous for their mechanized production, but modern de-skilled assembly-line work had not reached into Lowell's mills of the early 1940s. Power stitchers at the parachute factory needed some training; Remington work required little skills and, unlike highly organized automobile assembly-line work, could continue even when the line broke down. Nineteenth-century mechanization put workers' skills under owners' control; twentieth-century assembly lines eliminated many skills.

The Boston Navy Yard and other government operations provided more varied tasks for Lowell women. The image of Rosie the Riveter remains famous, and some women found work at the Navy Yard in traditionally male occupations. The percent of women in ship building and aircraft jobs doubled by March 1943.[26] Far more women, however, performed traditionally female occupations, but for new employers. These occupations, long open to many women elsewhere, often meant novelty and variety to Lowell women accustomed only to mill routines. Claire Contardo's life changed significantly when she took on accounting and bookkeeping at the Navy Yard in an office of 150 people, most of whom were women:

> I was working at the Navy Yard in Boston in a supply department. I was in the stock control division there. It had to do with the supplies that the Navy Yard had on hand to supply the ships or repair the ships. Everything was in our warehouse and we controlled the prices according to how many we had on hand and how many came in. . . .
>
> I asked for the transfer. I found out that the navy was going to open something in Lawrence, and being so close to Lawrence we thought this would be easier to get to, the commuting part of it. So both Doris [Poisson, her sister] and I applied for a transfer and it was effected without any trouble at all.
>
> Over there I was actually asked to come to work again in a stock control division because I had the experience. But when I got there that division was not ready, so the commander in charge there asked me if I'd like to help him on personnel work to interview people to set up the different departments. And after about six months of that, when all the departments were ready to open, I had become quite interested in personnel work and he asked me if I would like to stay on. And one day a week I went into the labor board at the Navy Yard to learn more about personnel work, and I enjoyed it tremendously.[27]

Her sister Doris Poisson worked first in the Navy Yard typing pool:

> I was in a production department and when a ship came in for repairs, all the repairs to be done to it were sent up to us and we would have to type it up. . . . That is what we did all day, just typing those job orders— job orders they called them.
>
> From there I was in the stenographic pool. And then I became secretary to the production officer, Captain Rush. Everybody feared him. I was enjoying working for him. There my job was all secretarial, but the confidential part of it was when a ship came in and it was docked, I was the

first one to be called. The docking officer would call me and tell me a certain ship was in. And I would have to make a notice and send it out to be mimeographed and send it out to responsible people who would have to do the repair work.

I stopped in '44. I transferred and went to Lawrence for the navy again. It was a redistribution center. All the materials, I guess it was left from the war, they were redistributing to various naval places, I imagine. I don't know really. I was secretary there. It was on a smaller scale: you know, you got to know everybody that you worked with. . . . Then we went to Boston for the Separation Center. . . . There I was supervisor for thirty girls. . . . I stopped working for the government in 1957.[28]

These two examples are not isolated cases: they illustrate the novel, yet common wartime movement of Lowell women into such jobs. In the first two war years, two hundred Lowell women signed up for civil service work in Washington, a far cry indeed from the century-long tradition of mill work.[29]

Equal Work, Unequal Pay

To a city that had suffered fifteen years of depression, the most important homefront development for women, just as it was for men, was the opportunity to earn a living. In Lowell, the standard depression wage is simple to establish and was remarkably uniform. Before war and the Fair Labor Standards Act of 1938, most mill women started—and stayed—at $13 a week. Yvonne Hoar recalled, "Everybody was getting that. As my husband used to say, it was like a deck of cards; they didn't need no name or anything else, they could just hand out the $13. Everybody got $13."[30] The average salary for Lowell women at $18.65 in 1941 was only slightly above the 40-cent-an-hour legal minimum in 1942 set by the Fair Labor Standards Act.[31]

Remington's demand for workers—offering women a minimum of 55 cents an hour to start—caused mills to steadily raise pay despite the semi-rigid national wage freeze. Lowell wages rose to $23.60 within a year and to $29.10 by 1943.[32] Lowell women recall wartime wages ranging from a low of $20 a week to $70 a week on piecework. The most common wartime starting pay was around $30 a week with steady raises. Remington paid women up to $37 for a standard forty-eight-hour work week in mid-1943.[33]

National women's wage rates in Lowell's principal industries rose about 50 percent from 1941 to 1944. As a city with old industries, however, this rise lagged behind the rise for manufacturing in general.[34] This made Lowell more inviting to marginal employers and less inviting as a city in which to live or work.

It wasn't just mill wages that were low; almost all traditionally female jobs paid little. Just before the war, Doris Poisson "was teaching school for $7.50 a week. I could have had a job for three lawyers for $6 a week." It was a simple choice to decide to take a government job: "I was making $30 at the Navy Yard."[35]

Just as significant as women's absolute wage is their wage compared to that of men. The War Labor Board allowed employers to grant raises to women to help equalize pay and Massachusetts was one of four states to enact equal pay legislation during the war.[36] Indeed, the ratio of women's weekly wages to men's in all manufacturing industries in 1941 improved from .54 in 1941 to .60 in 1944. Nevertheless, the same ratio only for Lowell's principal industries, all old and all with relatively little capital investment by twentieth-century standards, reveals a worsening position for women in every case. For example, in cotton textiles, women earned 74 percent of what men received in 1941; by 1944, they received only 68 percent of what men were paid:

Table 4. Ratio of Women's Weekly Wages to Men's

Industry	1941	1944
Boot and shoe	.67	.65
Cotton (North)	.74	.68
Silk and rayon	.72	.62
Wool	.74	.72

Source: International Labor Office, *War and Women's Employment* (Montreal: International Labor Office), 207, 210.

It should come as no surprise, therefore, that Lowell women ran to assembly-line work at Remington and other war industries. Yvonne Hoar recalled, "It was better money at Remington, so everybody was leaving the mills to go there and make bullets, ammunition, and all."[37] (Even at Remington, women had to fight for equal wages: for the first few months the plant was open, Remington's minimum wage for women was less than that for men.)[38] Lowell women (and men), who traditionally stayed inside the city's borders, now took trains and car pools to Boston and Waltham. Although "nobody knew how many" worked outside Lowell, wrote the *Lowell Sun,* "the number is perhaps staggering. Their 1918 antecedents all worked in Lowell."[39] Thus, war brought—indeed, almost forced—freedom and broadened opportunities by releasing women from a small-city, single-industry environment.

For women with husbands in the services, the federal government provided a small supplemental income: the monthly allotment. Although the amount was a bare minimum on which to live—$50 per month for a wife with no children, $22 of which came from the soldier's salary—the extra money certainly helped women pay higher wartime prices. Richard Lingeman in *Don't You Know There's a War On* considered this $50 sufficient. "The $50-a-month allotment was of course not princely, but a GI overseas, with nothing else to spend it on, would usually send part of his regular pay home."[40]

More common in Lowell, however, was the experience that women on allotment lived with either family or friends. Contrary to Lingeman's statement, Alice Swanton had to send money to her husband: "They couldn't really expect to live on the allotment, not at $50 a month, and $21 of that my husband had to pay out of his check. . . . So the boys over there didn't have much money, that we would usually have to send them money for extra necessities. . . . We sent them packages and foods that they really didn't get over there, extras if you could get any. . . . And nobody squawked about sending it."[41]

Rather than rely on friends or live solely on an allotment, many women chose to work. Dorothy Ahearn: "The allotment just wasn't enough. . . . [I didn't like working] because I worried a lot about the children. And then I had to come home and work, too, do my housework. . . . I think a lot of women like myself went to work because their husbands were in the service or they couldn't make ends meets on the allotment."

Thomas Ahearn: "My wife went to work after I went in the service. She worked in GE over in South Lowell for about three months, and one of the kids always got sick so she stopped working. Later on, in desperation, she went to work in the Breslee tent factory."[42]

Thus, women workers used their paychecks not as pin money, but to support themselves and their families. This was especially true in working-class cities like Lowell. Women's Bureau figures for Springfield and Holyoke again suggest what probably happened in Lowell: in those cities, 87 percent of a married woman's pay went to support her family, compared to 77 percent nationally. More than half the women contributed their entire paycheck to family expenses, compared to a third nationally.[43]

War also changed payday in less dramatic ways. At the mills, workers had always received weekly wages in cash. Similarly, in her first civil service job in Washington, Doris Poisson "had to stand in line and get paid in cash." At the Navy Yard, however, "they went into the check system." At Remington Arms, also, wages were paid by check.[44]

The change from cash to check was not a minor side effect; it further rationalized labor-management interactions, making the exchange of money for labor more impersonal and routine. In the future, checks could be printed by a machine with a standard signature, and it became more intimidating for workers to question deductions—for taxes, war bonds, union dues, insurance, or anything else.

Unprotective Legislation

Along with better hourly wages went the possibility of working "men's" hours. Nationally, women's average hours increased from 38.1 per week in 1941 to 41.2 in 1944. A Remington survey of thirteen Lowell companies in January 1943 showed that at three, women's hours increased; at eight the work week for women was 46 to 48 hours.[45]

Just as important as the total hours women spent at a workplace was *when* the hours were put in. Before the war, women worked only the first mill shift, even when mills ran two (rare after 1925) or three (almost unheard of after 1925) shifts each day. According to Massachusetts state law, women were limited to nine-hour workdays, six days per week, and forty-eight hours per week. The law also required a forty-five-minute lunch period in any six-hour period and prohibited women from working from 10:00 p.m. to 6:00 a.m. In practice, women did not work in the mills past 6:00 p.m.[46]

Early in 1942, said the state *Monthly Labor Market Report,* "Lowell cotton goods manufacturers . . . received a waiver permitting women over 30 years of age to work on the third shift."[47] The Massachusetts legislature passed a law allowing the Commissioner of Labor and Industries to suspend any regulation pertaining to women or minors "as he deems necessary to supply any deficiency in manpower." Twenty-three other states passed similar legislation. Further legislation allowed the governor to suspend rules regarding Sunday and holiday work if "necessary to expedite the production, processing or transporting of war materials." Similar acts allowed suspension of seating, weight-lifting, and lunch-period laws for women. Dressing-room, rest-room, and toilet regulations were unaffected, as were prohibited work periods due to pregnancy.[48]

Taken together, these changes "for the duration" represented a step backward in protective labor legislation. They also continued the New Deal trend toward increased relegation of legislative power to the executive branch. Finally, the modifications all tended to equalize working conditions for men and women at the lowest common point.

Legislative changes affected all areas in which women worked. Women worked all three wartime shifts at the Merrimack; the company simply had to ensure that women leaving in midshift had transportation home. Similarly, mill women lost fifteen minutes from their standard lunch period, supposedly to make the shifts more efficient. After the war, women continued to work until 11:00 p.m., and the shortened lunch period remained in effect.[49] By 1944, cotton manufacturers were expected to keep all women—except those "with bona fide household responsibilities which made them available for part-time work only"—at work forty-eight hours per week.[50] At Remington, said Alice Swanton, there were "three shifts; you alternated the shifts. Every two weeks you worked a different shift."[51]

Boston Navy Yard women had the most demanding schedules because the Yard ran three shifts a day, seven days a week. Doris Poisson relates:

> Once war was declared . . . there was always somebody at the Yard, seven days a week. So the hours were there. It was sort of a shift. I worked nights for two weeks and two weeks days. I worked an eight-hour day, but sometimes you'd go five days and have a day off and then you'd go fifteen days before you had another day off.
>
> I travelled by train. I took the train at 6:30 in the morning; we came back about 6 o'clock at night. And then for a couple of years I did it by car, and then I had to leave at 6:00 to pick up my car full of people. I'd come back at 6:30.[52]

Claire Contardo worked six days per week at the Navy Yard, plus one Sunday each month "because the phone had to be covered seven days a week.[53]

The net effect of these changes on war production is an open question. Undoubtedly, more workers working more hours meant more production. No one in Lowell reported decreasing efficiency as women worked longer, although the *Lowell Sun,* quoting a management source, reported high absenteeism in the mills.[54] Evidence from other parts of the United States varied. A Women's Bureau *Bulletin* article by Margaret Kay Anderson stated that "as months of war work lengthened into years during World War II, reports of increasing fatigue among women employees became numerous; absenteeism occasioned much comment; and in the summer of 1943 the War Production Board reported a slowdown of production." Directly contradicting this is Richard Polenberg's conclusion in *War and Society:* "As long as the work week did not exceed 48 hours, there was no difference in either the productivity or efficiency of men and women."[55]

It appears that Polenberg's statement generally describes Lowell. In woolen, worsted, and cotton goods, fewer workers made far more worth of products for their employers in 1945 than in 1940. Production per dollar of wages stayed relatively constant despite any increased fatigue or absenteeism.[56] (Unfortunately, the cotton industry was one of several for which the government did not report national output per worker-hour for the war years.)[57] The proportion of manufacturing costs represented by workers' wages, in fact, declined in all Lowell industries.

Discipline, Security and Their Limits

The atmosphere of war in the United States allowed a greater emphasis on "security" in the workplace. Ostensibly intended to prevent sabotage, such measures reinforced the already authoritarian atmosphere of the factory or mill.

In Lowell, Lawrence Mill manager Jesse Clark asked all employees their ethnic background, supposedly in order to expose potential "German agents." According to Clark, the war was when things began to tighten up in terms of knowing about everybody. Significantly, one Franco-American, angered at this mild inquisition, responded, "We are all Americans."[58] No one questioned the need for every worker in war industries to be fingerprinted. Indeed, guarding against sabotage and fingerprinting war workers were two major police jobs in wartime Lowell, despite the lack of evidence that either was necessary.[59]

As a war production plant, Remington had more security regulations than did textile mills. To get in each day, employees had to show a photo badge to guards posted at the gate. With each paycheck came an entry pass for the following week. Instructions in the employees' handbook included numerous rules governing security: the carrying of weapons was prohibited, visitors had to be authorized, passes were required in order to carry out any packages, and cameras were prohibited.[60]

Reality at Remington, however, did not always match theory. "There was a lot of security, [but] it didn't seem too worth a darn," said Yvonne Hoar. "You had to have your picture taken and you couldn't go in unless you had your picture and your number. [But] if you tell them you forgot it, you'd just walk in and that was it."[61]

Even more surprising is the experience of *Lowell Sun* photographer Dow Case. He wanted to tour the plant, but no one was at the gate to direct him to the Remington office where he could get permission and a guide. He decided to enter the grounds and start snapping pictures, assuming he quickly would get shown to the office. After a half hour of uninterrupted picture taking, Case gave up and returned to the newspaper.[62]

The Boston Navy Yard observed security regulations more strictly, as the results of disobeying the regulations indicated. Doris Poisson, through her confidential work, learned of the arrival of her brother's ship:

> Of course you were never supposed to tell, not even at home or anything. He came in to South Boston dry dock; I was in Charlestown. So I decided I wasn't going to tell, so by yard messenger I sent him a note saying meet me at the station for such a train and we'll come home together. Well, he had to appear before the intelligence [board], how I knew the ship had come in, because they thought he had told me. He said, "Don't ever do that again. You don't know how hard I worked to defend myself." They finally traced back and found out how he had done it very reasonably.[63]

In another instance, Poisson got in trouble for talking in French at work:

> Only English could be spoken. They put up signs and one day I slipped. I met somebody, French-speaking person. And the intelligence officer was next to me and he came over. He said, "Where's your badge?" We all had to wear a badge. It was under my lapel, so I showed it to him. He said, "What language were you speaking?" I said, "French." He said, "What are you discussing?" I said, "We're discussing what movie we're going to see tonight," which was true. He said, "Don't you know only English is being spoken?" Oh, they were very strict on that and they had all kinds of big signs, like "A slip of the lip will sink a ship."[64]

Similarly, Claire Contardo recalls that the Navy Yard monitored employees' telephone calls as standard procedure.[65] As a security measure, monitoring calls could provide little real benefit, but the procedure could serve to keep women working rather than talking on the telephone.

The same rationale that led to increased security also led to increased discipline over workers' lives in matters unrelated to security. Remington's employee handbook included instructions on smoking, eating, telephone calls, address registration, cursing, raffle selling, and the "passing of papers of any nature." Further, "Employees may be transferred from one Area to another when it is considered for the good of the employee or the Company." This last rule was often invoked: when there was a lack of work in one department, women were temporarily transferred to another.[66]

Some rules were strictly enforced. Yvonne Hoar: "You couldn't loaf [not come to work]. If you loafed, they'd send somebody to the house to find out why you were loafing, if you were sick or not. . . . It was like playing hookey from school." When returning to work after being ill, an employee needed clearance from the medical department. And "there was loads [of supervisors]. Everybody had a title in them days." Hoar, on the other hand, "ignored most of [the supervisors]. I didn't pay attention. As long as I got in and did all my work, I figured that's all that mattered."[67]

Several factors contributed to this disrespect for discipline despite the psychological and social pressures of a war effort. First, people understandably resented a paternalism and supervision reminiscent of Lowell's company-town origins and anti-union reputation. A further dent in worker morale and loss of supervisors' authority resulted from the fact that most Remington bosses were male. Alice Swanton: "In fact, men bosses in plants couldn't really control the help because nobody paid any attention. They just called them a 4-Fer. 'Who do you know that kept you out of the service?' And they resented them and they let them—gave them all a bad time. They had no picnic. Of course, a lot of them had reasonable excuses for not being in, something maybe they didn't want to talk about. But they got really quite a rough going over from the women." The disrespect also flowed from a cause more directly related to the work itself, as Alice Swanton said:

> We worked there about a year when the rumor came around: "You know what they're doing with these bullets? They're dumping them in the river. They're really not any good." We didn't know why we were manufacturing them. So everybody became completely indifferent. Wherever there was a dedicated worker, there wasn't after that. There never was really any proof of that, but that was the story that was passed around. There was a small write-up in the paper after the war about it.[68]

Yvonne Hoar added, "It was a farce and it was a waste of money and everything else. And of course, worst, it was a waste of public money."[69] Thus ended the need for patriotic dedication to the work.

At Boston Navy Yard, women showed the same lack of respect for the men who were supposed to supervise them. Problems also arose from male riveters making passes at the women to whom they were assigned to teach skills, as Doris Poisson related: "We had a lot of women riveters on the ships, and that created problems. . . . I remember that Captain Rush was very, very strict. If a Navy man went by, they would salute him. He was real military. And he'd be on the ship and a man would be making believe he was teaching the woman how to rivet, but he was actually holding her in his arms."[70]

Claire Contardo reported similar events in the yard offices:

> At first what I was amazed about was the sailors were allowed to come upstairs on our floor to check invoices. And there was an awful lot of

fooling around, an awful lot of time wasted at the time. And they finally put a stop to that and then the sailors could not come up on our seventh floor. They could only come into the warehouses downstairs to check on their invoices. Most of the women didn't like that because a lot of them, had met these fellows and were going out with them.[71]

While barring sailors from the seventh floor solved the immediate problem, it ignored social patterns that made it difficult for men and women to cooperate in a work environment. Instead, the notion that the sexes must be segregated for efficiency was further reinforced. Burying the problem enabled the system to function, but the basic cause remained to hinder effective positive change. This sex segregation benefited the employers: it removed a cause of inefficiency and avoided potential labor-management conflict should individual supervisors attempt to interfere with social contacts between men and women. Separating men and women did not benefit workers. They lost social contacts they saw as a positive fringe benefit as well as an opportunity to challenge patterns that condoned this type of segregation.

The Freedom to Choose

While war increased security measures to some extent, it immensely raised women's freedom to change jobs. During World War II, Margaret Mead observed that "an important experience women have had, while the men were away, is moving about." In the first three years of war-induced prosperity, three million more women went to work than would have in "normal" times. Nationally, the proportion of women textile workers who changed jobs reached a phenomenal high of 89 per 100 workers in 1943.[72]

Undoubtedly, many Lowell women would have deserted the mills sooner had any alternative been available. The war created the alternatives. Such was the case with Yvonne Hoar and several of her friends: although they had been actively involved in union organizing at the Merrimack, they immediately left the mill as a group to move to Remington.[73]

Women didn't just leave mills and take up permanent work at Remington. New types of jobs opened up to women both in the mills and elsewhere. At the Boott Mill, women gained the right and the opportunity to perform eight distinct jobs that previously had been reserved to men. At Remington, Alice Swanton "was a grease monkey for a machine. I knew nothing about machinery. They just handed me a pail and a couple of grease guns and showed me the machinery and they told me, 'It's a machine, put grease in it.' All the men were gone so they started using women in every job they could."[74]

A local bank replaced men with women as tellers. The *Lowell Sun* regularly featured "Women at War"—brief portraits of individual women in previously all-male occupations. The newspaper's "Man About Town" column on the editorial page featured the story of Marion Anderson, whose child had been born three months earlier and whose husband was missing in action: "Marion Anderson is the girl who went all out for the war effort by being one of the first employees at the Remington Arms Company when it came here, and later won a minor distinction by taking over a real man's job because of a manpower shortage by becoming the proprietor of a gasoline station at the corner of East Merrimack and High Streets."

Throughout the war women changed jobs in search of better conditions, more money, and perhaps simply a change of pace. This display of women's growing independence was especially obvious in Lowell, with the state's highest quit rate. Free from the threat of the draft, women quit their jobs twice as often as men.[75]

Alice Swanton was one of about a half-dozen women who pursued better jobs together. When war was declared:

> I was at the Merrimack making $20 a week. I went to Remington and made $90. I went to United States Rubber and made a hundred. I went to Waltham Watch Company in Waltham and made a hundred....
>
> I more or less was on my own, that I could investigate all the new defense plants that were coming in. I could travel where I wanted. I didn't have a family, children or anything. And most of the girls that I [changed jobs with] ... were newly married women that didn't have children or were living with their mothers maybe and they were free more or less to move about.[76]

Some women, however, were unable to enjoy this freedom, as one confided: "The thing that bugged me the most was that all my girl friends were going to defense plants and getting a lot of money, like at the parachute factory in Lowell and all that. And I had to stay with my dad with a small salary because all the boys had left and he needed me."[77]

World War II also improved women's job choices by helping lessen traditional limitations, imposed by mill corporations, based on ethnic backgrounds. The workers' fight against such bigotry continued up to the war: strikers against the Merrimack in early December 1941 cited the owners' ethnic prejudice as a principal grievances.[78]

The arrival of Remington changed the situation. Alice Swanton recalled:

The Merrimack Mills were the most prejudiced place you could work. You were one nationality and one religion. If you weren't, you just took the crummy jobs. You never could hold an office job. That was completely out.... And ... you took what you got because you had to. It was a question of survival. You were just grateful for a job and you held onto it. You took everything they threw at you, because you had no alternative. And they had their prejudices.

[At the defense plants there was] no prejudice at all.... It was like breaking loose when we got into the defense plant, because it was a different attitude. They was all nationalities and people intermingling at work, [no] question on your religion or nationality by any means. In fact, it didn't mean a darn what you were. It was a whole new world. When you went there, they didn't probe to find out what your background was. If you were a worker, you met the requirements that they stated on the sheet to employ you, that was it.

I think that that about—you know, when the war came and the mills began to decline, that turned the tide on [discrimination].[79]

The 1941 Merrimack strike reflected the increasing organized activity of Lowell workers. It also reflected the militancy of the women in the mills. The paid union organizers at the Merrimack were male, but the fight succeeded largely because of women's militance. Alice Swanton considered Yvonne Hoar the key to the Merrimack victory: "That woman, five feet, maybe one, took on the whole Merrimack and she fought them to a standstill. She was amazing and she had the heart of a lion, but she was fair. You could have attended some of the meetings, and it was really something to see that tiny woman on one side of the table and on the other side were all the big shots of the company, the agent, the boss's management. But she called them on every question and called them on their prejudice."[80] Nationally, more than eight hundred thousand women joined labor unions, increasing their number to more than three million.[81]

On the other hand, war also led to corporate attempts to limit job mobility. With labor scarce, employers and planners continually pushed for government controls on where people could work and when they could change jobs. Although a "labor draft" never developed, hiring controls announced on February 5, 1943, were intended to direct workers into essential industries and reduce the type of turnover practiced by Swanton and her friends.[82] To be hired in an essential industry, a worker had to present a certificate of availability from the previous employer or from the U.S. Employment Service.[83] When Swanton decided to leave Waltham Watch Company after a pay cut, she had to get an official release:

If you worked in a defense plant you just couldn't quit your job. You had to have a release and . . . a very good reason. Say you figured, "Oh, I think I'll go work in another defense plant. I hear they're paying more money." You had to go up before a board and they questioned you on why you wanted to leave and you really had to put up quite a battle to get out of there usually.

In Waltham I was working on bombsights. I was travelling six o'clock in the morning, I'd get home six o'clock at night, take a bus from the square. You paid your bus fare back and forth and Waltham gave us $100 a week promised by the employment bureau if we travelled there. . . . And then that contract ran out. So then they got some other kind of contract which paid less which meant our pay dropped to $50 a week. . . . So we went to the employment bureau again and told them we wanted a release from Waltham. We wanted to go back to Lowell and work down here because it wasn't worth while paying bus fare and the long hours.[84]

The actual flexibility of controls is indicated by the fact that Swanton was allowed to take to non-war work despite opposition from the Waltham Watch superintendent:

The personnel manager of Waltham Watch came down and put up a fight. . . . He wanted to keep us because Lowell people were good workers and fast workers. And we refused it. We wanted to go home at night to our own home. So they had to give us our release. . . .

Most of us moved around from one plant to another. Wherever we heard the money or the hours were better or conditions were better or you had two extra benefits, that's where you moved to.[85]

Controls, in the words of one government study, "depended entirely on voluntary compliance by employers" and were laxly applied to workers.[86] As George Flynn concluded in his study of the War Manpower Commission: "Not only did Americans gripe about [WMC director Paul] McNutt's restrictions, they frequently ignored them. They flaunted rules while simultaneously telling pollsters that they were willing to accept more regimentation to help win the war."[87]

As with so many aspects of women's work during World War II, job mobility's real effect, therefore, was complex. On the positive side, jobs opened up and some ethnic limitations disappeared. Knowing jobs and choices existed let women feel secure enough to turn down the worst jobs and sometimes challenge employers. However, improvements often made a great deal of sense from a business point of view: they alleviated tensions between employees and employers over narrow job choices and ethnic discrimination that had been brewing for decades. No rational economic reason existed for keeping women out of certain occupations.

Moreover, the changes did not fundamentally improve women's working conditions. The threat represented to male enclaves was temporary, and few opportunities opened up for vertical mobility, only for horizontal moves. The percentage of women in supervisory positions was essentially the same in 1950 as it had been in 1940: between 1 and 2 two percent in each year, both in the United States as a whole and in Lowell.[88]

From the workers' point of view, hiring controls *were* a threatening precedent. First, although rarely exercised, their existence had some intimidating effect, discouraging workers from changing jobs and challenging working conditions. Second, the introduction of hiring controls set a precedent for increased governmental authority over work, and official agencies could build upon that precedent in future years to hurt workers as much as help them. Similarly, the precedent of increased control for alleged security reasons was more important than the actual laxity of enforcement. The pattern for government intrusion into the lives of individuals was enhanced, just as it had been as a result of most social and economic legislation of the 1930s. Corporate control over mill women did not approach the direct discipline of the early nineteenth century, but responsibility for maintaining a disciplined working class was already shifting to the government, thus helping defuse labor-management conflict.

The Joys of Work

What women liked and disliked about wartime work reflected the conditions under which they worked. Undoubtedly, "the feeling that we were contributing to the war effort" against fascism made Doris Poisson's time at the Navy Yard more enjoyable, but few women could afford to be motivated solely by patriotic motives. "A lot of [those who worked for Remington Arms] said it was patriotism," recalled Yvonne Hoar, "but it really wasn't; it was more money."[89] Money, of course, meant economic subsistence and introduced a measure of security and even luxury after fifteen years of depression. It also could have meant new independence, self-respect, power: all that work is expected to bring to men. Clearly, confidential government work could be equated with an excitement and sense of purpose impossible in the mills.

Working at the Navy Yard had other enjoyable aspects—or diversions—separate from the excitement of a patriotic job. Doris Poisson said:

Sometimes, when a ship was launched, they would ask one of the girls to present the gifts to the launcher. I did that once, presenting a gift to the person who had launched the ship. . . .

They had big bond drives. They'd bring in entertainers, bond salesmen. You could sign up right there. They'd get you emotional. I think you could get emotional about that. It meant something to buy a bond. . . .

Another thing that was a big uproar at the Navy Yard was when they brought in the foreign ships, but especially the French. The girls went crazy over the French sailors. They'd exchange a packet of cigarettes for their red pom-poms on their beret. They'd still be on the ship. They'd throw the cigarettes and they'd throw the red pom-pom down.[90]

The novelty of having a choice of work beyond mills and Lowell meant a great deal in terms of social benefits. Claire Contardo:

This was my first experience in a big place to work. I had never been out of Lowell to work, and the two places I had worked were very small. . . . At that time, I didn't even mind the travelling, the commuting back and forth to Boston. We commuted by train, mostly, for a couple of years, and then we had a little car that we used just during the nice months. . . .

When I was at the Navy Yard in that supply department, [my future husband] was at the coast guard station on Broad Street and we actually spoke nine months over the phone without ever meeting. Because anything the coast guardsmen would need for their ships, their cutters, any supplies, they'd have to come through our office. And where he was, he had to make these calls and I was constantly talking with all of them. Until one day our building was giving a dance at the Hotel Bradford in Boston. And I asked him if he thought he would be there along with the other coast guardsmen. He said he would go only if I went as his date. So it turned out we started going out together from that day on.[91]

Relationships with colleagues provided another social network, as working outside Lowell exposed women to new ideas about themselves and their work. Doris Poisson contrasted good relations with workers to attitudes towards supervisors: "Some supervisors were on a friendly basis, but some were very stiff. They pressured you a little bit . . . . But among the co-workers everything was beautiful."[92] Some women even recall more about life in Boston during the war than about their hometown as the focus of their lives transferred to the big city.

Women made their work lives more pleasant in smaller, personal ways. Alice Swanton needed to wear coveralls for her Remington job as a grease monkey: "We decided the coveralls weren't very becoming to us so we took the sleeves out and wore ruffed blouses underneath. And we were supposed to have hair nets. Instead of hair nets, we tied ribbons around our hair. . . . It was more or less uniforms. You had to call it coveralls."[93]

Nevertheless, women recognized and complained about the many farcical and petty aspects of their work. Discipline and security measures annoyed the women at the Navy Yard, and much complaining resulted when telephone calling and other social contacts were stopped arbitrarily. Remington came in for even more abuse: for its extreme security regulations, for the lax enforcement of these rules, and for the rumors that its products were useless. These invasions of workers' privacy and the distrust they symbolized directly contradict reports of dedicated patriotism. Moreover, the corporations' need for increased control implied that workers asserted their independence despite the combined dictates of a war effort and employers' exhortations.

Significantly, little complaint existed on the surface about the temporary nature of many jobs. Most women were either content about or resigned to resuming the old economic hierarchy after the war. It was common knowledge that the Remington plant, symbolic of the increased options for Lowell women, had been built to last only five to ten years.[94] Hoar called Remington "one of those fly-by-night things."[95] In addition, while women's work roles did change somewhat, the changes usually never questioned the relationship between men and women either at home or at work. Still, when the Women's Bureau surveyed women workers in 1944 and 1945, more than three-quarters indicated they planned to continue to work after the war.[96]

Postwar Realities

The onset of war pulled women into the active labor force; the winding down of overt hostilities pushed them out. The decline began even before the war ended: from June to September 1945, one out of every four women in U.S. factories lost her job.[97] Immediately after V-J Day, 175 out of every 1,000 women employed in manufacturing were laid off, a rate twice that for men.[99] By August 1946, the proportion of women in the American labor force had declined from 36 percent to 29 percent, but remained over the 1940 level of 25.5 percent.[99] Nevertheless, official unemployment figures for women remained low as women reportedly abandoned the labor force and as economic conditions stayed above depression standards.[100]

Events in Lowell both match and explain the national trends. Some Lowell women gladly left work after their husbands returned and found employment; these women had only seen work as a temporary stopgap. Other women left work in the postwar baby boom. As Claire Contardo recalls, she had intended to work in Lowell after her government office closed down, but she stopped working "exactly three days before we were married":

> The center closed. The Naval Separation Center had been set up until most of the officers who were getting out after the war were separated. And that was the end of my job and I had looked around for others—I was hoping to get something closer to home because we were getting married and had decided that we would settle in Lowell. My husband was from Boston and we decided that we would settle here in Lowell and I was hoping not to have to commute too far, because at the time we did not own a car.
>
> But then, not long after we were married I was in the family way, and I just abandoned the thought of going back to work. And I didn't go for quite a few years with bringing up five children.[101]

Many women simply left the labor force when war plants and several mills ceased operations between 1945 and 1948. Other companies, such as Waltham Watch, lost their lucrative war contracts and cut wages, thereby leading many employees either to seek work closer to home or to stop working.

In the first few postwar years, work did exist for most of those women who sought it, albeit at lower wages. The availability of work for those who sought it is, no doubt, partly attributable to the large numbers who chose not to continue working, given postwar options. The United States Employment Service reported that "elderly and other marginal female workers in Massachusetts left the labor market rather than accept necessary wage and occupational adjustments."[102]

The memory of the 1930s helped women workers accept ideas that today often appear questionable. First, many women may have desired to hold their jobs—or find new ones—but with a resignation founded upon prewar conditions coupled with propaganda sending them back into the home, they withdrew silently from the labor market. Although little stigma attached to working-class women who worked, both sexes continued to express the belief and to act as though it were preferable for the husband to be the sole wage earner should only one job be available per family. Only slight protest greeted preferential treatment for returning servicemen over women with seniority.

Civil service workers were most secure and worried the least about retaining their positions or equivalents, although even they rated behind returning veterans. And despite its wartime threats to the contrary, Merrimack rehired many skilled women who had abandoned the company to work at Remington. Wartime replacements hired by the Merrimack also stayed on, but moved to less desirable shifts and job classifications. Because men sought skilled work, the state, returning to prewar standards of men's and women's work, actually reported an excess of men in the 1946 labor market and a shortage of women. That is, few jobs existed for skilled workers (men), while women now refused to fill positions reserved for "marginal" workers. Unemployed women reportedly had work experience limited to war jobs no longer in demand. Other workers found employment in Lowell's shoe factories or in new and/or expanded military contractors such as Sylvania, Raytheon, and AVCO.[103]

Male-dominated unions, perhaps also fearing a new depression, fought to protect their newly acquired strength by concentrating on bread-and-butter issues. These organizations ranked the rights of their female members low on the scale of priorities. As a result, employers could treat women as a continued source of cheap, plentiful, unprotected workers. In Lowell, women worked in the increasingly marginal textile industry until, by the mid-1950s, the major mills had all closed, moved South, or out of the country—a change unions were powerless to prevent. The depression had conditioned women to accept "the inevitable"; indeed, it was obvious in Lowell that only the war had provided a respite from depression and narrow choices for workers.

The city's mood also changed after 1945. The tension of wartime life disappeared, as did the massive numbers of servicemen from Fort Devens. Soldier-husbands who settled in their wives' hometown tended to offset women who married servicemen from other regions and moved away. Other people besides soldiers and wives moved away, and stories circulated of friends and neighbors moving to Detroit or California for better work. Regardless of their extent, these migrations constitute an important factor for Lowell citizens because people felt the movements to be both true and significant.

Balancing the departure of people from Lowell was the feeling that a new group was arriving: returning servicemen, often strangers in their hometown. Husbands and wives often needed time to get reacquainted. Alice Swanton: "When you're married three years and then you meet again after four years, that's a long interval. You're almost strangers. And you try to take up your life from there on. It took us a year to straighten ourselves out, to get to know each other again, to get back into the routine, which we fell right back into. Got our own home and began to make plans for the future. . . . It takes quite a readjustment and it did in every marriage; it was a real big adjustment."[104]

The case of Lowell contradicts divergent interpretations of the meaning of the war years for American women. On the one hand, it has been said that World War II changed little, that reconversion renewed prewar standards in terms of the number of women working and their status.[105] This view stresses the still strong ideology prohibiting women from working. But in Lowell, no strong ideology had ever kept women out of the factories; local custom only restricted their *competing* with men when the labor market tightened. Lowell was a working-class city; ideologies that frowned on working women were peculiar to the small middle class and the rich. The ideology did not change; conditions did. When work appeared, women grabbed it; when prewar depression became postwar recession, some women left the labor market. Because changes in ideology played a relatively minor role in such decisions, the crucial point in determining the domestic impact of 1941 through 1945 becomes not war, but the economic effect of war: the end of the Great Depression.

On the other hand, World War II has been viewed as the turning point in the role of women in the labor force.[106] Masses of women who would never have thought of seeking employment entered the labor force; they took jobs previously forbidden to the "weaker sex." With the experience of work—both novel and traditional—women would continue to assert their rights after 1945, although some retreat was inevitable. This attitude, too, denies the experience of Lowell's working-class women before, during, and after the war: given the availability of work, household economics dictated that all able members of a family bring home a wage. Further, this interpretation flies in the face of current conditions: women continue to earn less than men in equal jobs; women continue to be shut out of "men's" work; women rarely have the opportunity to find "equal" work. Again, the change was not in ideology, but in the fact that employment became a real possibility during and after World War II. Susan M. Hartmann concludes in her study of American women in the 1940s that "a substantial number of women acted under the sheer imperative of economic necessity: whatever the popular consensus, they were compelled to order their lives in response to their own material needs and those of their families."[107]

In other words, interpretations of the long- and short-term effects of war on women can't focus on ideology, on mystiques, on cults. This approach tends by its nature to focus on intellectual history and, therefore, on the few, on elites. Focusing on Lowell workers seems exceptional at first glance because of the city's peculiar history. But that history only appears peculiar: it is a history focused on the working class, on the many. It is a history in which individual lives are clearly and closely limited by day-to-day economic reality. For Lowell women, ideology was a largely unaffordable luxury.

Claire Contardo:

My father was a plumber by trade and always worked at his trade, even during the war. But my mother worked in defense plants such as the Breslee Company that made the tents. It was here in Lowell just during the war. And I remember she had to wear these heavy coveralls like men because these tents had some kind of oil or something in them that they would get terribly messed up ... and they did have to wear these real farmer jeans. I remember Mother going to work that way. But she did work right through the war. ... She started really during the depression days. With a family of eight she went to work as a stitcher; that was her work.[108]

The Bitter and the Sweet

War brought income to Lowell women for the first time in fifteen years. And war brought excitement unheard of in the city's history. With money and diversions came a measure of security, but these also compensated for hardships that occurred in practically every family.

The story of one women, in its intensity, epitomizes both the obstacles women overcame and the inadequacy of official and private welfare institutions. In her case, as in many others, solutions came from herself, from informal assistance by friends and/or coworkers, and from changing economic conditions.[109]

For six months after her husband was drafted in mid-1942, Alice Swanton tried to keep the farm she and her husband had rented in 1941. But when no allotment check came, she lost her home:

I sold the car to pay for the stove. And the stove I sold to pay for the furniture. And we ended up bankrupt. When I ended up bankrupt I went to the Red Cross. I won't speak of that. I have a lot of bitterness about the Red Cross. I certainly am not a Red Cross fan. When I went there, the head of the woman's bureau that I spoke to, she loaned me $15 to get myself out of the mess I was in, to get myself an apartment. A Red Cross loan.

And then about two weeks later she sent me a letter, she wanted her $15, so I told her I didn't have it. I hadn't got straightened out because I had to send him money for cigarettes and I had my own expenses. And I was alone at the time, trying to get squared away. And she actually began dunning me. She happened to live in the same district I did. She'd stop on the way home at night and knock on the door and ask for her $15.

So I went to my congressman and I spoke not actually to Mrs. Rogers, to her secretary. He was always in constant communication with Mrs. Rogers in Washington. ... She sent me a letter and said she would get in contact with the Red Cross and they would leave me alone and as soon as things were squared away for me, I would repay the loan. And

I wasn't to be annoyed or bothered until they heard from me. So I wasn't and when I got my first allotment check two days before Christmas, I went over and paid them the $15.

This story highlights several significant facts of wartime life. A husband's absence meant more than a romantic loss or a loss of supplemental family income; it deeply disrupted the social and emotional structure of many women's lives and removed the established means of economic subsistence. "I had lost everything and had to rebuild . . . waiting for him to come home and start a future again."

Like many working-class Lowellians, Swanton has a great disdain for the Red Cross, which from all accounts and from Red Cross records, consisted primarily of middle- and upper-class women. They had little understanding, sympathy, or interest in the needs of the citizens of their own cities, except during major "natural" disasters.

When the Red Cross failed to provide real help, Swanton went to Congresswoman Rogers for assistance, not to some "small-time politician. . . . That was where you got help." After a decade of the New Deal, the sources of power and some justice in Lowell lay, in Swanton's eyes, in the federal, not in the local, bureaucracy. "Anything the servicemen's wives needed, we went to Mrs. Rogers. . . . She was a tremendous woman. . . . The whole time she was in office, nobody went to anyone else except Mrs. Rogers."

Actually, Congresswoman Rogers did not solve the problem; she only removed the harshest aspects. The beginnings of a real solution came from Swanton's friends, who took her in when she became ill. They then gave her a home until her husband returned: "I had a small apartment for a while and I became ill. Then I went to live with Mr. and Mrs. Hoar for the duration. . . . My mother and father had just passed away when the war broke out; . . . I didn't really have any place to go. Thank God I had Mr. and Mrs. Hoar. When I became ill, they didn't think I should be living alone and they took me to live with them. Most women had to go back to their families." Even more than this friendship, Swanton's relief came when she found employment that allowed her to support herself in her husband's absence.

One last part of this personal World War II history reveals the resilience and generosity of Lowell's working women, including Swanton. She relates her story today saying: "I was one of the fortunate ones. I happened to have marvelous friends. People went out and got doctors for me. I had sort of a nervous breakdown when my husband left, and I lost my home and everything I owned and then I ran into no income except $20 a week from the Merrimack. I lost a farm. Yes, there was a great disruption in my life, but thanks to good friends, they stayed by me and saw that I was all right."

NOTES

1. *Lowell Daily Sun*, 3 November 1944, p. 24.

2. *Handbook for the Visitor to Lowell* (Lowell: D. Bixby, 1848), 30; United States Department of Commerce, Bureau of the Census, *Sixteenth Census of the United States, 1940, Population, Third Series, The Labor Force: Occupation, Industry, Employment, and Income: Massachusetts* (Washington: GPO, 1943), 31–33.

3. United States Department of Labor, Women's Bureau, *Changes in Women's Employment During the War*, Special Bulletin no. 20 (Washington: GPO, 1944), vi, 3.

4. Joan Ellen Trey, "Women in the War Economy," *Review of Radical Political Economics* 4, no. 3 (1972):44; United States Bureau of the Budget, Committee on Records of War Administration, War Records Section *United States at War* (1946; repr., New York: Da Capo Press, 1972), 174.

5. United States Department of Labor, Women's Bureau, *Women Workers in Ten War Production Areas and Their Postwar Plans,* Bulletin no. 209 (Washington: GPO, 1946), 30.

6. City of Lowell, "Record of Votes 1937 to 1943"; United States Department of Commerce, Bureau of the Census, *Population, Fourth Series, Characteristics by Age, Marital Status, Relationship, Education and Citizenship: Massachusetts* (Washington: GPO, 1943), 31; Women's Bureau, *Changes in Women's Employment,* vi.

7. Women's Bureau, *Women Workers in Ten War Production Areas,* 29; *Lowell Daily Sun*, 24 March 1943, 4.

8. Interview with Yvonne Hoar, 6 May 1975.

9. Interview with Sam Pollard, 7 January 1975; interview with Wilfred Pearson, 2 January 1975.

10. Interview with Doris Poisson, 15 May 1975; Bureau of the Census, *Population, 1940, Third Series,* 31; *Lowell Daily Sun,* 16 June 1943, 1; Sidonie Matsner Gruenberg, *The Family in a World at War* (New York: Harper and Brothers, 1942), 204.

11. Interview with Alice Swanton, 4 June 1975.

12. United States War Production Board, *Production Wartime Achievements and the Reconversion Outlook,* WPB Document no. 334 (n.p., 9 October 1945), 81; United States Division of Employment Service, Massachusetts and Massachusetts Division of Employment Security, *Joint Quarterly Statistical Bulletin,* April 1943–June 1943, 5.

13. *Lowell Daily Sun,* 24 March 1943, 4; U.S.E.S. *Joint Quarterly Statistical Bulletin,* April 1943–June 1943, 5.

14. United States Employment Service, Massachusetts, *Monthly Labor Market Report,* 16 March 1942–15 April 1942; oversize volume 9, Edith Nourse Rogers Papers, Schlesinger Library, Radcliffe College, Cambridge, Mass.

15. Interview with Dorothy Ahearn, 8 March 1976.

16. Interview with Verner Clark and Jesse Clark, 24 February 1975.

17. *Lowell Daily Sun,* 10 November 1944, 9.

18. WPB, *Production Wartime Achievements,* 81; interview with Hazel Fiske and Frank Fiske, 3 December 1974.

19. Interview with Yvonne Hoar.

20. *Lowell Daily Sun,* 4 March 1943, 1; 31 December 1943, 1; oversize volume 10, Rogers Papers.

21. Textile Workers Union of America, CIO, *Executive Council Report to the Fourth Biennial Convention* (n.p.: 1946), 13.

22. *Lowell Daily Sun,* 4 March 1943, 1.

23. U.S.E.S., *Monthly Labor Market Report,* 16 March 1942–15 April 1942, 13.

24. Interview with Yvonne Hoar.

25. United States Department of Labor, Manpower Administration, Bureau of Employment Security, *Dictionary of Occupational Titles, 1965,* 2 vols. (Washington: GPO, 1965), 1:786.

26. National Archives, Record Group 211, "Records of the WMC."

27. Interview with Claire Contardo, 16 September 1965.

28. Interview with Doris Poisson.

29. *Boston Herald Traveller,* 30 January 1944.

30. Interview with Yvonne Hoar; interview with Hazel Fiske and Frank Fiske.

31. *Lowell Daily Sun,* 24 March 1943, 4.

32. Ibid.; National Archives, Record Group 202, "Records of the NWLB."

33. Interview with Alice Swanton; interview with Claire Contardo; Record Group 202, "NWLB Records."

34. International Labor Office, *The War and Women's Employment: The Experience of the United Kingdom and the United States* (Montreal: International Labor Office, 1946), 207, 210; interview with Frank Fiske and Hazel Fiske; Remington Arms Co., Lowell Ordnance Plant, *Information for Employees* (n.p., n.d.), 10.

35. Interview with Doris Poisson.

36. Chester W. Gregory, *Women in Defense Work During World War II: An Analysis of the Labor Problem and Women's Rights* (New York: Exposition Press, 1974), 180–81.

37. Interview with Yvonne Hoar.

38. Record Group 202, "NWLB Records."

39. *Lowell Daily Sun,* 24 March 1943, 4.

40. Richard R. Lingeman, *Don't You Know There's a War On: The American Home Front, 1941–1945* (New York: G. P. Putnam's Sons), 92–93.

41. Interview with Alice Swanton.

42. Interview with Thomas Ahearn and Dorothy Ahearn, 8 March 1976.

43. Women's Bureau, *Women Workers in Ten War Production Areas,* 50–53.

44. Interview with Yvonne Hoar; Remington, *Information for Employees,* 10; interview with Doris Poisson.

45. Trey, "Women in the War Economy," 45; Record Group 202, "NWLB Records."

46. United States Department of Labor, Women's Bureau, *State Labor Laws for Women with Wartime Modifications,* December 15, 1944, Bulletin no. 202 (Washington: GPO, 1945), pt. 1, 36–39.

47. U.S.E.S., *Monthly Labor Market Report,* 16 March 1942–15 April 1942, 14.

48. Women's Bureau, *State Labor Laws,* pt. 1, 36–39, 108; pt. 2, 4, 19, 34; pt. 3, 2, 10; pt. 5, 27, 44.

49. Interview with Hazel Fiske and Frank Fiske; interview with Yvonne Hoar.

50. Report to members of the National Association of Cotton Manufacturers, 2 May 1944, NTA Papers.

51. Interview with Alice Swanton.

52. Interview with Doris Poisson.

53. Interview with Claire Contardo.

54. *Lowell Daily Sun,* 24 March 1943, 4.

55. United States Department of Labor, Women's Bureau, *Women's Wartime Hours of Work: The Effect on Their Factory Performance and Home Life,* Bulletin no. 208 (Washington: GPO, 1947), 1; Richard Polenberg, *War and Society: The United States 1941–1945* (Philadelphia: J. B. Lippincott, 1972), 146.

56. Department of Labor and Industries, "Census of Manufactures—Lowell—1950," 2–3.

57. United States Department of Labor, Bureau of Labor Statistics, *Handbook of Labor Statistics* (Washington: GPO, 1950), 170.

58. Interview with Verner Clark and Jesse Clark.

59. Geoffrey Perrett, *Days of Sadness, Years of Triumph: The American People 1939–1945* (New York: Coward, McCann and Geoghegan, 1973), 101; *Lowell Daily Sun,* 1 April 1943, 1.

60. Remington, *Information for Employees,* 10, 16, 20–22.

61. Interview with Yvonne Hoar.

62. Interview with Dow Case, 12 December 1974.

63. Interview with Doris Poisson.

64. Ibid.

65. Interview with Claire Contardo.

66. Remington, *Information for Employees,* 8, 20–22; interview with Yvonne Hoar.

67. Interview with Yvonne Hoar; Remington, *Information for Employees,* 13.

68. Interview with Alice Swanton.

69. Interview with Yvonne Hoar.

70. Interview with Doris Poisson.

71. Interview with Claire Contardo.

72. Jack Goodman, ed., *While You Were Gone: A Report on Wartime Life in the United States* (New York: Simon and Schuster, 1946), 284; Lingeman, *Don't You Know There's a War On,* 148.

73. TWUA, *Fourth Executive Council Report,* 16; interview with Yvonne Hoar.

74. *Lowell Daily Sun,* 24 March 1943, 4; U.S.E.S., *Joint Quarterly Statistical Bulletin,* January 1944–March 1944, 7; interview with Alice Swanton.

75. *Lowell Daily Sun,* 11 February 1943, 21; 8 November 1944, 6; 23 February 1943, 1.

76. Interview with Alice Swanton; interview with Claire Contardo.

77. Confidential interview, 9 June 1975.

78. *Lowell Daily Sun,* 7 December 1941.

79. Interview with Alice Swanton.

80. Ibid.

81. ILO, *War and Women's Employment,* 237.

82. United States Civilian Production Administration, Bureau of Demobilization, *Industrial Mobilization for War: History of the War Production Board and Predecessor Agencies 1940–1945* (Washington: GPO, 1947), 702.

83. Committee on Records of War Administration, *United States at War,* 435.

84. Interview with Alice Swanton.

85. Ibid.

86. Committee on Records of War Administration, *United States at War,* 436.

87. Flynn, *The Mess in Washington,* 256.

88. Bureau of the Census, *Population, 1940:* vol. 2, *Characteristics of the Population,* 49, 97, 98, 173, 174; *Population, 1950:* vol. 2, *Characteristics of the Population,* pt. 1, *U.S. Summary,* 1–101, 129–30.

89. Interview with Yvonne Hoar; interview with Doris Poisson.

90. Interview with Doris Poisson.

91. Interview with Claire Contardo.

92. Interview with Doris Poisson.

93. Interview with Alice Swanton.

94. *Lowell Daily Sun,* 4 March 1943, 1.

95. Interview with Yvonne Hoar.

96. Women's Bureau, *Women Workers in Ten War Production Areas,* 31.

97. United States Department of Labor, Women's Bureau, *Employment of Women in the Early Postwar Period with Backgrounds of Prewar and War Data,* Bulletin no. 211 (Washington: GPO, 1946), iv.

98. United States Department of Labor, Bureau of Labor Statistics, *Monthly Labor Review* 64, no. 3 (1947):411.

99. Lingeman, *Don't You Know There's a War On,* 158.

100. Women's Bureau, *Employment of Women in the Early Postwar Period,* iv.

101. Interview with Claire Contardo.

102. U.S.E.S., *Joint Quarterly Statistical Bulletin,* April 1946–June 1946, 3–4.

103. Ibid., 3–4; interview with Alice Swanton; interview with Doris Poisson; interview with Hazel Fiske and Frank Fiske; interview with Yvonne Hoar.

104. Interview with Alice Swanton.

105. See Mary McKinney Schweitzer, "Women in the Labor Force, 1940–1947," M.A. diss. University of North Carolina, Chapel Hill, 1977; Eleanor F. Straub, "U.S. Government Policy Toward Civilian Women During World War II," *Prologue* 5 (Winter 1973):240–54; and Karen Anderson, *Wartime Women: Sex Roles, Family Relations, and the Status of Women During World War II* (Westport, Conn.: Greenwood Press, 1981).

106. See William Chafe, *The American Woman: Her Changing Social, Economic, and Political Roles, 1920–1970* (New York: Oxford University Press, 1972) and Gregory, *Women in Defense Work During World War II.*

107. Susan M. Hartmann, *The Home Front and Beyond: American Women in the 1940s* (Boston: Twayne Publishers, 1982), 26–27.

108. Interview with Claire Contardo.

109. Interview with Alice Swanton.

4

Working-class Life

Just as war invades the world of work, so too does it enter the structure and the detail of other daily patterns. World War II altered the lives of the people of Lowell; the most dramatic changes occurred in the lives of the city's working-class citizens.

Two factors had the greatest impact on what Lowell people did in their hours away from their work place. One was the presence—of work. This provided money to purchase both necessities and luxuries. The second factor was the absence—of people and goods. Many men left for the services and what money could buy was in short supply.

The Men Who Left

In an emotional sense, prosperity did not define war; the draft did. Despite news from Europe, sometimes listened to avidly in a city dominated by immigrants, few people in Lowell consciously attributed shifts in city life to World War II until soldiers started to ship out to Europe or Asia. But when this change came, it was drastic: nationally, one-tenth of women war workers had husbands absent in the services. Three-fourths of these women were under forty years old, so the departure of so many men of their own generation irrevocably altered the rest of their lives.[1]

Of course, women joined the services, too. One woman tried, but ran into a double standard that was being obscured in the working world:

> After [my brothers left] I decided "I'm going to join, too." So I went to the office and joined the WAVES, because they were in the navy and I thought I wanted to be in the navy, too. Then when I wrote to my brother in the South Pacific and I told him I had joined and I was going to help fight this war, he answered back, "If you join, I'll disown you as my sister because your place is at home with Mom and Dad."
>
> So I went to the recruiting office and they tore up my application. Very nice, huh? I guess they understood. So then I felt, while the boys are

fighting, the girls should be back home doing something. So when I saw that, I joined the USO and I joined the Red Cross. And I did volunteer work at Devens with the boys coming back. And I worked with the blood bank with the Red Cross. And the USO: I went to all the dances I could get to at Devens, just to keep up their morale. I guess I was thinking of my brothers, my fiance, and I thought it was my share.[2]

A never-ending scene during the war was the separation of families, which put enormous pressure on all involved and affected families for years afterward. When her husband left Lowell, one woman determined she would not cry and make his departure more difficult. The moment after he left she burst into tears in the kitchen, only to have him return in a minute to pick up a wallet he forgot. Alice Swanton's husband, as already mentioned, was drafted soon after the couple had invested their life savings in a farm, which she soon lost while he spent thirty-six months in Europe. Claire Contardo prepared for her fiance's return by "join[ing] things like learning how to sew, learning how to cook. And I just wanted to learn an awful lot. . . . He was gone a year-and-a-half and that was just the good time for me to do it."[3]

War created special hardships for a woman with a husband, son, or boyfriend in the services. Obviously, the most important fear centered on death. How well women stood up to this pressure is almost impossible to measure: people tend to remember or relate only cases of brave and patriotic waiting. Yvonne Hoar remembered, "I know my mother worried a lot about my brother being in. The people worried, mothers and parents and sisters, they were all worried about their sons and daughters and all that were in there. But outside of that, they didn't seem to have too much—of course, they kept to themselves most that they worried, tried not to show it and all."[4]

Claire Contardo had five siblings in the services: "There was a lot of concern, but I never heard [my parents] being resentful. . . . But I do remember my mother really following this war every which way she could, because of the boys being here and there. And she had put a big map in the dining room and, oh, she just followed everything that was going on during the war."[5]

Complaints about loneliness were voiced more freely. Dorothy Ahearn said: "It was lonesome, damn lonesome. Of course, I used to write to Tom every single night, and of course I'd pour out my woes and troubles and all the rest of it to him. That was my—I had good neighbors, though, that were good to me and good to the children. And I had my father. But it was a damn lonesome time, I'll tell you, when I look back at it now. And I think I felt worse for the children because they missed him so much."[6] Another woman confided, "I went home to Mother because I was scared to stay alone."[7]

Getting information about men overseas absorbed much attention from friends and families on the home front. Letters provided the best news, and women would "wait for the mail" despite heavy official and self-censorship. Swanton's husband "griped his way all through it. . . . Most of the boys did."[8]

Sometimes, however, little or no news would arrive. To compensate for any paucity of direct news, families would closely read newspapers and listen to the radio in an effort to pick up information. Lydia Howard, the wife of the mayor, recalled, "It was constant, the war news. You heard that the first thing every day." In 1944, NBC devoted 20 percent of its airtime to news, compared to 3.6 percent in 1939; CBS devoted 30 percent.[9]

Media cooperation was central to official desires to manipulate the wartime atmosphere. Radio stations and newspapers donated hundreds of millions of dollars worth of advertising space and time for wartime propaganda; they donated more than $400 million worth for war bond campaigns alone.[10]

To the donated ad time should be added biased news reporting; all media freely cooperated with the government in this. One *Lowell Daily Sun* reporter recalled, "It was very important to the government for the papers to get out the news." Therefore, the *Sun,* which had a daily page-one feature on Lowell people killed or wounded in the services, had no trouble getting supplies despite rationing. As the only surviving daily in Lowell, the *Sun* also received a great boost from plentiful government advertising.[11]

Lowell's movie theaters did their part not only by housing and running war bond campaigns, but also by showing special "public service" films. The head of the Lowell Red Cross wrote to the Somerville, Massachusetts, Red Cross about one such activity: "I have the film 'Women of America' which we used in the theaters and will be glad to loan it to you for your campaign. . . . The Lowell theaters were most cooperative in showing it several times each day during the campaign [to recruit nurse's aides]."[12]

The importance that people placed on war news makes the conclusions of reporter Phillip Knightley about the filtration of wartime journalism especially noteworthy: "With what were, no doubt, the best of motives, most Allied correspondents in the Pacific acquiesced in a system that gave the illusion of providing a free and open coverage of the war and its conduct. In fact, the result was the same as the system adopted in Japan—the public received only the news of the war which its government considered advisable to tell it."[13]

Inside Lowell, Victor Luz, a high school student during World War II, later reflected on the same phenomenon and compared it to what happened during the Vietnam War:

> People were informed more or less—or led to believe they were informed—the patriotic thing to do was to back the war. The communications system was so completely different then. The reaction now [1975] as compared to then was diametrically opposed because [now] you get an awful lot of kids reading, I think, about that [Vietnam], and I think probably it's because of the communications system. They didn't get that [during World War II]. They'd have to go to the movies or something. And everything was edited and geared, even as far as the newspaper was concerned, and the radio. Where we don't have so much now, almost like censorship.[14]

For those whose sons and husbands and brothers survived, reunions were the joyful side of separations. Claire Contardo:

> All of a sudden there seemed to be so many more people because of all the fellows that had suddenly come back. I don't remember it being a let down.
>
> We were just married and started a new life for ourselves and everything, so there was nothing let-down personally for me or for my husband. I'm sure that it wasn't for him either because to us it was such a good life and everything. . . .
>
> And while they were gone, you could have easily found an apartment and you [now] found that there just wasn't one to be had. . . . We were always looking, looking for an apartment, because we did live at my folks until maybe a year-and-a-half and then finally we found our own apartment.[15]

Being the one to tell a family about a death was perhaps the most difficult homefront task:

> I think we were just living on anxiety, waiting for letters. . . . And then, I'll never forget, one day this man came from the telegram office and he said, "Is your name ———?" And I said, "Yes." And I nearly collapsed there. And he said, "We try not to deliver telegrams. We try to find the right relative so that it's easier to give the bad news." And I just grabbed the telegram. I says, "Which one is it?" And it was my cousin who lived on the same street that was killed at Iwo Jima. And he said, "Would you go and tell his mother?"
>
> So I took the telegram and was shaking. It was just the anxiety, you know, we just lived with tension and yet there were no tranquilizers in those days. We just prayed and hoped that when the bad news would come, we'd accept it.

I had to take the bus to save on gas. I went to the priest of the parish and I said, "I can't do this. You have to do it." He said, "No, it's better if it's a relative."

So I knocked at the door, and I said to my aunt, "When's the last time you heard from him?" And she said, "I got a letter yesterday. He's fine." That didn't help. I said, "Well, I have the telegram here and it was bad news. He was killed at Iwo Jima." I'll never forget that day. She threw me out of the house. She said I had no right to do that, that it wasn't official. I left the telegram and I just went home and prayed and cried.[16]

One women remembered that events surrounding the return of wounded men "were done very quietly." In other cases, wartime furloughs and the final release ended war's tension, but rarely ended its effects on men and their relationships with the women. And for a few couples, years of separation were too much stress, and a long engagement ended in nothing:

My fiance was an m.p. and was sent to Italy to bring back the prisoners. And it turned out that he stayed two-and-a-half years. During the time he was there, his jeep went over a cliff and he lost his memory. So he came back with amnesia. That was the end of the engagement. It took me a long time to get over it, but there must have been a reason. . . . I had kept all the letters he wrote until when the letters stopped coming, I suspected something. But no one would tell me. I didn't know if he was missing. I didn't know if he was dead. I just didn't know. They were afraid to tell me, but when he came back and he didn't recognize me, then they had to explain things to me.[17]

In almost every case, husbands and wives had to learn to become accustomed to each other again. Divorce rates, which climbed slowly through the 1930s, rose faster in the early war years, then jumped dramatically as the "boys" came home. The rates then declined steadily until 1960:

Table 5. Divorce Rates per 1,000 Population

	1940	1941	1942	1943	1944	1945	1946	1947
U.S.	2.0	2.2	2.4	2.6	2.9	3.5	4.3	3.4
Mass.	1.1	1.1	1.3	1.3	1.6	1.7	2.3	2.2

Sources: Interview with Alice Swanton; P.H.S., United States Department of Health, Education, and Welfare, National Center for Health Statistics, *Vital Statistics Rates in the United States 1940–1960* (Washington: GPO, 1968), 102, 110–11.

From Birth to Death

Like divorce, other normal parts of life—birth, death, marriage—did not stop for war. Of course, births and marriages declined after Pearl

Harbor, then rose markedly after 1945. On the other hand, deaths peaked in 1943, but, outside of that year's high figure, remained relatively constant from 1936 to 1946.

Surprisingly, substantially fewer people died in Lowell in 1941, 1942, and 1944 than did in non-war years, although the opposite was true for the nation. Most likely, Lowell's decreased death rate reflected improved health care, better mental health due to employment, better diet, and other benefits that come with higher income. War dead contributed little to the overall mortality. Even for the United States as a whole, the death rate due to war hit 1 in 10,000 only in 1942 and 1945. Machinery caused at least ten times that many deaths each year.[18]

Economic factors seem to have significantly influenced births and marriages as well as reducing the causes of death. Almost surely, improving family finances led to the increase in births from 1937 to 1942. But even throughout the war, the birth rate stayed higher than the 1941 level. The security of a job apparently more than balanced the insecurity of war. In the postwar baby boom, all factors—economic prosperity, reunited families, and alleviated war tensions—worked together.

The vital statistics for a single parish, St. Michael's on Bridge Street in Centralville, reflected the city's overall pattern. As a working-class neighborhood, the statistics for this parish reinforce the image of the effect of prosperity. As in all Lowell, prosperity in St. Michael's meant more children despite war. It also meant more marriages than during the depression. Only limited figures for deaths are available for this parish, but the peak comes in 1944 as opposed to 1943 for all of Lowell. Perhaps working-class St. Michael's furnished a higher percentage of casualties as war persisted (Table 6).

Cooperative Solutions

While many married Lowell women had long been accustomed to working outside their homes, the war accentuated the need to cooperate to accomplish daily tasks. By December 1942, the active labor force had absorbed almost all available single women in the United States. This left married women—with and without children—as the only available reserve. Twenty percent of women workers and 32 percent of married workers had children under fourteen in their households.[19]

There are several ways women could have taken care of the extra burdens. No evidence exists that Lowell's working women gained much from *Redbook* magazine's advice on how women in war jobs could

Table 6. Life, Death, and Marriage, 1936–48

	All Lowell*			St. Michael's Parish**			United States*** (1/1000)		
	Births	Deaths	Marriages	Births	Deaths	Marriages	Births	Deaths	Marriages
1936	1843	1393	990	—	—	—	—	11.6	10.7
1937	1700	1431	991	—	—	—	18.7	11.3	11.3
1938	1882	1422	949	113	—	44	19.2	10.6	10.3
1939	1905	1368	1133	114	—	52	18.8	10.6	10.7
1940	1916	1440	1229	130	—	77	19.4	10.8	12.1
1941	2038	1326	1191	142	—	101	20.3	10.5	12.7
1942	2407	1320	1459	173	—	79	22.2	10.3	13.2
1943	2280	1524	909	157	105	60	22.7	10.9	11.7
1944	2192	1334	940	155	117	50	21.2	10.6	10.9
1945	2096	1408	1182	130	101	58	20.4	10.6	12.2
1946	2994	1401	1627	208	75	87	24.1	10.0	10.4
1947	—	—	—	236	87	69	46.6	10.1	13.9
1948	—	—	—	232	—	63	24.9	—	12.4

* Compiled and supplied by the City Clerk's Office, Lowell, Mass., August 1975.
** Compiled from St. Michael's Rectory parish records and supplied to the author, 19 May 1975.
*** P.H.S., *Vital Statistics Rates*, 105–6, 114, 316.

get housework done faster by giving up bridge games. Nor did the magazine's opinion that "about half the things women do could be done in about half the time or none at all" mean much in Lowell.[20] Instead, women turned to friends and family for support and security. Indeed, the depression had already taught the necessity of such community solutions in the face of crisis.

One form of cooperation widely practiced involved housing: families or single women would take in a woman whose husband was in the services, or several women might share a home. Yvonne Hoar, whose family invited Alice Swanton into their house, recalls that during the war people "felt more compassion for one another and tried to help one another out as much as they could. They were closer it seems. They were always willing to help out one another."[21]

Cooperation also contributed to childcare and housekeeping. When several members of a household had jobs, they would often plan work shifts so one person could be home. Mr. Hoar worked double shifts, while Mrs. Hoar and Mrs. Swanton alternated shifts.[22] In Dorothy Ahearn's house, her father "stayed with the children while I worked."[23]

Cooperative child care was especially prevalent in a factory town such as Lowell, where it built on tradition. Despite having eight children, Doris Poisson's mother "went to work [in the 1930s] because some of us were old enough to take care of the house after school. She went to work at the Lawrence Mills, but during the war she worked at the parachute [factory where]. . . . she worked the night shift, 12 in the morning, so that my sister-in-law, whose husband had been drafted, could go to work days. There was a baby, and they each took care of it."[24]

Although some federal and state child-care funding became available in 1942 and 1943, few families in the nation benefited. According to a War Production Board memo, "It seems as though most women found individual [i.e., nongovernmental] solutions to the problem."[25] Lowell's emphasis on extended family ties apparently matched that of the nation: "Care when the mother was away at work was given these children [under 14] most frequently by adult relatives living in the household."[26] The *Daily Sun* contained little news or ads about child-care options. Accurate figures for child-care arrangements are not available for Lowell, but can be assumed to resemble those for the Springfield/Holyoke area (Table 7).

In some cities, public day care did exist: "Federal government and local authorities," reports Karen Anderson in a 1981 study of women during World War II, "collaborated on a wartime day-care program unprecedented in its scope and level of commitment to public child

Table 7. Child-care Arrangements for Children under Fourteen of Women War Workers

	10 Areas in the U.S. (percent)	Springfield/ Holyoke (percent)
Husband on another shift	12	18
Older children in school	5	5
Other relative in household	36	32
Relative outside household	11	9
Maid in household	4	1
Neighbor	7	6
Nursery school	5	8
No care when worker absent	16	12
Other	4	9

Source: Women's Bureau, *Women War Workers in Ten War Production Areas,* (Washington: GPO, 1946), 56.

care. . . . The community had to assume responsibility for 50 percent of the cost of operating the centers." However, Lowell does not appear to have had any public child-care programs and, in any case, Anderson notes that even in cities that had centers, programs were often underutilized due to poor quality, inconvenience, and a continued preference for "time-honored methods of child care."[27]

In Lowell, household members shared marketing duties just as they did child care. Doris Poisson, working at the Navy Yard, was often saved from standing in long rationing lines by her mother or co-workers taking over the chores.[28] However, Margaret Kay Anderson of the Women's Bureau came to a different conclusion for the United States as a whole:

> In a few instances the marketing was turned over to other members of the family. Usually, however, it had to be done on Saturdays, if that day were partially free, or the women shopped during lunch period or took time off from work during the day to do marketing. The dinner hour was advanced under the longer hour schedules, and this later dinner hour left little time for other tasks after dishes were washed. Often Sundays became a day of laundering and cleaning, rather than a day of relaxing.[29]

Neither solution—cooperation nor adjusted, busier schedules— emerges as conclusive, although a safe guess would be that reassignment of tasks to others increased during the war. An answer might lie in food-market-item sales by the hour and by the day, if such figures had been kept. But Anderson's conclusions seem stereotyped and assume that women ran the family alone, that women had not already been accustomed to non-house work, and that women previously could relax on Sundays.

Transportation

Lowell had been designed in the early nineteenth century to allow workers to walk to the mills. World War II changed this pattern and forced workers to find new ways to travel. By 1944, approximately five thousand Lowell workers commuted to other cities, with most going to General Electric in Lynn, the Boston Navy Yard, and the Watertown Arsenal.[30] However, gas rationing made driving difficult; it meant carpooling to work and little pleasure driving. Claire Contardo: "When we did start commuting by car, it was the rationing on the gas. These coupons were very dear and when you were given your allotment, it was pretty hard to get more. So I do remember coming home every evening and even if we wanted to go anywhere with the car, we had to be very careful because these coupons had to be saved so we had enough gas for the week."[31]

Robert Lynd and Helen Lynd, in their 1929 study of Muncie, Indiana, *Middletown,* said the automobile was a major element in town life. In Lowell, however, cars still had not become necessary, even in 1941. For many people, wartime prosperity presented for the first time the financial means to purchase a car. But few cars were available for families still on a tight budget, quality of used cars was poor, spare parts were difficult to find, and Detroit had suspended production of new cars for the duration. John Zawodny bought his first used car in 1944 for $200. It fell apart one week later, and he waited until 1949 before buying another. Paul Santilli, a union business agent, had better luck: he bought a new Pontiac in 1941 for $1,400; because of the severe postwar shortage of automobiles, he sold the Pontiac in 1946 for that same price.[32]

During the war, Santilli used his car daily to carry several people to Boston and back to the Navy Yard: the government encouraged people to carpool whenever possible, with commendations to companies that sponsored successful programs. In Lowell, Abbott Worsted, Massachusetts Mohair Plush, and John Pilling received government citations for their workers' high car-sharing averages. As a convenience to workers who travelled by car to night jobs, Lowell repealed its overnight ban on parking as a War Emergency Measure.[33]

Many more workers relied on public transportation than did on private automobiles. Bus service changed considerably under the demands of the war. Nationally, busses carried 692,000,000 passengers in 1942, 75 percent more than in any peacetime year with only a 25 percent increase in the number of bus-miles operated.[34] The Lowell city council deliberated several petitions for War Emergency Certificates from bus companies who wanted to operate intercity lines, and asked the Lowell bus company to extend its 5 cent fare limit to include the Remington plant in South Lowell. To attract workers, plants in other cities ran busses into Lowell for a nominal fee.

The gas shortage presented some difficulties for bus companies as well as for automobile owners: half the prewar stops had to be eliminated. But despite fewer stops, busses were quite convenient. Yvonne Hoar: "The busses were run until 11:30 every night. And then of course when Remington come in you'd have busses at all hours, because we worked from 3:00 to 11:00 at night, I think. So it would give you time to get down to the square to get in the last busses that would be pulling out at 11:30."[35]

Bus riding in 1943 in Lowell was up 44 percent over prewar levels until the ending of a WPA subsidy for a run to Devens; thereafter, it was about 30 percent over prewar levels. The increased business caused one bus company to take out large newspaper ads describing its "4 Point Program . . . to hasten war-time transportation pace." The ads admonished riders to avoid unnecessary rush hour use; have exact fares ready; move to the back; and get off quickly—all standard practice, but encouraged as a patriotic activity. Lowell's increase in bus riding was, however, the smallest in the region: in Lynn, bus riding increased 90 percent, indicating a basis for Lowell workers' reputation of working close to their homes.[36]

Trolley service in Lowell had been dormant for years when war began, and the advent of hostilities led to the enactment of a proposal put forth long before Pearl Harbor: the removal of the old trolley tracks. Proposed initially as a WPA project, trolley tracks were finally pulled up in the drive to collect scrap metal. Eastern Massachusetts Railway Corporation sold the tracks to the Metals Reserve Company, although before the war had created a demand for metal, the Railway Corporation had intended to donate the tracks. But a month and a half after the sale, the city council voted to stop the removal unless the disruption of city streets could be minimized. The rails continued to be ripped up, however, as the council simply moved to follow the matter closely. (In another metal-conservation move, Massachusetts eliminated the second license plate on automobiles.)[37]

Railroads, like busses, found war good for business. Nationally, railway passenger-miles were 83 percent higher in 1942 than in 1941 with virtually the same equipment use. In Lowell, rail traffic doubled in the first two years of the war. One indication of the greater number of Lowell people working outside their home city was a request to the B&M Railroad to change its 3:05 p.m. Boston-to-Lowell train to 3:30 to accommodate work shifts that ended at 3:00.38

Leisure Time

The radio not only held center stage as a source of war news, but it also provided the major entertainment. The result was a booming radio business. Advertising budgets rose from $195 million in 1942 to $390 million in 1944, and per-station income rose 125 percent.[39] One woman claimed "*That* was our entertainment."[40]

Doris Poisson best remembers listening with the family to Gabriel Heatter's "Sad News Tonight": "There was one commentator who was very dismal and pessimistic. He would cast a gloom on it, I'll always remember. . . . But he always gave the bleak side of the news every night. My mother used to listed to him religiously, and she was really affected by it."[41] Heatter's pessimistic radio broadcasts depressed many families, and are far better recalled than any "good news tonight."

Another diversion came when Lowell working-class families invited Fort Devens servicemen into their houses on holidays. The city's French-Canadian community became famous for entertaining French sailors. When two French ships, *Le Terrible* and *Le Fontasque,* docked at the Boston Navy Yard, Claire Contardo responded to a general request and took several French sailors home. "It was quite an experience. . . . [It was] unusual to hear Parisian French [and I] picked up new words. . . . It seemed as though everyone had a son or cousin . . . so there was a lot of talk about it."[42]

More traditional family activities persisted, with wartime modifications. For example, many women living with parents returned home earlier because of blackouts. Alice Swanton, living with the Hoar family, often drove Mr. Hoar to the beach on weekends or went to ballgames with the Hoar's young son. Playing-card sales went up 1,000 percent during World War II. Claire Contardo found extra time to learn to cook and sew while her fiance was overseas. When he was in town, on the other hand, furloughs were like a holiday. The couple spent most of their time in Boston—at outdoor concerts along the river, at movies with stage shows, and dancing once a week at the Hotel Bradford.[43]

Nothing distracted and diverted Lowell's citizens and visitors more than the goings-on at local movie theaters: bond rallies, shows, and the movies themselves. Even the woman who claimed radio was her family's sole entertainment spent Thursday nights dining out with friends and then taking in a movie. Hollywood produced more movies, shown to larger audiences, than in any prewar year. As with news, the government considered movies as part of wartime propaganda and therefore imposed few restrictions on output, while attempting to have Allied war aims infused into as many pictures as possible.[44]

However, war films enjoyed only limited popularity, and comedies, love stories, and adventure films consistently outdrew them. Nevertheless, Hollywood produced and distributed many pictures concerned with war. Of 1,313 pictures made between 1942 and 1944, 28 percent had war-related themes. This emphasis peaked in 1943 at one-third of all pictures produced. Thereafter, Hollywood responded to a national rejection of depressing and/or propagandistic reminders of daily problems. A *Daily Variety* headline on July 7, 1943 announced "Studios Shelve War Stories as They Show 40% Box Office Decline."[45]

Clayton Koppes and Gregory Black have written that government desire to tailor films to propaganda contributed, instead, to the studios' move away from message films altogether:

> The 1944 Academy Award winner, Bing Crosby's *Going My Way,* reflected the shift to non-ideological, frequently religious, entertainment pictures in which war and rumors of war seldom intruded. Several reasons contributed to this shift, among them increasing war weariness and a sense that the war would end soon. But another important cause of the decline was what [Nelson Poynter, head of the Bureau of Motion Pictures, Office of War Information Hollywood liaison office] had predicted: the alliance between OWI and the censor made the studios shy away from significant themes.[46]

War movies may not have been a big draw, but bond rallies at theaters were major social events, as this announcement of a 1944 rally suggests: "The policemen of this city will demonstrate their bond-selling flare for the sixth time during the next few weeks in connection with the gala Sixth War Loan premiere to be held at the Strand theater on Wednesday night, November 29. . . . Nathan Silver, manager of the Strand theater, warns that the last show of this kind, held in June, was a complete sell-out 10 days in advance."[47]

Downtown—in Lowell and in Boston—provided more amusements than just movies. Even though some women claimed that they didn't know what to do with themselves with the fellows gone, Lowell's city center was active late into the night. With people finishing work at all hours due to late shifts, recalls Yvonne Hoar, "The city was always jammed with people every night of the week. And the stores would be open." Victor Luz agrees: "One of the things that were happening in Lowell was fantastic activity downtown because people had to depend on busses and it was always crowded downtown."[48]

With many men away, women often went to a restaurant in a group, then on to a show or a nightclub. At the posh Commodore Ballroom, women reportedly outnumbered men five to one. Despite a severe liquor shortage nationwide, nightclub "business was up 40 percent over the 1941 boom period to $250,000,000 annually" in 1945. A local musician, ineligible for the draft, found his profession in great demand, with high pay at classier Lowell and Boston clubs. But even the presence of Devens servicemen in Lowell did not compensate for men lost to the draft, so elderly men were in great demand as dance partners.[49]

For men, the choice of clubs in Lowell started at the Commodore Ballroom away from the center of town on Thorndike Street, whose business drop in early 1943 was reportedly due to the lack of men in town and servicemen's preference for cheaper places. From there, the range dropped to the infamous bars and whorehouses of Moody Street nearer the industrial section. The fame of this street spread around the world to wherever servicemen from Devens travelled. As would be expected from Moody Street's reputation, reported cases of venereal disease peaked from 1942 to 1946.[50]

Soldiers filled the city every night. On weekends, the crowds could be excessive, and conflicts repeatedly arose between the town and the military. Going beyond the usual fights of a nighttime entertainment district, the issue of race confronted Lowell. Although ethnic antagonisms had long underlay city affairs, racial problems had not, for the simple reason the local black population had never numbered more than a hundred. During the war, tension often ran high at church or USO dances when a black soldier would ask a white woman to dance.[51]

Overt racial confrontations were, however, the exception rather than the rule. Black officers and white officers shared the same club at Devens, although a white man commanded the all-black 366th infantry regiment until a protest was made. The black commander later stated that, "The people of the state were most kind and always cooperated with the 366th. They knew we had a job to do and the inconvenience it caused them at times was accepted graciously. Our time at Fort Devens was a happy time."[52] A black officer who lived in Lowell during the summer of 1942 wrote that he knew of no disturbances involving black troops and white troops, but he acknowledged that some may have occurred. On the other hand, a black man drafted out of Harvard

Law School reacted more critically: "When I was assigned to Fort Devens reception center casual barracks, there again was racial separation." From his induction until he entered OCS, he had nothing "like an integrated military experience." Only after the war did the army officially desegregate.[53]

Perhaps the most novel wartime entertainment came during air raids. Alice Swanton:

> The only time the lights were out in Lowell was when we'd get the precautionary air raid and all the lights went out and people were supposed to cover their windows. They had mock air raids.
>
> The funny part of that was—it was quite a joke around the city—Remington Rand was a munitions plant with a munitions dump out there. And most people went to Fort Hill. . . . It was a big park, a city park. Most people congregated up there if anything happened in Lowell, fires. So when we had the air raids, those who had cars and those who could walk—everybody—went up there to see what the city looked like blacked out.
>
> Well, you couldn't see a light, but the munitions plant, which would be the main target of any real air raid, was lit up like a Christmas tree. You could pick it out right away. And when I was working in the plant, when there was an air raid [warning], we used to laugh because we said, "Boy, if there was a real thing and anyplace was going, we were going to get it for sure. . . ."[54]

Lowell's busier nightlife led many people to think the city should augment its police force; both civilian and military authorities responded. In case of a big disturbance in town, city police also could call on the twelve-man outside guard at the Merrimack Mill as an auxiliary police force. George Ashe's inaugural address as mayor in January 1942 referred to recommendations for increased police and fire appropriations. Again in 1943, with factories running late shifts and a busy entertainment industry, more police were requested for the late shift. In 1944, the city council recommended neighborhood police patrols on the 11:00 p.m. to 7:00 a.m. shift to stop night prowlers. Also in 1944, Mayor Sweeney connected the increased need for police with Fort Devens: "With the War and a camp 15 or 16 miles [away] with many soldiers coming here, we need police protection."[55]

Assistance from Devens military police wasn't always welcome. The *Lowell Sun* in 1943 reported that "military police from Fort Devens manhandled, detained and pushed around Lowell citizens." The following year the city felt compelled to ask MPs to "use discretion between Lowell men home on furlough or leave and those simply visiting from the nearby Camp Devens."

Only in 1941 and 1942, however, did crime—measured by the number of arrests—rise significantly. As the economic situation improved and morale rose, arrests fell to below the prewar level in 1943, 1944, and 1945. (Arrests by military police—which didn't appear in city statistics—balanced the lower city arrest rates somewhat.) Rates for most crimes showed little change, although police arrested significantly fewer people for economically motivated crimes, such as breaking and entering, robbery, and larceny. Despite the expressed need for increased police funds, police work actually centered on mundane chores: chastising dim-out violators, guarding against sabotage, and fingerprinting war workers.[56]

One side effect of the combination of wartime anxiety, leisure time, and more money was a drinking problem (in some people's eyes, at least). In 1943, a Lowell priest began running classes for women on the evils of liquor consumption. Lowell alcoholic consumption rose 70 percent in the first two years of the war.[57] The number of arrests for drunkenness rose dramatically in 1941 and 1942 as the shock of war first hit, but declined thereafter. Drunk driving (and auto thefts) diminished considerably as gas and cars became scarce.[58]

Drunkenness and crime probably declined for obvious reasons. People felt more purpose in life, and they identified more with national goals. Moreover, they had more money, reducing the need to commit economic crimes, and faced increased community pressure to behave moderately. Finally, more hours spent at work left fewer for less approved activities.

Beyond Lowell

It made us more conscious that Lowell wasn't the only place on the map, that there were other states we didn't know about. . . . Before the war, it seemed like Lowell was just a small community, but then we met people from all over the United States and I think it sort of made us branch out, like girls met fellows from Colorado, like my girl friend. . . . She was my closest friend and her brother introduced her to a boy from Colorado.

I remember, "Oh, I hope she doesn't marry him, she's just going to go away to Colorado." And she did. So you see it broke our friendship. . . . Then the brother who had introduced her to this soldier was killed in action.[59]

War took men to foreign nations, but to many women, also, war brought an education about life beyond the borders of Lowell. For Navy Yard workers, the escape from Lowell meant a whole new social world. Many of these workers spent little time in their hometown, spending time, instead, exploring the bigger city with friends. Even the commute to Boston on the train provided a fresh opportunity to extend contacts with people outside Lowell.

A significant portion of any person's life concerns the opposite sex. Although husbands and lovers may have left, war brought a new crop of eligible friends to town. At the Navy Yard, as already noted, women and sailors, said Doris Poisson, "got to know each other pretty well .... A lot of these girls ended up married to those fellows," (as did Poisson).[60] The proximity of Fort Devens gave Lowell women an opportunity to meet men from all over the country.

Alice Swanton valued the opportunities presented by the fort, but also recalled that the different origins of Devens men resulted in a major, overt racial clash, as well as other problems:

There were servicemen from all parts of the United States here. At first it was from the eastern part of the country. Then they were just from the West. Then we had an Indian division here. Most of the boys were welcome. They were *made* welcome, got along very well. Until they moved the Southern boys—the Southern companies didn't go good in Lowell. In fact, there was a lot of turmoil in Lowell with the Southern boys. They caused an awful lot of trouble, so they declared they were off limits. ... Well, it was their manners—attitude towards the women.... The boys from the West were well-behaved, well-mannered, courteous, caused no trouble. They put every woman on a pedestal.

When the Southern boys moved in, it was a racial situation. There were quite a few colored fellows in Lowell; they gave no trouble, and there was no trouble here until they came in from the South. Like at a dance or night club ... the Southern boys didn't like the white people mixing with the colored people, which they weren't *too* much, but there was quite a bit of it. And there was this street brawl and an argument and it became so bad they declared Lowell—they pulled them out of Lowell. ...

The Southern attitude of the Southern fellows that came here—like Downtown Lowell was full of young women, older women. And servicemen never bothered them. Young people kid back and forth, but the older women were left alone. But when the Southern boys came in, they approached any woman, no matter who it was. They treated the women of Lowell as though they were beneath them, just as though *they were tramps,* more or less. They just say anything they felt like to any woman. In fact, you got kind of upset about going through the square, which was something that was very unusual for us. Their manners were terrible.[61]

Women joined the USO, as did Claire Contardo, and "went to dances. We had a big USO here in Lowell on the corner of Appleton. And they used to bring truckloads of boys from Devens and find different places for the dances."[62]

In 1944, the *Lowell Sun* told of a woman who married one serviceman too many:

A 21-year-old girl, found guilty in district court today of polygamy, was sentenced to one year in the house of corrections by Judge Arthur L. Eno. . . .

Testimony . . . disclosed that the girl was married in October, 1942 to William H. Brown in East Hartford, Conn., and on Oct. 5 of this year to Christian Botelho of Haverhill.

After the latter marriage, it was shown, she lived here and during that time frequented many night spots with servicemen, a habit which prompted the police probe of her activities.[63]

The ability to meet men from all over did not obscure some obvious difficulties war placed on relationships. One woman confided: "I was right at the age where, you know, you could have dated and had a normal courtship. And we weren't having normal courtships. We were going to Devens to entertain these boys, and in our hearts we knew we might never see them again even if it was just to go for a dance and coffee with them for one weekend. They didn't know if it were their last or if it were our last time that we saw them. It wasn't a normal time for us, especially at our age."[64]

In addition, many women feared walking in parts of Lowell, especially Moody Street. An article in the *Lowell Sun*'s "Man About Town" column told of a woman who used a flashlight to find her way home at night near the center of town: "After observing her precautionary measure we wondered if the light, heavy as it was, didn't serve a dual purpose both as an aid to finding her way home and as a weapon to ward off potential attack." Another newspaper item reported a case, apparently typical, of a Fort Devens soldier charged with assaulting a Lowell woman.[65] The extent of such crimes against women remains difficult to determine. Arrests for rape and related crimes ranged between one and six per year, not significant enough to attribute a rise or fall to the war, but such incidents are historically underreported. Cases of assault were high in 1941, 1943, and 1945, but not as high as in 1946.[66]

Still, on the whole, the people of Lowell had reason to greet soldiers warmly. Regardless of where they came from, servicemen spent a good deal of money in Lowell. Even more than this economic factor, people became attached both to individual soldiers and at times to entire companies. Alice Swanton: "They'd be here for so long, and they'd be on their way. Everybody knew it was temporary they'd be in. And when an outfit would have been with us for say a month or so at the most or two months at the most, then they'd leave, it was almost like a loss to the people. You got to know them so well. So many boys passed through Devens. And if they passed through Devens, they passed through Lowell."[67]

Volunteering

One of the most revealing separations between economic classes was the amount and type of volunteer activities in which people engaged. The previous accounts of workers' leisure time should be considered within the context of a daily routine of factory and house work that left little free time. Work defined daily life, and family, friends, and relaxation had to fit into its prescribed routine. When she wasn't at work, Yvonne Hoar "always had plenty of housework. . . . Once in a while we'd go out to eat or something like that, but we were never great for parties or anything like that, clubs. We had no social life whatsoever." Asked about his leisure, pipefitter Everett Harris answered, "When I wasn't working, if I was loafing? Well, when would that be [laughs]? Well, I wasn't loafing at all in that period. I was always busy."[68]

Whereas middle-class women contributed to the war effort through continued or increased participation in social clubs and welfare groups such as the Red Cross, such organizations related much less to working women's lives—either before or during World War II. Yvonne Hoar described this class differentiation:

> I don't know of anybody that did volunteer work, only that most of the wealthier people, those in the higher bracket, might help towards the Red Cross or something. . . . They had the time, but other people were working. . . . Like I worked nights. At Remington you'd have two different shifts. You be on two weeks days and two weeks nights. So you really didn't have time to give up any volunteer time. Now, that is the working class. As I say, the wealthier ones would perhaps go into Red Cross or something like that.[69]

Within these tight limits, however, most working-class people did contribute to the war effort. They may not have spent time with amateur theatricals like the Paint and Powder Club, but they did give blood. Claire Contardo "gave quite often to that because they used to have the drives at the Navy Yard and places we worked."[70] As noted, Lowell families of all classes invited servicemen into their homes for Sundays and holidays. In keeping with class separations, less affluent families apparently entertained enlisted men while the wealthy entertained officers. Women who volunteered with the USO did so to ease servicemen's lives as much as they did it for their own pleasure.

Almost all Lowell citizens, except the poorest, purchased savings bonds to support the war effort. The number purchased, of course, depended greatly on wealth. If the rich man could later make a down payment on a daughter's house by selling his bonds, a working family might buy smaller items or do home repairs. The tendency was to sell the bonds gradually as needed, although one woman did splurge and buy a fur coat when her engagement fell through.[71]

Because bonds were most often purchased through work, purchases were not *wholly* voluntary—several companies encouraged workers to buy bonds on payroll deduction. At the Merrimack Mill, bosses would approach each worker approximately every six months and ask him or her to purchase a bond; almost all said yes.[72] Bond drives at the Navy Yard, with famous entertainers participating, could be exhilarating emotional experiences.

Finally, it must be stressed that working people directly contributed to the war effort eight or more hours each day at their jobs. What the economically secure did to fill time and to help the nation, these men and women had to do out of economic necessity. It is not apparent that patriotism motivated one group more than the other. But there is a great deal of evidence that the contributions of workers were more directly valuable.

Religion and Tragedy

On Pearl Harbor Day, December the seventh ... at 4:00 p.m. I was conducting a worship service in the Fort Devens chapel. And during the service, the commandant and his wife and several officers walked into the service, into the sanctuary, sat down, and listened to the remainder of the service.

The choir of the Matthews Memorial Church, of which I was the pastor—Methodist church; the name Matthews is for Mrs. Hiley's father who built the church and was founder and was pastor for thirty-three years—we had thirty people there, thirty voices. They sang several selections at this service. Our church organist, Arthur Thompson, gave a brief organ recital, and I preached a sermon.

And after the benediction, the commandant came up to me and informed me and the rest of the congregation of the attack on Pearl Harbor. We then had a prayer service with several members of the congregation participating and members of the officers participating also.[73]

As with so much in Lowell's history, religion was planned into the city by its corporate founders. In 1824 the Merrimack Company paid $10,000 to have St. Anne's Church built, and they deducted 37.5 cents each month from each worker's pay to support the church. That building still stands at the city's central physical spot, at the west end of the downtown near the high school, city hall, public library, and YMCA. That location was also the meeting point of two ethnic enclaves, the French Canadian and the Greek. Unlike most Lowell churches, St. Anne's congregation, therefore, had a certain diversity yet still served mostly middle-class Yankees: professionals, low-level managers from the mills, small businessmen, a wartime mayor.[74]

Most Lowell churches, however, served a distinct neighborhood, ethnic group, and class. Except for a few churches for the elite and St. Anne's, the rest were primarily oriented to the working class, and the role churches played in wartime life usually reflected their ethnic orientation. For example, Holy Trinity Church, serving Lowell's Greek community, used the city high school to run a benefit for Greek relief work in 1942. Similarly, the local B'Nai B'rith sponsored a Jewish Welfare Board that functioned as a USO, running parties for Jewish soldiers from Fort Devens.[75]

The connection between ethnicity and church activities was most evident at St. Jean the Baptist Church, located in the heart of Lowell's French-Canadian community. With an estimated three thousand families of French descent in Lowell—most of whom spoke French at least as fluently as English—St. Jean's became home to sailors of the Free French fleet in the United States, and Charles de Gaulle appointed St. Jean's Father Armand Morisette as chaplain to the fleet.[76]

Along with public schools, churches served as centers of war-related volunteer activities. St. Jean's, in addition to its work with French sailors, sponsored war bond drives. Reverend Arthur Hiley of Matthews Memorial Church, a more elite institution, asked the members of his congregation to write servicemen once a month:

> We had a League of the Golden Pen in the church. And once a month I would publish mimeographed the names of all of the young men in the service. That would be passed out to the congregation. And we'd ask them to send letters to each of the boys or a card to each of the boys on the list. Then at Christmas time, we always sent them boxes. We took up offerings for the month of December—the months of November and December—and we sent boxes with all sort of things in them: razors and shaving cream, talcum powder, soap, washclothes, toothpaste, toothbrushes, all that sort of thing. We sent them all over the world, as a matter of fact. One year, we sent them all $15 a piece in a money order, but I guess a lot of those were lost.[77]

Established church groups redirected some of their activities toward the needs of soldiers stationed in the area, including providing light food for USO dances and for soldiers spending the night at the YMCA.

Members of church women's groups also helped with various USO and Fort Devens dances. At the first Devens dance, the League of Catholic Daughters was one of several women's organizations that sent fifteen girls each. And most churches did as St. Jean's did, inviting soldiers into the homes of members of the congregations for weekends and holidays.[78] Arthur Hiley:

> During the war years ... the various churches would provide hostesses for the USO Club in Fort Devens in Ayer, which was held at the Federated Church in Ayer. Each Saturday evening the local churches would provide food—sandwiches, cakes, pies, coffee, candy, and so forth. The hostesses, young women, would go up there and serve it to the soldiers and they'd have a dance. And, in fact, several of our young women met soldiers there and married them and are very happy with them. . . . [The YMCA] provided lodgings each Saturday evening. The Protestant churches would invite the soldiers to come and visit their church on Sunday morning and the parishioners would take them home for dinner.

Naturally, churches saw their main function as acting as support for members of their own congregations during a time of crisis. According to Hiley, "people were eager to get to church, to come to church. They wanted something to lift—to give them a lift. And we tried to be—most clergymen tried to be helpful in that way in their sermons, in their prayers, in directing their worship services, to give people something to take home to remember and to lift them up, lift their spirits up, keep them lifted up."[79]

In general terms, this meant that people attended church more often, and some sermons dealt with the war, "always in a comforting vein," as one resident said. However, churches apparently contributed little to people's daily specific needs. Ministers were often asked, and sometimes agreed, to deliver the news of a serviceman's death to his family.[80] But Constance Case recalled that "the religious of that day were . . . isolated from society."[81] Yvonne Hoar, who belonged to St. Louis Catholic Church, said, "They used to pray for the soldiers and the dead every Sunday. But as far as talking about it or into anything political or anything about it, no, there was never any talk about it. We were just praying for the dead and for peace."[82] As did local government, churches declined to answer a wartime need many churches currently take upon themselves: establishing day-care centers for working-class children.

One woman, who took part in a church program for women with fiances in the services, confided a special bitterness:

This priest saw that we were very depressed and he said, "Well, don't waste your time. Let's start a marriage course to prepare you for when the boys come home."

I was against that at first. I wasn't too holy-holy and I didn't go for this religious bit. But he told me, "Hey, if you're going to sit home and wait for your boyfriend to come back, why don't you take a marriage course?" It was a ten-week course. Finally, I gave in. It was a doctor and a nurse and a lawyer and a priest who gave the course.

Then he said, "Why don't you send the course to your boyfriend?" And so that made it interesting. . . . .

But I remember when my boyfriend came home and it was finished for us, I resented that time and I blamed it on that. You always have to blame something, right?[83]

Perhaps because wartime activities of the religious community focused on what Morisette termed "praying very hard for our soldiers," it seems natural that, as Hiley lamented, "as soon as it was over [the people of Lowell] forgot [religion]."[84] On both V-E and V-J days, churches were jammed, and this was the basic definition of being religious. On those days, up to six hundred people worshiped at St. Anne's, which had a victory altar. But, as Father Cantwell, then of St. Rita's Catholic Church, said, "the minute the war was over people went back to their regular way of living without even a thanks to God." Arthur Hiley expressed much the same sentiment:

People went to church more during the war, of course. I think a lot of them went out of fear, except those that were in the church before. And some of them left after the war was over. Some stayed, of course, but a lot of them just went out of fear and hoping that the prayer of the minister or the prayer of the rabbi or the prayer of the priest would save their son in the war, of course, and that's ridiculous, I think. . . . They came out of fear, which is a tragedy, I think, a real tragedy.[85]

Ethnicity: "We Are All Americans"

Not only in their religion, but also in almost every facet of life—work, leisure, politics—people in Lowell kept awareness of their own and other people's ethnic heritage at the forefront—before, during, and after World War II. Rarely does anyone in Lowell talk for long before observing in passing that someone lives in the Greek part of town, or that a church is Polish, or that a certain job has been reserved for French Canadians. Yvonne Hoar: "There was the nationality bit that always came in and in those days was quite strong. We're the French, and the Irish, or the Greeks, or the—they'd all have their little clique.

Like the French didn't like the Irish and the Irish didn't like the French. Or they'd say, 'Oh, the Greeks, don't bother with them.' But I hear that's still going on. I was surprised to hear that, because in this day and age to think that that is going on, it's ridiculous."[86]

Interest in European events depended largely upon a person's ethnic group, although for all ethnic groups the European war and its potential impact on either American or Lowell life remained distant until December 1941. Louis Vergados:

> The war influenced them as far as they were attached to their mother country. At that time [1940] the Italians had invaded Greece, so of course the Greeks were totally involved because of all the relatives they had. Many of them had come from the old country: the overwhelming majority of them, the ones ranging from forty years old to about seventy, were immigrants, and of course had been involved in the Balkan Wars of 1912–13. So they were more keenly interested in the war. And of course the Irish—I mean the intellectual ones—were very concerned with the war because what was happening to the English was joyful to them. . . . But the rest of the community, and even the groups that I talked about, during that period . . . just went about their business. No great botheration, as we say. They seemed to have a feeling of invincibility.
>
> It was after a while that war created a unity among these people, especially amongst the Greeks. World War II created a unity that did not exist. You see, before, during my years I was growing up, if you were from one part of Greece, one state of Greece, and you married someone else from another state, man oh man, that was like scratching yourself out of the family name. In other words, if you came from Crete and I came from Sparta and somebody else came from Macedonia, from Thessaly, you know, they looked at each other as if they were not worth the other's hand. But the World War . . . at least amongst the Greeks in that community, bonded them together. . . . Now they were Greeks.[87]

Indeed, Philip Gleason has written that "cultural pluralism in all its ambiguities and complexities is the crucial legacy of World War II in respect to American identity."[88] However, ethnic identity continued to play a role in Lowell. Doris Poisson got her first job because she grew up speaking French as naturally as English: "I graduated in August '40. I taught school waiting to be called to Washington. . . . I wasn't a qualified school teacher. What happened, I was in the parochial school, a Catholic school, and we had Canadian nuns who were coming on to speak French. And because of the war, somehow they wouldn't let them through. So they hired three of our graduating class to take the smaller grades, and I just taught from September to May."[89]

At the intersection of religion and ethnicity, Armand Morisette's position as chaplain of the Free French fleet in the U.S. made him a focal point for war-related activities of Lowell's French-speaking community. French sailors, living on ships or in South Boston barracks, would often visit the homes of Lowell's French Canadians. Armand Morisette:

> I was traveling all the time. I was a real commuter, mostly to Boston, very often to New York or Washington, made a couple of quick flights. But my job was really over here and that's where I played some kind of a role. . . . I went to Boston sometimes—not very often, but as many as three times the same day—but very often I went twice to Boston the same day. I would say on an average I was in Boston half a dozen times a week and New York very often three. That's where the French sailors were. . . .
>
> Then of course I interpreted for them quite a bit. For instance, if they were in hospitals I'd go there and interpret for those who didn't know English and I found people who knew French to befriend them and visit them, invite them into their homes. . . . I talked over the radio a couple of times to France telling the people not to be worried about their sailors, those that were in the United States, because they were well taken care of.[90]

Lowell's French Canadians maintained connections to sailors loyal to both Vichy and Free France; in fact, Morisette thought that initially Lowell's French-Canadian families, one of the city's more conservative ethnic groups, tended to sympathize with the Vichy government, only gradually siding with de Gaulle:

> The French Canadians didn't care for de Gaulle. They thought he was fresh and they liked the old man Petain. They thought he was so nice. It was too bad that the Germans had overridden part of France, but that it wasn't Petain's fault, after all. He stood, you know, for family life, while de Gaulle was just fooling around with Churchill and Roosevelt there. . . .
>
> The people here don't mix too much with the politics of France itself, because for one thing, the French Canadians have been in America for three hundred years and as a matter of fact they feel that France abandoned them, and besides that, when they came here they were Royalists, it was the time of the kings. . . . I had a great time convincing the French-Canadians or the Franco-Americans of French-Canadian origin that de Gaulle was the right one.[91]

Just as important as convincing Lowell's French Canadians to support de Gaulle was convincing Americans that many people in France—the Free French—sided with the Allies despite Vichy's collaboration with Germany. Armand Morisette:

> Some people organized a group called France Forever. That was organized all over the world, but we had chapters in the United States and a good

one in Boston. And I was approached and I was asked to organize one in Lowell, and we organized a chapter of France Forever in Lowell which was very successful. And that was to keep the two nations friendly. That was the idea of the chapter: France and the United States.

France was the enemy really, Vichy France, was the enemy. It was such a thing that we could not fly the real French flag anymore in the United States. . . . And myself, I had a uniform and I wore the cross of Lorraine on my uniform all the time to make sure that they knew I was a Free French. So the point was the make sure people understood that there were some Frenchmen still on our side, thanks to de Gaulle.[92]

A Footnote on Electoral Politics

To be in Lowell's working class was essentially synonymous to being a partisan of the Democratic party. Only the French-Canadian community—the most skilled workers and therefore the elite of the working class—shared the Yankee middle- and upper-class preference for the GOP. One mill worker believed that to vote Republican would be to starve his own children. "I'm a working man. . . . [FDR] put in NRA and . . . came out for the working man." Even many middle-class Republicans voted for Roosevelt, as did John Albert Notini, a cigarette wholesaler: "I thought Roosevelt was a wonderful man. . . . My family is Republican. I'm a Republican. . . . I voted for Roosevelt. . . . I thought he could handle anything that came along and I think he did."[93] By contrast, Edward Larter, whose father founded the Wannalancit Mill, thought "Roosevelt was the root of all evil obviously. All these giveaway programs. . . . Well, it all depends on how you think, I guess."[94]

As a local politician said, Roosevelt "took this area like Grant took Richmond." In every wartime election, registered Democrats outnumbered Republicans almost three to two. In 1940, Roosevelt received 30,000 votes to Wilkie's 16,000. In 1944, as interest in presidential politics waned, he polled 27,000 to Dewey's 14,500. (Blank ballots showed the only increase, from 872 to 1,103.) In each election, Lowell voted against the tide in Middlesex County and Massachusetts. In elections for governor and U.S. senator, the city repeatedly countered county and state trends by voting Democratic even in landslide victories for Republican Leverett Saltonstall. Republican Henry Lodge, Jr., barely managed a victory in Lowell in 1942, although he won the state and county easily. As would be expected, Democrats dominated less affluent wards, while Republicans won in the "respectable" third, fourth, sixth, and eighth wards.

The exception to Democratic loyalty was an opposing one to Republican Congresswomen Edith Nourse Rogers (and to her husband before her, from 1913 to 1925). Despite her tight family connections to the mill elite, her election victories were even more impressive than Roosevelt's. Serving in Congress from 1925 to 1960, she won in 1940, 31,000 to 14,000. In 1942 she ran unopposed, and in 1944, won 25,000 to 16,000. Time and again Lowell returned her to Washington because they believed she delivered on her promises, often contrasting her to local politicians in this respect. This disdain for the ability of local politicians to produce results was another result of expanded federal power during the war.[95]

Riding on Rogers's coattails would have been difficult, however. Several people expressed the—questionable—opinion that the conservative congresswoman, later a supporter of Joseph McCarthy, was more Democratic than most Democrats.[96] And she does have detractors. James Ellis:

> You see the greatest problem Lowell had was it just couldn't get itself to diversify simply because the people that controlled, had the reins of power in Lowell weren't interested in diversification. They wanted to maintain the status quo: the textile mills, the low wages, the same conditions. Don't forget Mrs. Rogers was the congresswoman in that area. She could have done a lot for Lowell. She wasn't interested in doing very much for Lowell because her relatives controlled the Boott Mills. . . .
>
> She succeeded her husband, John Jacob Rogers, and he was there for many, many years. The people that succeeded Mrs. Rogers were Rogers people: Bradford Morse, a good boy, good friend of mine, became the congressman after Mrs. Rogers; [he] was administrative assistant to a Saltonstall, who was very closely tied in with the Rogers. . . . You've got to remember that for fifty years, the Fifth Congressional District, Lowell being the largest city, was controlled by the Rogers.[97]

Not until 1975 did a liberal Democrat, Paul Efthenios Tsongas, successfully challenge an arch-conservative, Yankee incumbent.

Perhaps Congresswoman Rogers's major wartime achievement related to women's rights. As did every congresswoman during the war, Rogers worked for legislation in this area. Writes Susan Hartmann, "She shepherded legislation [regarding women in the services] through the House" beginning in May 1941 when she introduced a bill to establish the Women's Army Auxiliary Corps.[98] Nor was her advocacy superficial. According to Hartmann, Rogers maintained

> that women were better qualified than men for certain kinds of work. . . .
> Moreover, Rogers had observed the inadequate care provided for women serving in France during World War I and had campaigned without success to obtain veterans' compensation for them. "I was resolved," she said, "that our women would not again serve with the Army without the

protection that men got." Finally, Rogers urged passage of her bill on the grounds that women both wanted and deserved equal opportunity to serve their country.[99]

Going Nowhere

Lowell's social history during World War II, like its economic history, was an interlude, a respite from a slow descent. Nothing happened in the city to establish wartime progress as a lasting improvement. Just as families resumed prewar patterns centered on a father's work role when men returned, so, too, advances in public transportation soon disappeared in the shift to reliance on automobiles. Neither the churches nor the electoral system prepared Lowell to take control over its own destiny, to counter the pessimism with which people approached the postwar world. Experience in the outside world and fading ethnic separatism could have been steps toward building a modern city, but they seem rather to have loosened bonds that had made Lowell a stable community.

As prosperity faded and Fort Devens shrank, so did the brief glory of Lowell's downtown: from a half-dozen theaters in downtown Lowell, none remain today. The Commodore Ballroom, closed for several years, later housed occasional rock concerts. The population of the city continued to decline; no one expected the young to stay. In essence, Lowell's postwar social history simply reflected its economic history. Temporary wartime advances gave way to a return to "normalcy."

NOTES

1. United States Department of Labor, Women's Bureau, *Women War Workers in Ten War Production Areas and their Postwar Plans,* Bulletin no. 209 (Washington: GPO, 1946), 45–46.

2. Confidential interview, 9 June 1975.

3. Interview with Leo McCue, Sr., Helen McCue, and John McCue, 7 January 1975; interview with Alice Swanton, 4 June 1975; interview with Claire Contardo, 16 September 1975.

4. Interview with Yvonne Hoar. 6 May 1975.

5. Interview with Claire Contardo.

6. Interview with Thomas Ahearn and Dorothy Ahearn, 8 March 1976.

7. Confidential interview, 17 May 1975.

8. Interview with Alice Swanton.

9. Interview with Barbara Notini and Andrew Notini, 27 January 1975; interview with Lydia Howard, 18 March 1975; Richard Lingeman, *Don't You Know There's a War On: The American Home Front, 1941–1945* (New York: G. P. Putnam's Sons, 1970), 223.

10. Jack Goodman, ed., *While You Were Gone: A Report on Wartime Life in the United States* (New York: Simon and Schuster, 1946), 437.

11. Confidential interview, 27 February 1975.

12. Lucy Church to Mrs. Henry A. Kind, 5 January 1945, Lowell Red Cross Papers.

13. Phillip Knightley, *The First Casualty, From the Crimea to Vietnam: The War Correspondent as Hero, Propagandist, and Myth Maker* (New York: Harcourt, Brace, Jovanovich, 1975), 301.

14. Interview with Victor Luz, 23 April 1975.

15. Interview with Claire Contardo.

16. Confidential interview, 9 June 1975.

17. Ibid.

18. P.H.S., *Vital Statistics Rates,* 594.

19. Joan Ellen Trey, "Women in the War Economy," *Review of Radical Political Economics* 4, no. 3 (1972)42; Women's Bureau, *Women Workers in Ten War Production Areas,* 55.

20. Sidonie Matsner Gruenberg, ed., *The Family in a World at War* (New York: Harper and Brothers, 1942), 206–18.

21. Interview with Alice Swanton; interview with Yvonne Hoar.

22. Ibid.

23. Interview with Dorothy Ahearn and Thomas Ahearn.

24. Interview with Doris Poisson.

25. Trey, "Women in the War Economy," 46–47.

26. Women's Bureau, *Women's Wartime Hours of Work,* 5.

27. Karen Anderson, *Wartime Women: Sex Roles, Family Relations, and the Status of Women During World War II* (Westport, Conn.: Greenwood Press, 1981), 122, 124, 141, 145.

28. Interview with Doris Poisson.

29. Women's Bureau, *Women's Wartime Hours of Work,* 4.

30. *Baltimore Sun,* 16 January 1944.

31. Interview with Claire Contardo.

32. Interview with John Zawodny, 22 March 1976; interview with Paul Santilli, 21 January 1976; Lowell, "City Council Journal," 1 December 1942; 15 December 1942; National Archives, Record Group 188.

33. National Archives, "Records of the Office of Price Administration, Rationing Department."

34. Annals of the American Academy of Political and Social Science, *Transportation: War and Postwar* (n.p.: AAPSS, November 1943), 72.

35. Interview with Yvonne Hoar.

36. Lowell, "City Council Journal," 6 June 1942; 1 September 1942; 27 August 1945; interview with Frederick Burtt, 3 November 1975; *Lowell Daily Sun,* 3 March 1945, 5; 2 November 1944, 18.

37. Lowell, "City Council Journal," 21 April 1942; 15 September 1942; 3 November 1942; 17 November 1942; *Lowell Daily Sun,* 2 November 1944, 1.

38. United States Bureau of the Budget, Committee on Records of War Administration, War Records Section, *United States at War* (1946; repr., New York: Da Capo Press, 1972), 162; *Lowell Daily Sun,* 3 March 1943, 1; Lowell, "City Council Journal," 1 May 1944.

39. Lingeman, *Don't You Know There's a War On,* 120; Goodman, *While You Were Gone,* 284.

40. Interview with McCue family.

41. Interview with Doris Poisson.

42. Interview with Claire Contardo.

43. Interview with Doris Poisson; interview with Alice Swanton; Lingeman, *Don't You Know There's a War On,* 272; interview with Claire Contardo.

44. Clayton R. Koppes and Gregory D. Black, "What to Show the World: The Office of War Information and Hollywood, 1942–1945," *Journal of American History* 64 (June 1977): 89.

45. *Lowell Daily Sun,* 29 April 1943, 1; Lingeman, *Don't You Know There's a War On,* 205–6.

46. Koppes, "What To Show the World," 103.

47. *Lowell Daily Sun,* 18 November 1944, 2.

48. Interview with Yvonne Hoar; interview with Victor Luz, 23 April 1975.

49. Lingeman, *Don't You Know There's a War On,* 281; interview with Barbara Notini and Andrew Notini; *Lowell Daily Sun,* 12 February 1943, 1.

50. *Lowell Daily Sun,* 12 February 1943, 1; Commonwealth of Massachusetts, Department of Public Health, *Annual Report of the Department of Public Health,* Public Document no. 34 (Massachusetts, passim).

51. Interview with Wilfred Pearson, 2 January 1975.

52. Mary Penick Motley, comp. and ed., *The Invisible Soldier: The Experience of the Black Soldier During World War II* (Detroit: Wayne State University, 1975), 335, 337.

53. John Martin to author, 5 October 1976; Motley, *Invisible Soldier,* 295.

54. Interview with Alice Swanton.

55. Interview with Patrick Gill, 3 February 1975; Lowell, "City Council Journal," 5 January 1942; 15 June 1943; 31 January 1944; 21 February 1944.

56. Commonwealth of Massachusetts, *Annual Report of the Commissioner of Corrections,* Public Document no. 115 (n.p.: passim); *Lowell Daily Sun,* 4 May 1943, 1; 1 May 1943, 14; Lowell, "City Council Journal," 1 May 1944.

57. *Lowell Daily Sun,* 7 June 1943, 1.

58. Massachusetts, *Report of the Commissioner of Corrections,* passim.

59. Confidential interview, 9 June 1975.

60. Interview with Doris Poisson.

61. Interview with Alice Swanton.

62. Interview with Claire Contardo.

63. *Lowell Daily Sun,* 21 November 1944, 1.

64. Confidential interview, 9 June 1975.

65. *Lowell Daily Sun,* 21 November 1944, 6; 17 November 1944, 16.

66. Massachusetts, *Report of the Commissioner of Corrections,* passim.

67. Interview with Alice Swanton.

68. Interview with Yvonne Hoar; interview with Everett Harris, 17 September 1975.

69. Interview with Yvonne Hoar.

70. Interview with Claire Contardo.

71. Interview with Doris Poisson.

72. Interview with Hazel Fiske and Frank Fiske, 3 December 1974.

73. Interview with Arthur Hiley, 20 March 1975.

74. Margaret Terrell Parker, *Lowell: A Study of Industrial Development* (1940; repr., Port Washington, N.Y.: Kennikat Press, 1970), 71–72; interview with Frank Fiske and Hazel Fiske; interview with Lydia Howard.

75. Lowell School Committee, "Minutes," 5 August 1942; interview with Allan Gershon, 17 September 1975.

76. Interview with Armand Morisette, 16 June 1975.

77. Interview with Arthur Hiley.

78. Interview with Armand Morisette; interview with Arthur Hiley; interview with Wilfred Pearson; interview with William Pepin, 24 February 1975; *Boston Herald Traveller,* 12 April 1941.

79. Interview with Arthur Hiley.

80. Interview with McCue family; interview with John Cantwell, 6 May 1975; confidential interview, 9 June 1975.

81. Interview with Constance Case, 14 December 1974.

82. Interview with Yvonne Hoar.

83. Confidential interview, 9 June 1975.

84. Interview with Armand Morisette; interview with Arthur Hiley.

85. Interview with Arthur Hiley.

86. Interview with Yvonne Hoar.

87. Interview with Louis Vergados, 18 September 1975.

88. Philip Gleason, "Americans All: World War II and the Shaping of American Identity," *The Review of Politics* 43 (October 1981):518.

89. Interview with Doris Poisson.

90. Interview with Armand Morisette.

91. Ibid.

92. Ibid.

93. Interview with John Albert Notini, 12 April 1975.

94. Interview with Edward Larter, 22 March 1975.

95. Interview with Patrick Gill; confidential interview; Lowell, "Record of Votes"; Commonwealth of Massachusetts, *Election Statistics,* Public Document no. 43 (n.p.: passim.); Mary H. Blewett, "The Mills and the Multitudes," in *Cotton Was King: A History of Lowell, Massachusetts*, ed. Arthur L. Eno, Jr. (n.p.: New Hampshire Publishing, in collaboration with the Lowell Historical Society, 1976), 182.

96. Edith Nourse Rogers Papers, Schlesinger Library, Radcliffe College, Cambridge, Mass.

97. Interview with James Ellis, 16 June 1975.

98. Susan M. Hartmann, *The Home Front and Beyond: American Women in the 1940s* (Boston: Twayne Publishers, 1982), 151, 314.

99. Susan M. Hartmann, "Women in the Military Service" in *Clio Was a Women: Studies in the History of American Women*, ed. Mabel E. Deutrich and Virginia C. Purdy (Washington: Howard University Press, 1980), 197.

5

The Mill Elite

The Lowell elite—good Yankees all in a city of Greek-Americans, Irish-Americans, and French-Canadian-Americans—reflect traditions dating back to Lowell's earliest history. The Ames Worsted Company descended from Benjamin Butler's Civil War creation, the U.S. Bunting Company. As his name suggests, Ames Stevens, the company's World War II chief executive, descended, through near or distant relationships, from two major American textile families: Ames and Stevens.

Similarly, ancestors of the local owners of the Boott Mill arrived in Lowell in the nineteenth century. That mill was established by one of Lowell's founders, Kirk Boott. The Boott's last treasurer and general manager, John Rogers Flather, took over from his father, Frederick Flather. Frederick, originally from Lowell, had married a Lowell woman, Alice Rogers, and then, in 1900, moved to Chicago to become director of McCormick Harvester. But Alice Rogers Flather was unhappy in Chicago, so when the Boott Mill reopened in 1905 (having failed in the depression of 1893), the Flathers returned, and Mr. Flather became "manager of the works." In addition, Frederick Flather served on the Merrimack's board of directors during the 1930s and was its president in 1936. And the importance and power of this family to Lowell goes beyond their mill connections: another family member was Congresswoman Edith Nourse Rogers.[1]

While the elite families may have recorded a century of leadership when World War II arrived, they must have felt their ranks to be depleted. Only a few mills survived the long, slow decline that began in 1925. One survivor, the Ames Worsted Company, in moves later called "gambles" in company promotional literature, purchased three other mills during the depression, including the Lawrence, founded in 1828.[2] The Merrimack survived, but lost between $320,000 and $2,300,000 each year between 1925 and 1938. The Suffolk, Hamilton, Columbia, Tremont, Appleton, Ipswich, and Massachusetts Cotton mills all closed. Even those mills that survived had old equipment: in

1940, one-sixth of the Merrimack equipment (measured by cost) had been installed before 1914, and the average age of the machinery was almost twenty years.[3] For most of the mills in Lowell, the 1930s had represented the final crisis. Says Edward Stevens, the son of Ames Stevens and now president of Ames Textiles, "The textile industry [at the beginning of World War II] was just about to go through a major liquidation."[4]

The War Boom

World War II seemed to present an opportunity to escape the inevitable. As the war approached, the Boott got a fresh start when the elder Flather jumped to take advantage of expected war contracts. As early as 1937, the Boott made samples of uniform cloth that was eventually sold to the navy. When war broke out, says Edward Stevens, the surviving mills "all immediately had all [the business] they could use."[5] In 1942, Frederick Flather described the Boott success for the *American Wool and Cotton Reporter*: "In November, 1938, we filled a little contract for the Navy [8,000 yards], and then began to devote our long experience and skill to their coming needs. In 1939 we made what then looked like a large product. In 1940, we doubled the product of 1939. In 1941, we doubled the product of 1940. In 1942, eight months, we have doubled the product of 1941, eight months."[6]

The Boott, having "got in on the ground floor," says J. R. Flather, ran three shifts a day, an event unheard of for decades before the war. Eventually the company won an armed service E-Pennant for converting so much production to war work so soon. From 1937 to 1945, the Boott was the navy's largest supplier of bleached white twill.[7] Other mills followed the path beaten by the Boott. Ames Worsted produced serge for army jackets and trousers.[8] The Merrimack made corduroy for military bathrobes, jungle cloth, and, until nylon replaced their product, cloth for aircraft pilots' jackets.[9]

Edward Larter's father founded and owned the Wannalancit Textile Company:

> You must remember we were in the midst of the depression, and the war brought a lot of mills out of the depression. . . . [We were making] parachute cloth . . . for the aviators and sending it down here to Atlantic Parachute Company down the street and they were building a personnel suit. The government arranged it, for everybody then. They told us we were going to [make parachute material]. That's what we did. There wasn't any civilian business coming out of the mill during the war because the government took over all the looms. . . .

> It was subcontract, no prime contracts. Atlantic Parachute got the prime contract and subbed their business out. You submitted your price to Atlantic and Atlantic would come in with their price. . . . It'd be a problem sometimes to get the price.[10]

Conversion to government contracts had drawbacks despite the prosperity they brought. Government contracts often meant government inspectors, the complaint of every corporate administrator. One mill supplier recalled a government inspector trained at the Lowell Technological Institute who often rejected his company's products. (Rejected items, however, were shipped out of state, where they did pass inspection.)[11]

Government-corporate negotiations over quality were continuous. "We never satisfied them," says Flather, although the government "was constantly after us to make more cloth." Flather slept with an overnight bag handy because he had to travel to Washington or Brooklyn almost weekly to settle disagreements over specifications.[12]

Ames Worsted Company did not send a representative to Washington as often, possibly because the elder Stevens served there for the duration. Because of his prominent position in the textile industry, Ames Stevens, the company's chief executive, was appointed to the Textile, Clothing and Leather Bureau of the WPB as a dollar-a-year man. That is, his salary was only a dollar, although he did have an expense account. On one occasion he was accused of overspending, but vindication proved easy considering the "salary."[13]

In addition to hassles satisfying government quality standards, government business necessitated endless, aggravating paperwork. For example, in order to help the government direct workers to the most needed jobs, mills had to prepare "manning tables" in 1943 for each task, stressing training time to replace workers transferred to more essential industries or drafted. Managers listed male employees by draft status, with a special notation for jobs that women or handicapped workers could fill.[14]

A more important drawback to government work was that the Boott and Merrimack management had to bid competitively against Southern mills for contracts. In contrast, local arms factories often had lucrative "cost-plus" contracts that guaranteed a high profit. Only one Lowell mill—Ames Worsted, a knitting not a manufacturing mill—had significant cost-plus contracts. Fortunately, plenty of work existed for all mills in the country, North and South.

Given such complaints, the question arises why the Boott and Merrimack managements dealt in contracts of apparently limited profitability. If mills could have made a fortune by satisfying the great civilian demand, why did only a fraction of their business remain in civilian production?

In fact, mill owners would have preferred selling on the civilian market. But despite the lack of an official prohibition on this, companies actually had little choice. Rather than rely on industrialists' patriotism, in 1942, the government instituted a plan to allocate raw materials from Washington on a strict priority basis. Mills only received supplies when they showed the War Production Board a contract for war-related services. Similarly, the government had the power to allocate workers. General Electric in South Lowell, making rocket launchers, had a priority rating of 97 out of 100 in 1944; the Merrimack, despite a shortage of workers, had a rating of only 38.[15]

Even civilian production profits were somewhat controlled. A strict price ceiling existed for the products of the mills, although Chester Bowles, then administrator of Office of Price Administration, complained to Russell Fisher of the National Association of Cotton Manufacturers (NACM) about lack of corporate cooperation: "It seems evident that many members of the Cotton Textile Industry do not fully understand the laws and regulations under which OPA is operating and the reasons for some of the OPA policy decisions."[16] On the other hand, Bertrand McKittrick, president of the McKittrick Company, which dealt in used textile machinery, says that ceiling prices "never bothered us much because the average price never reached the ceiling price."

Government-induced prosperity lasted throughout the war, ending suddenly with the immediate cancellation of contracts at war's end. When Japan surrendered, the government abruptly ended more than one hundred thousand contracts and orders for $23 billion in war goods across the nation.[17] For a few years, demand for civilian goods unavailable during the war kept textile mills profitable, but the war, says Edward Stevens, had simply "delayed the inevitable." The Merrimack, like many mills throughout New England, was sold to entrepreneur Jacob Ziskind, who owned the mill until it finally closed in 1956. J. R. Flather supervised the closing of the Boott Mills in 1946; even during the war, he knew it would be a "case of closing down, selling out" when the artificial boom ended. He says that he tried to delay that final end—the Boott was Lowell's last major manufacturing mill—because its local management cared about the city, the workers, and history. The renamed Ames Textile Corporation remained headquartered in Lowell, but moved most of its operations overseas to Holland, England, and Northern Ireland. One small cotton manufacturer, the

Wannalancit Textile Company, operated until 1980 in part of the Suffolk Mill buildings.[18]

The Mills and the New War Industries

With the arrival of various war industries, the same conditions that workers welcomed made mill managers' jobs much more difficult. Based in part on cost-plus contracts, the new companies and government bases offered higher wages than the minimum standard for most mill workers, thus attracting the textile industry's best employees. Even a year before Remington arrived, some mills reported a shortage of workers. When Remington moved in, mill executives accepted an offer to discuss Remington's wage policy. The Remington representatives promised that their company would pay only "on the high side of average wages." The success of this attempt to keep wages from rising abruptly was limited, however; all attending realized that "the high side of average wages" meant that skilled textile workers would rush to Remington's assembly line.[19] "At one stage in 1944," says J. R. Flather, "we hired 5,000 employees to maintain a payroll of 2,500 employees.[20]

In response to the high turnover, as well as to try to stave off unionization, mill managers began to revise longstanding company labor-relations policies. The Boott, noted for its history of labor-management conflict, took the lead. The nurse's office grew, previously the material focus of the company's limited paternalism. Especially in 1944 and 1945, it became the primary duty of the nurses, using both rational arguments and "feminine charm," to change the minds of people who wanted to leave the Boott. The 1942 National Association of Cotton Manufacturers convention featured a talk by B. M. Selekman of Harvard Business School on the need for enlightened labor relations: the Boott's J. R. Flather chaired the convention's program committee. In cooperation with the Massachusetts Department of Vocational Education, Flather also established classes in which supervisors and overseers learned how to avoid certain offensive practices and concentrate on encouraging workers to remain with the company. The classes, according to Flather, started from the proposition that "what we are trying to do is hold onto people. . . . How can we train our foremen, not in technical skills . . . but . . . how to hold onto their employees?" Eventually, the program succeeded enough to become the subject of a government pamphlet on increasing production, and the Boott earned another star for its E-Pennant. The education program was indeed a distinct step forward from the favoritism previously shown to key workers, a practice that led to one of the few wartime strikes in a Lowell mill. The Boott also began training potential employees—primarily women and children—in cooperation with the WMC and WPB. In three years, two thousand people with no prior textile experience attended this school.[21]

Referring to competition from war industries, one mill owner complained persistently to the city council that the chamber of commerce, in its attempt to attract new types of industry to Lowell, granted Remington and other arms factories favors that were previously reserved for textile manufacturers. On the other hand, rumors issued from the city manager's office that textile companies defended themselves by refusing to rent vacant mill space to companies that might compete in the labor market. In March of 1942, the Merrimack Manufacturing Company was accused of refusing to sell their weave shops to General Electric. Although the Merrimack denied the charge, a city councilor remarked, "Happy Day when the Merrimack Manufacturing Company and the Boott Mills move out of Lowell. . . . In their set up they guard against industries coming in that pay higher wages." Eventually, the Merrimack rented the weave shops to the government for storage, but the mill's vacant space went otherwise unused. Again, in June of 1945, the city council voted to deal with the problem of "getting the Nashua Manufacturing Company to rent, lease or sell floor space in its Lowell Plant to some other industry."[22]

In a more publicized example of the textile elite's apparent resistance to competition, Lowell received national attention. Soon after Remington closed at the end of 1943, Undersecretary of War Patterson and the War Manpower Commission's outspoken director, Paul McNutt, accused Lowell of hindering the movement of three to five thousand people to a Bristol, Connecticut war plant, New Departure, severely in need of workers.[23]

Even before Remington announced its closing, the United States Employment Service had said Lowell had a pool of surplus workers and recruited people to work in other states. With Remington's closing, many workers began making plans to move to the West Coast. Then, in November, the U.S.E.S. cooperated in New Departure's campaign to attract workers to Bristol. The company ran exclusive interviews at the U.S.E.S. office in Lowell while bombarding the city with propaganda—including billboards, window cards, street signs, radio ads, sound trucks, full-page newspaper ads in English and French, and handbills that high school boys distributed to all Lowell houses. New Departure expressed itself happy with the results.[24]

In late November, however, Congresswoman Rogers announced that U.S. Rubber would be coming to Lowell. To the pleasure of local textile leaders, she admonished residents not to leave.[25] In a surprisingly frank interview with a Boston newspaper, "one prominent business man declared the scheme to keep labor here at home was based on a desire to maintain a surplus as a technique for keeping wages down in the postwar period."[26] However, even with U.S. Rubber, the U.S.E.S. said Lowell would have a pool of 1,500 to 2,000 available workers, and beyond the announcement of the arrival of U.S. Rubber, the defense against McNutt's charges referred principally to a *Life* magazine statement that Lowell had the largest rate of lives lost in the war of any American city.[27]

Eventually, the new industries that did arrive, coupled with the depression exodus of the mills, changed Lowell from solely a mill town into one with a choice of occupations for workers. Even though most war-oriented companies closed after the war, the mill elite had lost their hold as workers finally broke the tradition of mill work—or even work in Lowell.

It is not clear, however, that wartime diversification was a significant improvement. Companies coming in were, like the mills, low paying and labor intensive. And higher percentages working in non-textile industries were as much a function of old business leaving as of new opportunities coming to Lowell.

The Corporation "Family"

The mill owners' attitude toward their companies, their employees, and the city of Lowell can best be described as paternalistic. In this they followed in the footsteps of prominent Lowell leaders back to the planners of the city's industrial core more than a hundred years earlier. Frederick Flather, says his son, considered the Lowell mills as the foremost institution for "Americanizing" immigrants, because cotton mills hired any job applicant. The Boott managers claimed they ignored "good business practice" (i.e., closing the mill) when they sought war contracts in 1937 to keep the factory open.[28] In 1944, the Boott cited its dedication to Lowell (as well as the fact that few of its workers were male heads of households) in a plea to the National War Labor Board to allow it to continue paying wages below family subsistence levels: "The people of Lowell need Boott Mills, and will need it badly after the war. Boott Mills' chief aim is to fulfill that need, and requests that the National War Labor Board consider its plea in the light of a management that has a high sense of local responsibility . . . and which is imbued with the determination to provide steady and good employment opportunities for the City of Lowell for its second hundred years."[29]

At the ceremony marking the Boott's first army-navy E-Pennant, the six employees who had worked at the mill longest—each with the company more than twenty years—were honored as though they were the elders of a family. "We had a celebration in the mill yard," says Flather, adding, "The accomplishment was very rewarding to me. . . . Money wasn't that important since my pay didn't increase." Flather retained great pride for the several E stars "his" company received for contributions to the war effort.[30]

Wartime labor-management troubles at the Ames Worsted Company can be partly attributed, Edward Stevens believes, to the absence of his father. A warm friend of his employees, says Edward Stevens, Ames Stevens could not settle disputes personally while working in Washington for the government: "We acquired a union, the only one we ever had . . . because my father wasn't here." That the owner's paternalistic trust in workers' loyalty may be well-founded is indicated by the fact that only one Ames division unionized, albeit by a vote of eight to one.[31]

Edward Larter describes how local mill management effectively resists unionization:

> You take most organizations that are—the labor and management work very close together, don't have very much of a labor problem. Whereas these corporations where management is far removed from labor, doesn't understand their problems and does not work with them, you'll find usually you're going to end up with a union. I think it all depends upon the attitudes the company presidents and top execs have, whether they are removing themselves from labor or working with them.[32]

Workers had a different view, and union success in organizing Lowell during the war illustrates the lack of faith they placed in management paternalism. Even with the establishment of unions, mills cooperated with each other secretly through the National Association of Cotton Manufacturers to resist Textile Workers Union pay demands in mid-1945.[33]

At no point during the war did paternalism extend to paying much more than minimum wages to almost all mill workers. When war companies raised the wage scale, the Boott attempted at first to keep up, then couldn't. Instead, the Boott and the Merrimack both relied heavily, as their predecessors had, on personal attention and on the loyalty of old employees to hold staff. Flather continually emphasizes that the Boott, unlike Lowell mills that had failed, was a local family business. In his view, people who cared about Lowell and about their employees ran the mills; they would, after the war, try to keep jobs for the workers who had remained loyal.

This traditional emphasis on local ownership exists despite the fact that controlling interest in not only the Boott, but also the Hamilton, Tremont, Appleton, and Suffolk mills, rested in the hands of a few Boston families. Local managers and their families controlled only a minority interest.[34] The family that owned Ames Worsted lived near Lowell, but that company gradually closed almost all its New England plants and opened new plants in the South and in other countries. Management of the Merrimack, always dominated by Boston stockholders, moved in 1938 entirely out of the hands of Lowell businessmen. The directive to close the Lowell mill came from the corporation's New York office. Most factories serving the mills were, indeed, locally owned, but hired relatively few workers.[35]

Paternalism appeared most clearly when it failed to control workers. Those employees who quit to find higher wages elsewhere were considered traitors to the "family" feeling upon which the owners depended. After the war, one disgruntled employee who had left Parker Bobbin Company to work at Remington took his former employer to court in an attempt to regain his old position. Parker owner Charles Fairbank proudly states that the company fought successfully to prevent the worker's return.[36]

Double Time

The managers' own workdays reflected the Yankee heritage of Lowell's civic leaders. J. R. Flather arose at six every morning six days a week to walk the mile from the rich enclave of Upper Belvidere to the mill office, where he would remain for at least twelve hours. After returning home for dinner, he made the rounds of his neighborhood as a volunteer air raid warden, then either called it a day or attended—as a good example to others—the labor relations classes he had founded. Sundays after services at either Matthews Memorial Church or Christ Church United would also often be spent at the mill. "I never knew what it was like not to work Saturday or take a vacation," said Flather. The textile-machinery supply company owner never took a day off during the war, except for his Saturday morning golf games and one trip to Florida—by train to save gasoline.[37]

Long workdays were not unique to the war years, but had existed in less hectic times also. One factor that did make an executive's day busier was the draft. When selective service drained off supervisory or managerial staff, those executives remaining, top management included, had to take on extra duties. Fred Burtt, superintendent of Abbott Worsted, would get home from work at 5:00 p.m., but then went back to the mill at 7:00 p.m. to run the spinning room because of the scarcity of supervisors.[38] Although most report they would have served in the armed forces willingly, managers who took on these extra tasks were exempted from the draft as key civilian employees.

Appointments to government boards outside Lowell complicated the executives' workdays. The Merrimack's Bertrand Hawkins and the Boott's J. R. Flather were appointed to OPA's Cotton Weavers Advisory Committee. Hawkins also chaired OPA's corduroy and velveteen subcommittee. Officials of both the Boott and the Merrimack met with government representatives in 1941 to make recommendations on price ceilings.[39] In general, such industry-government cooperation followed the pattern set by this letter from OPA's placement officer to the NACM three days after Pearl Harbor: "Surely you will be able to supply me with with names and addresses of a dozen or more persons in the Textile Industry who would be more than willing to serve their nation in the hour of need as price executives or assistants to price executives in the Office of Price Administration."[40]

By mid-1944, 744 U.S. business men served in Washington as dollar-a-year or without-compensation employees. Of these, 467 came from manufacturing industries and 19 percent were top executives of their company. Seventy-nine served on the Textile, Clothing and Leather Bureau of the War Production Board, or 22 percent of the board's total employment.[41]

Lowell businessmen also worked in industry associations that lobbied in Washington. In addition to his OPA position, Ames Stevens in 1944 became a vice-president of the National Association of Wool Manufacturers (NAWM). Three other Lowell executives served on NAWM committees. Among the key activities of the NAWM was an active effort to "attempt to get adequate ceiling prices."[42]

The participation of businessmen in government decision making for the textile industry led to a major conflict of interest issue. In the Guthrie affair—named after the controversial resignation of Robert Guthrie as chief of the WPB Textile, Leather and Clothing Bureau—the board's industry representatives were accused of hindering the war effort with their self-protective conservatism. In addition to other charges, Guthrie alleged that "Kenneth Marriner, chief of the wool fabric section of the WPB, [failed] to formulate and carry out a mandatory wool blending policy for the woolen industry." Two congressional investigations issued conflicting judgments.[43] A postwar study of the WPB severely criticized the influence of these businessmen and the behavior of the textile industry in general. Textile officials, the study asserted, consistently rejected or blocked the need to create priorities in their industry: "The cost of such action would clearly have been the elimination of many luxury and less essential products and, to the extent that they were unwilling or unable to convert, of the producers of these products. The harshness of such actions was accepted as necessary in the interest of winning the war in the metal trades. It was never accepted in the textile industry."[44]

Because of the intransigence of textile executives, the report blamed them for wartime shortages of low- and medium-priced civilian clothing. "Only the abrupt ending of the war avoided the most acute squeeze on the domestic front."[45]

In other cases, too, the relationship between businessmen and government retained the love-hate character typical of regulatory agencies. Although businessmen participated in setting price ceilings, the National Association of Cotton Manufacturers prepared a statement—which it decided not to issue—that "it is quite apparent that the position of OPACS [Office of Price Administration and Civilian Supply] to arbitrarily set ceilings on certain constructions is based on historical data rather than factual information."[46] The NACM appeared to accept the ceilings only with great hesitation. The conflict between the NACM and OPA officials (especially John K. Galbraith) reached a high point at a 1942 meeting. Russell Fisher, president of the NACM, brought up the question of "whether the OPA was dealing fairly with the industry. Mr. Stix [of OPA] chose to resent the implication and asked if I thought OPA was dealing off the bottom of the deck. I told him we hoped not, but the decision in this case would indicate to the trade whether or not they were, and that we raised the question of whether OPA was to be trusted."[47]

The next year, noting that war had halted the decline of Northern textile industry, the NACM threatened to close those mills unless ceiling prices were raised:

> The trend of northern mill liquidation diminished with the outbreak of the war. This was not only because their production was needed, but because it appeared that the demand would be sufficient to enable them to operate profitably. Whether the refusal of the Office of Price Administration to recognize the increased cost of manufacture, through increased ceiling prices, will tend to make some of the manufacturers feel that there is no use endeavoring to continue, remains to be seen.[48]

Although the OPA was industry's chief villain, other agencies also drew attacks. Mills complained that United States Employment Service regulations, by giving textiles low priorities for workers, hindered textile production. Industry representatives believed that the WMC manpower utilization programs—focused on a longer work week—avoided what these businessmen saw as the real obstacle to more efficient use of workers: labor organizations, or, as they termed it, union rules.[49]

At least one Lowell businessman, Bertrand McKittrick, refused to serve on an allocation board when invited. He felt his central position in his industry left him too vulnerable to pressure from friends. Although the government representatives insisted that these ties were the reason he had been selected, he still refused.[50]

Politics: Belated Progressivism

Despite their hostility to liberal government domestic policies, many of the mill elite professed rather liberal political opinions on international wartime issues. Some of this derived from their English ancestry that doubtlessly contributed to early interest in the European war and a desire for the United States to do all it could, short of declaring war, to aid the Allied cause. Several local leaders now claim to have seen American entry into the war as inevitable and to have encouraged preparedness. Few people other than the rich gave such early support to war efforts.

On the other hand, few members of the mill elite ever broke faith with the Republican party in this predominantly Democratic city. Feelings about Franklin Delano Roosevelt were, at best, ambivalent. Although respecting Roosevelt's war leadership, McKittrick stated, "You always had the feeling he made deals we didn't know about." They recognized the Democrat's efforts to revive the economy, but also realized that only the onset of world war ended what one man still calls the "recession." Opinions of FDR ranged from this mild, almost grudging respect to "You mean for print?"[51] Fond memories still exist throughout the upper class for the first President Roosevelt.

The pet local political project of respectable upper-class Republicans actually preceded the war. As had been true in many American cities since the turn of the century, the Lowell elite wanted to reform the local political system, which they saw as corrupt and increasingly out of their control. This progressivism, in Lowell as elsewhere, aimed to "professionalize" government, in this case by reducing the power of elected mayors and placing it in the hands of appointed city managers.

Such efforts in Lowell came to fruition late in 1942. Capitalizing on a scandal that sent Lowell's last strong, elected mayor, George Ashe, to jail, a coalition of mostly Yankee well-to-do lawyers and corporate men successfully pushed through a change in the system of city government. In the new arrangement, called Plan E, most government power lay with a city manager whose salary was set at a level supposedly high enough—although far from overly generous, despite some accusations—to protect the city's primary official from being tempted by more corrupt sources of income. The idea was to eliminate the Irish-controlled ward and boss system, instituting in its place good, clean, efficient city government.[52]

Plan E elections did, in fact, increase the role of Greek-Americans and Polish-Americans in city politics, but did not threaten elite economic control. The first Plan E mayor was one of the Yankee's own: lawyer Woodbury Howard, a leader of the movement for the change.[53] Upper-class influence on all significant government boards was never questioned, and Howard, who, his wife says, "blamed FDR for everything that later happened in this country," certainly echoed manufacturers' political views.[54]

Samuel Pollard, a city councilor under both the new and the old systems, saw Plan E not as a reform, but instead as "the trickery of proportional representation" brought in by "British old-line settlers who had lost their political perch."[55] Charles Fairbank, a Republican who considered the move to Plan E a pet project, concedes that all but two ward bosses were reelected under the new system.[56] The progressive impulse to modernize and rationalize local government in Lowell produced little real change.

Money and the Obligations of Class

Far more than subjective social position, income is the common objective indicator of class. Lowell's successful citizens proved reluctant and vague—much more so than workers—about revealing the sources and amounts of personal and corporate income. In the aggregate, between 1939 and 1945, the American textile industry increased its net worth by 43 percent. Profits before taxes rose 345 percent and after taxes 107 percent; sales rose 102 percent. Although production wages rose 74 percent, salaries of non-production workers rose 115 percent. Return on corporate net worth rose from an average of 5.4 percent between 1936 and 1939 to 24 percent in 1944.[57]

In Lowell, the income for the Ames rose from $202,000 in 1939–40 to a high of $500,000 in 1942–43 and below $300,000 only in 1943–

44. The Boott showed a very modest profit of $30,000 in 1939; in 1943, it earned $235,000. J. R. Flather recalls the excess-profits tax, but says the mills never earned excess profits to be taxed. In any case, the allowed profits of 7 percent were significantly higher than had been typical in the textile industry.[58] The effect of the war was most dramatic at the Merrimack under the new "professional" management of "outsider" Bertrand Hawkins. During most of the 1930s, the Merrimack posted net losses. Between 1942 and 1945, its annual income was consistently more than $1 million (Table 8).

If personal income is taken into account, Lowell's hometown elite might be merely upper middle class in most big cities, certainly not the movers and shakers of society. At the Boott, J. R. Flather's salary from the mill as assistant general manager and assistant treasurer never rose above $15,000 during the war years.[59] Frederick Flather left an estate of $750,000 when he died in 1967.[60] The salary of Bertrand Hawkins as president of the Merrimack was higher, and rose from $30,000 in 1938 to the remarkable amount of about $70,000 per year during the war. To his salary can be added an income as a stockholder in a corporation with earnings in the vicinity of $1 million each year. Hawkins's share of the Merrimack rose from zero in 1938, 1939, and 1940 to more than 12 percent by 1945. The vice-president of the Merrimack received about $20,000 a year.[61]

These incomes were certainly very comfortable, but not those of titans of industry. The ancestral family homes in Lowell, like many

Table 8. Merrimack Manufacturing Company, 1935–45

Year	Total Income	Total Income Tax	Excess Profits Tax	Lowell Property Tax	Adjusted Net Income Before Taxes
1935	408,924.51	0	0	93,012.31	−483,600.49
1936	461,215.48	0	0	49,612.68	−468,379.73
1937	726,343.26	0	0	46,192.74	−692,271.16
1938	190,040.57	0	0	52,747.92	−758,879.58
1939	1,518,980.22	42,976.49	1,043.72	49,113.90	262,493.41
1940	2,453,553.45	190,383.73	701.84	47,742.91	809,932.23
1941	3,482,198.81	293,769.07	0	42,353.05	950,985.86
1942	4,612,838.35	241,854.73	0	49,366.90	2,260,620.88
1943	3,900,841.12	237,452.99	0	50,654.08	1,721,219.89
1944	3,332,244.25	221,999.75	1,910.32	78,975.60	1,528,645.02
1945	2,631,072.54	225,642.86	0	67,216.04	1,103,659.41

Sources: Federal Income Tax returns, 1935–45, Merrimack papers.

New England houses, were quite spacious, but few were mansions. Most were located on or near Andover Street in Upper Belvidere, a stable neighborhood until after the war when the exodus of Lowell's successful citizens accelerated. All had a 1941 tax value of less than $16,000 and were situated on about a half acre of land valued at $5,000.[62] Family economic life was always secure and comfortable, but rarely opulent.

By hometown social position, however, the mill elite are certainly an authentic elite, as their leadership in the Plan E campaign illustrates. Through social networks built up over decades, Lowell reveals itself most clearly, as both Lowell natives Charles Fairbank and Jack Kerouac describe it, as a large town rather than as a small city.[63] A few dozen mill owners, bank officials, successful businessmen, and professionals all meet in the same clubs and sit on the boards of the same community organizations. From their point of view, all Lowellians gave generously of their time and fortunes to the war effort. "Lowell's a cooperative group," said Fairbank.[64] An extremely close-knit group, most of Lowell's social leaders know each other well, even if they were not always close friends.

Mill representatives naturally sat on the boards of Lowell (and Boston) banks and thereby took formal part in the active financial life of a city at war. Savings rose and the loan market was extremely busy. Practically every local company applied for and received loans to get old machines going again and to expand for new war business. Guaranteed by the government, these loans were all repaid promptly. The ratio of deposits to withdrawals improved during each war year, followed by a wave of withdrawals in 1946 as people spent their war savings. All Lowell savings banks showed a significant annual increase in the size of accounts between 1941 and 1946. The banks' assets, of course, rose also.[65]

As would be expected of the upper class, Lowell's elite took the public lead in wartime home-front activities. A week after Pearl Harbor, Mayor Ashe called a meeting in city hall attended by representatives of "all public utilities, key city departments and big mill and business interest. . . . On motion of Walter B. French, agent of the Appleton Company and a selective service board member, the group organized into the Lowell Permanent Defense Strategy Board, with Frank G.W. McKittrick [of Frank G.W. McKittrick Textile Co.] as chairman." Within ten days, a hundred Lowell citizens had signed up as volunteer auxiliary policemen to guard property during blackouts and air raids.[66]

As did labor leaders, corporate leaders served on all major boards overseeing wartime activities in Lowell such as the draft, manpower allocations, and rationing. The difference was that while labor representatives might have to deal with cases of individuals they knew, business representatives sometimes dealt with *companies* they knew. For example, corporations, like individuals, had to apply for priority ratings for gas rationing. The application of the McKittrick Company was an excellent example of New England thrift and upper-class cooperation: the chair of the rationing board, upon reading the application, called the president to mention that the request was barely a third of what could have been allowed. The board, however, was permitted to grant only the requested amount; nevertheless, the company even purchased and operated a new car left in a showroom from before auto manufacturers shifted production to war vehicles. Workers preferred less luxurious cars, so permission for the purchase was obtained easily. Even the high price proved a partial blessing: it ensured that the corporation stayed well within the bounds of the excess profits tax.[67]

In more personal ways, gas rationing reflects the obligations on social leaders. Most upper-class sacrifices because of rationing were undertaken voluntarily for the war effort or under social pressure. Gas rationing presented little real hardship and reflected the petty side of class advantages. In Stevens's case, "Father had a special car because he was a businessman [and] could always get the gas he needed."[68] Ames Stevens's nephew, Reginald Pawle, as personnel director at U.S. Bunting, was in charge of gas rationing for the mill; "being a conscientious soul," he says, he gave himself the least possible rating and therefore he walked to work and could use his car only on weekends. Homer Bourgeois, president of Union National Bank, bicycled to work.[69] Although "coupons were so easy to get," Bertrand McKittrick used the train for business trips because "it was embarrassing to drive." The Flathers even kept a horse and buggy rather than use a car and used this conveyance for an overnight trip to an inn in nearby Andover. They caused quite a stir; it had been many years since the inn had had facilities to handle a horse.[70]

Similarly, war rationing affected the vacations of Mayor Woodbury Howard, as his wife Lydia recalls:

> We went vacationing up to Hancock, New Hampshire, [because] there was an inn there and we could stay.... We never would take a trip in those war years where you had to tour around because there wasn't gasoline....
>
> I do also remember now that once we went up to the Hancock Inn and that was wartime and I forgot to pack his white shirts. And that was the day where you couldn't have appeared in the dining room without a white

shirt. We had to go down to Fitchburg, which used gasoline we shouldn't have used, and buy some shirts that were inferior and more expensive. . . . But that's the way you did it: you went to one place and stayed there.[71]

J. R. Flather's most public voluntary contribution to the war effort came in his work on the Middlesex County draft appeal board, work that demanded several of his already busy mornings each month. He served on the board throughout the war with a Lowell doctor, a local labor leader, and several others from cities throughout the county, and proudly remembers siding with the labor representative in most disputes. (The overwhelming majority of cases were unanimous.) Requests for exemptions came primarily from employers seeking to retain key help. "We looked with a jaundiced eye on some of these" because board members all had to contend with employees and co-workers being drafted. In Flather's opinion, the board never veered from strict impartiality, and he recalls no requests for religious or conscientious objector exemption, nor reclassifications to I-A being used as punishment.[72]

The chair of the local Red Cross chapter also ran a family corporation dealing in used textile machinery. As early as December of 1941, Lowell citizens were called upon "to show their Americanism . . . by voluntarily contributing to this great humanitarian cause."[73] On the other hand, the value of Red Cross work in Lowell, like the value of paternalism in benefiting workers, has been questioned. Philip McGowan, a successful store owner, considers the Red Cross was more talk than action compared to the more significant contributions of the less class-bound and less classy YMCA and Salvation Army.[74]

Early Red Cross war work centered on fund-raising for relief projects in Europe. For this, contacts within Lowell's upper class counted highly. Later, as a result of Lowell's proximity to Fort Devens, the local chapter became one of the most active in Massachusetts, devoting the greatest part of its energies to determining the whereabouts of missing servicemen.[75] For this effort, administrative and executive skills proved useful, although not nearly as much as skill in fund-raising.

Another favorite charitable activity was to sit on the YMCA board of directors. As with the Red Cross, the efforts of the directors centered on raising money for the wartime expansion of Y activities. With Lowell as the major liberty town for Fort Devens soldiers, the Y provided sleeping facilities for countless servicemen throughout the war. In addition, the physical fitness program was greatly expanded to take care of the many young men who wanted to prepare for the draft physicals and for boot camp. Traditional Y programs had to be shortened so that participants could complete them before being drafted.

The Lowell Boys Club, of which J. R. Flather was director, "built character" and "contributed to good morale" in the cause of the war.[76]

A good deal of soliciting for donations to the Red Cross and other social service organizations occurred informally at the Yorick Club, Lowell's exclusive luncheon club for three hundred men of respectable position and income: mill owners, managers, a few doctors and lawyers, "successful" businessmen, with the temporary addition of a few officials from Remington and other war industries. John Albert Notini, who ran a wholesale cigarette business, was one of the few men who actually had more time during the war to spend at the Yorick: "Because of the fact we didn't have the merchandise to sell and we could move things quicker, we had more leisure time on our hands. And I remember spending a lot of time [at the Yorick] during the war because we didn't have as much to do. You had to do your work in the morning, and then by afternoon, probably, you didn't have any more stuff to do."[77]

Charles Fairbank, a long-time member, describes the Yorick as "just a luncheon club where mill people met. Anything that happened was informal because managers, etc., met here. [The club] always had a full membership." At the Yorick, a public-minded citizen not only could ask comrades for donations, but could also discuss establishing programs—there was one at each mill—for employees to buy war bonds and contribute to the Red Cross, both individually and through payroll deductions.

More than social service business occurred in the Yorick, of course. Away from government priorities and prying, mill managers could dabble in local politics, discuss business and war conditions, and deal informally with friends who would provide their mills with supplies. Fairbank notes that he "didn't have to compete in price back then" because he could deal personally with Flather and others.[78]

To a lesser extent, Vesper Country Club and the Rotary Club played a similar informal role. Business at the Vesper, however, suffered during the war because of both the draft and transportation difficulties in reaching the club on the outskirts of town: to get to his weekly golf game, McKittrick carpooled.[79] Even the gas shortage, however, could not keep many executives from golf games that were important for personal or business reasons. Lowell was represented at a wartime annual meeting of the New England Textile Club held in Connecticut. "Despite the gasoline shortage, rubber conservation and other inconveniences, the meeting was well attended, about fifty appearing on the golf links during the afternoon."[80]

William Doherty, in the metals business, told how informal ties benefited both him and the Merrimack:

> We had forty tons of straight tin. . . . Merrimack Mills . . . needs tin to line chemical vats and the like. They came to us and they said, "Can you give us five ton of tin?" They knew we had it, because we were their supplier. We didn't declare it. They said declare all your inventory, but we only deducted a minimum part of inventory, and I was sitting on this thing. I can't use it.
>
> Now Merrimack needs the stuff, because they can't buy it. I sold five ton of tin and I had them charge it back as cast iron. And I delivered it to them, I remember, on a Sunday. I went with the truck driver, and he made the purchasing; the master mechanic and his guy unloaded down there, because we didn't want anyone to see what the hell we were doing.
>
> And it was a legitimate thing. They needed it; we had it. If the government knew it, Jesus, we'd be right in the soup.[81]

Finally, mill managers were necessarily involved in all corporate voluntary contributions to the war effort. The Merrimack Mill established a payroll deduction program for the workers to purchase war bonds, with administrative expenses absorbed by the company. The Boott chief executive personally walked through the mill often—and requested other executives to do likewise—encouraging his employees to buy bonds, contribute to the Red Cross, and bring scrap metal to the collection in the millyard. All well-to-do Lowellians bought a good many war bonds themselves. The president of the Parker Bobbin Company, Charles Fairbank, later sent his daughter through college and paid for her wedding and a down payment on a house when he cashed them in.[82]

Women's Contributions

Social position implied special duties for wives of successful mill executives as well as for their husbands. (Few Lowell women—14 in 1940 compared to 266 men—held positions of major responsibility in manufacturing.)[83] Through membership in the Middlesex Women's Club, the female equivalent to the Yorick, women participated in fund-raising, collected Christmas gifts for Fort Devens, and heard lectures on "Why America Fights."

Women from practically all of Lowell's women's clubs did volunteer work connected with Fort Devens. Several groups sent fifteen girls each to the first dances for Devens soldiers. Seton Guild members served breakfasts at the USO. Representatives of the Paint and Powder Club and Seton Guild served as telephone operators for mock air raids.

The women's pages of the *Lowell Daily Sun* featured such timely items as "Second World War Styles," including an air-raid warden outfit.[84]

Lydia Howard described a few elements of wartime life from her perspective as mayor's wife:

There was the Red Cross. I learned home nursing and first aid and band-aging. These were all separate things. . . . [Learning home nursing] was done very thoroughly, the idea being that it was hard to get doctors. And you might have a severe illness at home, and we were trained by trained nurses. And it was a really serious course. The idea was that if you had then a sickness at home, you'd be able, in a fairly professional way, to take care of them. . . . My daughter had pneumonia when she was a little girl, and I remember that I could take care of her very professionally. . . .

I presume I was always home in the morning. Then in the afternoon if I had one of these Red Cross things to do, or anything related with the war effort, bandaging, whatever, then I had a babysitter and went out. I did my own work. And then evenings—of course, I did have to go a great deal with [Woodbury Howard] to political things: dinners and whatnot. So probably they were very active years. And I think probably because you had to maybe, I sewed a lot then, made almost all the clothes, and lots for myself, too. So that it was just very busy. And you did things like, my husband was never good at fixing things, but you know he tried. He tried to fix the washer because it was hard to get plumbers . . . because in every profession, every type of work, somebody was gone, which meant a doubling up of work. . . .

I think there was more entertaining at home because people were closer to each other, it seemed to me. We had an awfully good time, but then most of our friends were not in the service. . . . As far as I was concerned, it was a very positive, happy, active time, and sacrificial years, but not when I think of sacrifice—I'm not such a fool that I don't know we've never ever sacrificed as we would have if we'd lived in Europe or in Asia, the Middle East.[85]

One woman's major contribution remained hidden throughout the war from all except her husband. Even today few of Elizabeth Flather's neighbors or relatives know of her secret government work.

Near the war's beginning, a woman she did not know asked Flather to serve the government voluntarily by reporting any suspicious activities in the city. The anonymous woman gave Flather a Boston telephone number to call if she had information; no clue was ever given as to whom she was working for. Flather never learned what agency she reported to, only that it was not the FBI.

Disbelief that she could be of any use was her first reaction, but Flather never doubted the authenticity of the assignment, nor did she ever ask to see the credentials of the woman who enlisted her. The government apparently wanted information on the loyalty of Lowell's ethnic groups, about which this mill owner's wife knew little. Eventually it developed that Flather was to listen at bridge clubs and other social gatherings to find out if anyone spoke against the president of the United States. In addition, because the neighborhood children tended to gather in the family's yard, she listened to their conversations. The government's interest focused on the loyalty of foreign-born servants, especially several Mexicans working in the small stables of some wealthy Upper Belvidere residents.

Given the wartime atmosphere, Flather willingly agreed to this informal spying upon her friends. Fears that refusal might impugn her own loyalty played little role in her cooperation; to her it represented a way to contribute to the war effort, although she never expected to contribute anything of importance.

The task proved highly unrewarding, even frustrating: Flather never knew if action came of her reports; she received no pay, and only brief thanks at the end from a man in the State House in Boston. She rarely saw disloyal, or even unusual, behavior, although "I did see a Jap watching the mill once." Her reports centered mostly on the Mexicans, but she found "most of them were loyal," as were all Lowellians she observed. "I never had anything drastic to report." The Irish, although not altogether happy about fighting England's war, gave no signs of real discontent or trouble. All in all, although Flather frequently called the anonymous telephone number, she did not report a single incident she regarded as really important.

The real significance lies in the fact that, so far as Flather is aware, few Lowellians then or now realized that their neighbors had been organized to spy on them. Although it is unclear how many Lowellians—of either sex or from any class—performed a similar task, Flather (and women like her) had special entree that others didn't. She had unique social ties and mobility. And in addition to her extensive cultural network, she had time to volunteer her services.[86]

Obligations aside, war brought at least one luxury to wealthy families and especially to women. Sizable numbers of black servicemen were stationed at Fort Devens, and many of their wives temporarily lived in Lowell. To many long-time citizens, these women of a different race were the most highly visible difference in the wartime city. Many black women worked in Lowell's mills, but many others became domestic servants in homes of the well-to-do. Bertrand McKittrick remembers that "to get a woman to do one or two days' work in your house was easier," and when one left, as they did when their husbands left Devens, the worker would find another "colored" friend to take her place.

McKittrick's family "had some excellent ones. . . . Help was easier to get than after the war or before . . . . In general they were pretty good. We were sorry to see the end of it."[87] Parker Bobbin Company's Charles Fairbank noted the same "infiltration of colored help" from Devens.[88] The move to black household servants had begun, but was still far from significant.[89]

Conclusion: No Tomorrow

Looking back on the war years, Ed Stevens now calls it a "knights-on-white-chargers sort of thing."[90] The elite profess a pride in "their" city's contribution to the war effort. Lowellians, not loudly patriotic, "took their time to be of some genuine help," believes Charles Fairbank.[91]

Yankee honesty prevailed in the self-reports of Lowell elites. There was, indeed, a "big black market, but we would have nothing to do with it because life is short." A strong tinge of just reward pervades memories of those who succumbed to temptation only to be caught and prosecuted. Lowell citizens of high social status simply "lived from day to day as New England always did." Despite the excitement of war and the busy economy, their Lowell remained "a big city and a small town."[92]

On the other hand, Lowell remained, in fact, a city in which the views of mill owners—whether by custom or necessity—played the central role. Despite this ideology of deference, and despite prosperity and profits, the elite did little to prepare Lowell for the postwar years. Profits were not—and, because of government regulations until V-J Day, could not—be reinvested in the mills to modernize the plants and make them again technologically competitive. After two decades of decaying machinery from 1925 to 1945, this capital investment would have been necessary to halt the imminent closing of remaining mills. Further, mill corporations continued to adamantly fight unionization, although cooperation between well-organized labor and well-organized management might have helped to redevelop Lowell. Louis Vergados, union activist:

> At that time the Boott Mill refused to agree to the national contract that was negotiated. That's shortly, right after I returned [from the services]. So I was assigned to take care of the strike. . . . Everybody signed, the Boott Mill refused to sign. Everybody in New England signed, but the Boott Mill refused to sign to give the benefits that were negotiated. So we had a nine-month strike. We went through the winter, the summer, but we won the strike and a complete contract with all the benefits that were negotiated with the other plants throughout the United States.[93]

No major textile firm showed a significant tendency to reorganize during the boom, streamline itself, or broaden Yankee management. Fred Burtt says that Abbott Worsted changed little precisely because it was a closed, family-owned corporation. He adds that, as superintendent, he held the top spot possible for a someone not a family member.[94] The Merrimack had already shaken up its management in the late thirties, bringing in a suburban Boston president to replace Frederick Flather, who was then running both the Merrimack and the Boott, both at a loss.[95] Only one company, Ames Worsted, began to move operations out of Lowell, but this move followed the war. Says Edward Stevens, "war accelerated abrupt change."[96] Significantly, only the Ames still survives as a corporation, while the Boott and the Merrimack closed.

Finally, mill corporations continued to hinder any broadening of Lowell's industrial base—especially in their hostility to Remington and its successors. They viewed a threat to their local monopoly over labor as a threat to the city. Although resigned to closing the textile mills after the war, they acted during the war to prevent the establishment of substitutes. As community leaders professing a paternalistic interest in the welfare of the working class, the mill elite proved itself unwilling or unable to do more than protect its own short-range hegemony. Its actions essentially ensured that Lowell's steady industrial decline would continue in the postwar years.

NOTES

1. Merrimack Papers, Baker Library, Harvard Business School, Cambridge, Mass.; interview with John Flather and Elizabeth Flather, 13 January 1975.

2. *Ames Textile Corporation, 1865–1965* (n.p.: Ames Textile, 1965), 1–4.

3. Merrimack Papers; Margaret Terrell Parker *Lowell: A Study of Industrial Decline* (1940; repr., Port Washington, N.Y.: Kennikat Press, 1970), 105–8.

4. Interview with Edward Stevens, 26 November 1974.

5. Ibid.

6. *American Wool and Cotton Reporter* 56, no. 44 (1942):31.

7. Interview with John Flather, 9 December 1974.

8. Interview with Edward Stevens.

9. Interview with Frank Fiske and Hazel Fiske, 3 December 1974; Merrimack Papers.

10. Interview with Edward Larter, 22 March 1975.

11. Interview with Charles Fairbank, 19 December 1974.

12. Interview with John Flather.

13. Interview with Edward Stevens.

14. Frank McSherry to Russell Fisher, 27 November 1942, Northern Textile Association Papers, Museum of American Textile History, North Andover, Mass.; Fisher to J. Colby Lewis, 4 January 1943, NTA Papers.

15. "Priorities Regulation No. 10," National Association of Wool Manufacturers Papers, Museum of American Textile History, North Andover, Mass.; National Archives, Record Group 211, "WMC Records."

16. Chester Bowles to Russell Fisher, 24 April 1942, NTA Papers.

17. United States Civilian Production Administration, Bureau of Demobilization, *Industrial Mobilization for War: A History of the War Production Board and Predecessor Agencies 1940–1945* (Washington: GPO, 1947), 949.

18. Interview with Edward Stevens; interview with Frank Fiske and Hazel Fiske; interview with John Flather; *Ames Textile Corporation,* 5.

19. United States Employment Service: Massachusetts, *Monthly Labor Market Report,* 16 February 1942–15 March 1942, 15; interview with John Flather.

20. Interview with John Flather.

21. National Association of Cotton Manufacturers, *Transactions, 1933–1942* (n.p.: NACM, 1943), 673, 686–99; *American Wool and Cotton Reporter,* 31; interview with John Flather; *Lowell Daily Sun,* 24 March 1943, 4.

22. Lowell, "City Council Journal," 17 March 1942; 4 June 1945; Merrimack Papers.

23. *Lowell Daily Sun,* 26 January 1944, 1.

24. Record Group 211, "WMC Records"; *Boston Herald Traveller,* 21 November 1943; *Newsweek,* 5 February 1944, 22.

25. Record Group 211, "WMC Records."

26. *Boston Herald Traveller,* 30 January 1944.

27. Woodbury Howard scrapbooks, Lowell Historical Society, Lowell, Mass.; *Christian Science Monitor,* 22 January 1944.

28. Interview with John Flather.

29. National Archives, Record Group 202, "NWLB Records."

30. *American Wool and Cotton Reporter* 56, no. 41 (1942):32; interview with John Flather.

31. *Textile Labor* 6, no. 9 (1945):9; interview with Edward Stevens.

32. Interview with Edward Larter.

33. Telegram from NACM Clearing Committee to all CIO mills, 20 July 1945, NTA Papers; telegram from Frederick Flather to Clearing Committee, 20 July 1945, NTA Papers; L. N. Hale to all Northern mills, 18 July 1945, NTA Papers.

34. Interview with John Flather and Elizabeth Flather, 13 January 1975.

35. Merrimack Papers; *Boston Herald Traveller,* 11 December 1957, 18; interview with Edward Stevens; interview with John Flather; interview with Charles Fairbank; interview with Frank Fiske and Hazel Fiske, 3 November 1975.

36. Interview with Charles Fairbank.

37. Interview with Elizabeth Flather and John Flather.

38. Interview with Fred Burtt, 3 November 1975.

39. Memo, 20 July 1943, NTA Papers; memo, 22 August 1941, NTA Papers; Paul Halstead to J. Holmes Daly, 15 November 1943, NTA Papers; interview with John Flather.

40. Roberts Chickering to NACM, 12 December 1941, NTA Papers.

41. United States Civilian Production Administration, Bureau of Demobilization, *Dollar-a-Year and Without Compensation Personnel Policies of the War Production Board and Predecessor Agencies,* Historical Reports on War Administration Special Study no. 27 (Washington: WPB, 20 April 1947), 56–59.

42. National Association of Wool Manufacturers, *Bulletin of the Wool Manufacturers,* 1941; Russell Fisher to Robert Loper, 26 September 1941, NTA Papers.

43. *Daily News Record,* 17 June 1942; 19 June 1942.

44. David Novick, Melvin Anshen, and W. C. Truppner, *Wartime Production Controls* (New York: Columbia University Press, 1949), 266–67.

45. Novick, Anshen, and Truppner, *Wartime Production Controls,* 242.

46. Statement on ceiling prices, 14 August 1941, NTA Papers.

47. Russell Fisher memo, 2 December 1942, NTA Papers.

48. Russell Fisher to Frank Walton, 10 August 1943, NTA Papers.

49. Russell Fisher to Thomas Bancroft, 5 July 1944, NTA Papers; Russell Fisher memo, 28 September 1944, NTA Papers.

50. Interview with Bertrand McKittrick, 3 February 1975.

51. Interview with Bertrand McKittrick.

52. Mary H. Blewett, "The Mills and the Multitudes: A Political History" in *Cotton Was King: A History of Lowell, Massachusetts* (n.p.: New Hampshire Publishing in collaboration with the Lowell Historical Society, 1976), 161–89.

53. Blewett, "The Mills and the Multitudes."

54. Interview with Lydia Howard, 18 March 1975.

55. Interview with Samuel Pollard, 7 January 1975.

56. Interview with Charles Fairbank.

57. Textile Workers Union of America, Research Department Economic Report, *The Nation's Most Prosperous Industry: An Accounting of the Postwar Financial Experience of American Textile Manufacturers* (New York: TWUA, 1948), 20; *Labor's Monthly Survey* 6, no. 3 (1945):3.

58. Ames Textile Corporation, "Auditor's Financial Statements," typescript, passim; *American Wool and Cotton Reporter* 56, no. 5 (1942):95–99; *American Wool and Cotton Reporter* 58, no. 30 (1944):111–15; interview with John Flather.

59. Interview with John Flather.

60. *Boston Herald Traveller,* 19 September 1967.

61. Merrimack Papers.

62. City of Lowell, *Tax List* (n.p.: 1941).

63. Interview with Charles Fairbank; Jack Kerouac, *The Town and the City* (New York: Harcourt, Brace, Jovanovich, 1950).

64. Interview with Charles Fairbank.

65. Interview with Homer Bourgeois, 5 December 1974; *Boston Herald Traveller,* 19 September 1967; Department of Banking and Insurance, *Annual Report,* passim.

66. *Boston Herald Traveller,* 16 December 1941; 27 December 1941.

67. Interview with Bertrand McKittrick.

68. Interview with Edward Stevens.

69. Confidential interview.

70. Interview with Bertrand McKittrick; interview with John Flather.

71. Interview with Lydia Howard.

72. Interview with John Flather and Elizabeth Flather.

73. *Lowell Daily Sun,* 1 December 1941, 1.

74. Interview with Philip McGowan and Edward Doherty, 22 April 1975.

75. Frederick W. Coburn, "Typical Extracts from a History of the Lowell Chapter, American Red Cross," paper read before the Lowell Historical Society, 13 February 1946, typescript.

76. Interview with Wilfred Pearson, 1 January 1965; interview with John Flather.

77. McCarthy to author, 23 August 1977; interview with John Albert Notini, 12 April 1975.

78. Interview with Charles Fairbank.

79. Interview with Bertrand McKittrick.

80. *American Wool and Cotton Reporter* 56, no. 26 (1942):42.

81. Interview with William Doherty and Philip McGowan.

82. Interview with Frank Fiske and Hazel Fiske; interview with John Flather; interview with Charles Fairbank.

83. United States Department of Commerce, Bureau of the Census, *Sixteenth Census of the United States: 1940, Population, Third Series, The Labor Force: Occupation, Industry, Employment, and Income: Massachusetts* (Washington: GPO, 1943), 31.

84. *Lowell Daily Sun,* 8 December 1942, 8; *Boston Herald Traveller,* 12 April 1941; 11 October 1941.

85. Interview with Lydia Howard.

86. Interview with John Flather and Elizabeth Flather.

87. Interview with Bertrand McKittrick.

88. Interview with Charles Fairbank.

89. Bureau of the Census, *Characteristics of the Non-White Population, 1940,* 6; Bureau of the Census, *Population: The Labor Force,* pt. 3, 506, 509; *Population, 1950,* vol. 2, *Massachusetts,* 230–31.

90. Interview with Edward Stevens.

91. Interview with Charles Fairbank.

92. Interview with Charles Fairbank; interview with Bertrand McKittrick.

93. Interview with Louis Vergados, 18 September 1975.

94. Interview with Fred Burtt.

95. Merrimack Papers.

96. Interview with Edward Stevens.

6

The Shifting Center

One of World War II's ironies was that it split Lowell's middle class, accentuating its two contradictory identities. At the top, some male professionals such as doctors and lawyers benefited, moving closer to the elite in status and wealth. Even a few small businessmen would base postwar growth on wartime renewal and prosperity. On the other hand, most members of the middle class, such as teachers and shop-keepers, saw their self-interest move close to that of workers.

One reason for this division is that the men and women of the middle class defy simple definition, especially in contrast to the clearly delineated community roles of workers and bosses. The variety of middle-class economic and social functions is immense, yet relatively few individuals perform any single occupation. Whereas thousands of Lowell people during the 1930s could be classified simply as operatives and laborers, less than 10 percent of the labor force fell into standard middle-class categories—proprietors, managers, officials, or professionals. At the other limit on the income scale, the middle class did not control the Lowell economy; that privilege was reserved for the select few who owned and operated the textile industry.

Money alone did not separate the middle class from either the elite or workers. The income of foremen or families with two wage earners was higher than that of self-employed shopkeepers, while in the the upper ranks of the middle class, some proprietors and professionals were rich by local standards.

The paradox is that despite its small numbers and its lack of direct economic power, the popular image—in movies, advertising, magazines—of an entire community is identified with its middle class. Popular images of wartime life—as during other periods—reflected middle-class activities and standards even though war contracts affected middle-class enterprises only at second hand.

One explanation for the importance of the middle class in the popular mind functions as a definition of that class. The middle class is composed of those whose livelihood derives from acting as intermediaries between people and the necessities (and luxuries) of life. Thus, membership in the middle class derives largely from economic roles rather than income or social position, although these categories obviously overlap. The bourgeoisie delivers services—health care, legal services, education, religion—and goods—food, clothing, shelter. The day-to-day effects of war on Lowell were most obvious in the ability of the bourgeoisie to provide these necessities. Simply, city life focuses on the highly visible shops and offices of the middle class.

Professionals comprise one component of the bourgeoisie. The 1940 Lowell census included 2,500 professional men and women in occupations ranging from student nurses to surgeons. What is immediately striking is the duplication of the working-class sexual divisions of labor: men dominate prestige positions, and women are concentrated in the lowest-paid and subservient positions. Doctors and lawyers border on the upper classes; teaching and nursing border on working class.

Even more than professionals, middle-class proprietors conjure up images of typical bourgeois, upstanding community life. Members of this group sell the citizens of the city food, clothing, radios, cars, liquor, furniture, jewelry, and other material goods. Traditionally, middle-class proprietors are men working for money; their wives work at home (Table 9).

Neighborhood Groceries

The grocery business through the end of World War II was primarily a family affair, and each store served a distinct and limited neighborhood. Even outlets of national chains such as the A&P repeated this small, decentralized model. Thus, in 1939, Lowell had 673 stores that sold primarily food; only 1,114 employees worked in these stores, or less than two per store. Food stores that sold no meat averaged less than one employee per store, supporting the image of small family businesses. Gross sales in 1939 averaged only $19,000 for stores selling meat and $11,500 for other food stores. This was significantly less than the average of $25,000 for all Lowell stores.[1] Certainly, a corner grocery was a very difficult way to make a fortune. In terms of income, geographical location, and social networks, food stores most often were part of the working-class neighborhoods they served, even though they were the most numerous and most visible enterprises of the middle class.

Food stores also demonstrated to their neighborhoods the changed wartime delivery of services: shortages of many sorts plagued groceries

Table 9. The Lowell Middle Class, 1940

	Male	Female
Professionals		
Teachers	143	762
Clergy	107	0
Dentists	37	2
Judges and lawyers	110	6
Pharmacists	69	2
Physicians and surgeons	101	8
Nurses and student nurses	3	541
Proprietors		
Food businesses	320	30
Shoe store	21	0
Clothing stores	42	19
Variety stores	59	26
Filling stations	68	1
Car dealerships	50	0

Source: United States Department of Commerce, Bureau of the Census, *Sixteenth Census of the United States, 1940, Population, Third Series, The Labor Force: Occupation, Industry, Employment, and Income: Massachusetts* (Washington: GPO, 1943), 31.

throughout the war. Understandably, people remember this part of home-front life well because they faced shortages almost daily by necessity; unlike many other purchases, eating could not be postponed until after V-J Day. Food shortages affected families much more immediately than did the unavailability of major appliances (such as refrigerators) or automobiles and gasoline, all of which were relative luxuries in Lowell, even before 1941.

Everett Harris, a pipe fitter, recalled the potato shortage: "Potatoes were hard to get, very, very hard to get. I know one fellow, says, 'Come up to the house,' he says. 'I got some white potatoes.' And I went up, and he gave me two or three and that was a big thing during the war. I remember Campbell beans, you couldn't find them at all. . . . At that time, we didn't have a car, so I wasn't really affected by gas rationing."[2]

Demand for food could neither decline nor rise significantly from prewar levels. Depression or boom time, people had to eat. Eating habits did change somewhat, but total consumption stayed the same.[3] The result was increased shortages as production of all civilian items declined and stocks of storable basic commodities were severely depleted.[4]

The solution, in part, was rationing, and although it was primarily a war measure, it was also a social program. Little could be done in the 1930s to alleviate maldistribution of essential goods, but war and crisis let New Dealers institute rationing to prevent the rich from hoarding items that were in short supply. For all classes, rationing presented a hardship but not a great one, and it was rarely resented. Lowell's elite and working-class women alike accepted sacrifices willingly, if regretfully, with a bit of informal cheating to get by.

The difference between rich and non-rich lay in the point at which sacrifices appeared, which in turn referred back to prewar standards. For example, Charles Fairbank ended the war with five or six thousand meat coupons. He had the good fortune to run a business that used raw material obtained with meat coupons, and the company received far more coupons than it needed. He complained mildly that despite having coupons, he could only get the best cuts of meat at swank Boston hotels.[5]

Most citizens made do with hamburger or with less meat. Alice Swanton:

> I had a grocer before the war started and he would just put aside a pound of hamburger. Steak? Forget it, you didn't get it—or some liver, the cheaper cuts of meat. And when you went to get your groceries, if there were people in the store that maybe weren't regular customers, you didn't say nothing. You just bought a few groceries and he went in to the back and put it in—automatically put it into your bag without saying anything. And then you paid for what you got; it was added when you rang it up, the meat you had. But it was done undercover, put it that way. But there was no price gouging. Butter was the same.[6]

The Case family conserved meat coupons by using blood sausages and horsemeat, saving the valuable coupons for days when guests came to dinner. The daughter, Constance, was amused when relatives were served horsemeat steaks and not told after the meal what they had eaten.[7]

Thomas Ahearn, president of the Lowell Central Labor Union, was labor's representative on the local rationing board:

> You issued the blue stamps for meat and food depending on how many were in the family. Each person was entitled to so many stamps. . . . We had two different types of stamps. Like you couldn't buy a pound of bacon unless you had so many stamps, and different types of meat called for a different number of stamps. You weren't going to use up all your stamps buying a couple of pounds of bacon and not have any red meat for the month. Sugar, you had to have coupons. Sugar was rationed, shoes

were rationed, bicycles were rationed, tires for cars, automobiles were rationed, gasoline was rationed.

They had what they called A, B, and C stamps for gas. "A" stamp: if you owned a car, you're entitled to "A" stamps. . . . And you were only given so many for pleasure. If you worked in an occupation and had to travel . . . they'd allow you the mileage down and back each day. . . .

The ration board was divided into subpanels. They had a full-time secretary and full-time office help, which was civil service people, clerk, and so forth. . . . I'd say there was four panels, and each one had a secretary. There were three to five people [on each]. Labor had to be on each panel. And then they had the people in the office: the clerks and so forth and the counter girls. I'd say they maybe employed twenty or twenty-five people. . . . They were hired by the city, but the federal government approved.

Most of those girls were on civil service and asked for a transfer. There was a councilor, his sister worked up in Devens. She asked for a transfer down and took a cut in pay to work in the rationing board because the people coming in were meeting her. They'd get their "B" book or whatever it was because they were entitled to it, but she was on the counter so her brother was getting a lot of credit for things he didn't have nothing to do with.

Ahearn also described how the board regulated prices in order to keep shortages from pushing inflation:

We also had price control, which the rationing board handled complaints on. . . . A baker couldn't raise the price of a loaf of bread from a certain date. So if that baker tried to cut down the weight, he was in violation because he was going up in his price for the ounces he sold. We got complaints and everybody had to give a receipt with the name of the store and what was purchased and how much and what he charged. A lot of them wouldn't give it and people didn't ask for them. But if you asked, they had to give it to you. It was the law.

Now, if they charged more, that person brought it up to the ration board. What we usually used to do was we'd call this person who's running the business up and talk to them and straighten him out. The second time we'd get a complaint, we turn him over to the regional office and investigators would turn up. They'd come from out of town. Regional office'd send them in to investigate. If found guilty, they were fined and so forth.[8]

Lucille Cordeau's account of rationing is from the consumer's point of view: "We cast ourselves in an unusual situation because we had a young baby, and he had to have evaporated milk. We had tried numerous formulas. And we had to use our meat stamps in order to get him evaporated milk for his formula. We found that sort of difficult because he'd go through a case in a few weeks."[9]

The Office of Price Administration branch in Lowell regularly distributed the coupons that customers had to give grocers. This office also monitored as many stores as possible, reporting weekly to the Boston headquarters about compliance with regulations.

Rationing was a major item in newspapers. People wanted to know about events abroad, but they needed to know what foods were rationed, when stamps were valid, and what was in short supply. The newspaper answered this need with daily columns of rationing news; in addition, many foods ads dealt with shortages, as did this one by del Monte:

"HERE'S OUR FINAL ESTIMATE ON WHAT CANNED FRUITS AND VEGETABLES WILL BE AVAILABLE THIS WINTER—and what you can do to make the best of the situation[10]

In the annals of American government planning, rationing was a remarkably successful phenomenon. It epitomized potential government's ability to control economic affairs for the common good. Despite griping, by and large rationing minimized hoarding and increased the equitable distribution of food. Yvonne Hoar compared the two world wars: "They didn't seem to sacrifice to much of anything [during World War II]. I remember World War I we had no sugar. It was hard getting different things like sugar or butter. And I think there was a little of it during World War II, but not like in World War I."[11]

Just as shortages of major food items presented some minor problems for grocers, so, too, did the shortage of employees. The small size of most food stores and the decrease in limitations on work for young people, however, tended to lessen the draft's impact. In 1937, the A&P had begun moving from corner stores (16 in Lowell before 1935; 15,000 nationwide) to supermarkets, but still had three small stores in Lowell when war began.[12] Although staffed primarily by men before 1941, during World War II, most of the chain's employees were women. Almost all male workers were high school boys.[13]

The connection between World War II and dramatic changes in the postwar food business is difficult to determine. Clearly, the transformation from corner stores to chain supermarkets increased during the war and accelerated greatly after 1945. Of 201 groceries listed in the telephone book in 1941, only 170 remained in 1945 despite four years of wartime prosperity.[14] The *Lowell Sun* in 1943 reported that the war was hurting small businesses because containers for produce were sold to large coops before small, independent farmers.[15] Other factors contributed to the move toward supermarkets. The shortages of many food items led stores expand the range of products sold by introducing

non-food items into their merchandise. The increase of women working in factories and elsewhere stimulated the creation of larger markets
where a woman could quickly purchase all needed items.[16] One local
food store developed into a major New England chain after the war,
but its economic basis for the expansion is not clear. It could have
been war profits, outside legitimate investments, or even—as one ru-
mor asserts—a sellout to the underworld. The present owner of this
chain declined to be interviewed or to allow a look at wartime company
records.

By 1948, the average sales of Lowell food stores had risen to $61,404,
but the average number of employees was still low at 2.34. More important, only 433 of the 673 prewar stores remained. The trend to
supermarkets intensified as the number of all-purpose grocery stores
increased slightly from 171 to 176 despite the decline in the total
number of groceries. The proportion of women managers had increased, but only because of a greater attrition of male managers: from
the 321 male managers in 1940 to only 112 in 1950, and from 30
female managers in 1940 to 19 in 1950. In all, this part of the middle
class shrank from 350 to 131 in just a decade.[17]

Victory Fashions

Because food is such a basic need, wartime social pressures hindered
the open display of grosser inequities, such as eating hard-to-get items
like steak in a public restaurant. These same criteria applied to dress.
Lydia Howard, the wife of a wartime mayor, recalled, "I do remember
my husband saying he'd prefer I dress very simple at all, you know,
public places, so there wouldn't be any, you know—I don't think we
had anything that would have been too showy, but the idea was that
you just didn't do it. But, as I say, just about everyone we knew was
in the same boat, so it didn't seem sacrificial."[18]

In a wartime crisis—or any other crisis—food shortages appear to be
divided relatively equitably: government control to avoid favoritism
for the rich improves morale and community commitment. But clothes
are a slightly different issue. Although they also are a necessity, families
did not face daily pressures to purchase new clothes. Thus, retailers
in the clothing business stood on the border between providing necessities that had to be rationed and luxuries that did not.

Although larger than the neighborhood standard for food stores,
apparel stores in Lowell were still relatively small by modern, metropolitan standards. In 1939, 134 stores employed 599 people and
averaged $30,000 in sales per year. Only two-thirds were owner-op-

erated in contrast to food stores, which were 90 percent owner-oper-ated.[19] More than the small-scale grocers, clothing merchants worked out of substantial downtown Lowell storefronts and identified with city, rather than neighborhood, life. Some of these men even partici-pated in the fringes of the local elite social network, maintaining per-sonal contacts with both political and textile industry leaders.

Two wartime conditions determined the activities of clothing stores during the war: shortages—of cloth, finished products, and employees—and the relative abundance of money in the Lowell economy.

As in most areas of work, one visible change in the wartime clothing business was the proportion of women employed in it. Between March 1940 and March 1944, women trade and service workers in the United States rose from 42.8 percent to 54.9 percent of the workforce. Al-though the increase in the proportion of women was much greater in manufacturing—from 22 percent to 36.6 percent—women did not leave service jobs as suddenly after the war. In December 1945, 47.7 percent of trade and service workers were women, whereas in manufacturing, the number had fallen to 22.6 percent, virtually the prewar level.[20]

In Lowell, heavy wartime business compelled even a men's store to hire two women, augmenting a previously all-male staff of 15. The proportion of female managers improved slightly between 1940 and 1950, from 19 out of 61 to 20 out of 57.[21] But not all clothing stores hired women as a solution to the employee shortage; McGowan's em-ployees just worked harder. Philip McGowan remembered that "I had two that had to go [into the services]. I didn't [replace them]. We worked harder—three: I was forgetting one of my tailors. We worked harder and kept their jobs for them and had their jobs for them when they got out of the service. . . . There wasn't any question of working overtime, unless you considered taking shorter dinner hours. But they were on salary and commission, so it didn't make any difference to them."[22]

From the consumer's point of view, getting food presented some hardships, but clothing shortages were more difficult to overcome. Demand for clothing far exceeded the abilities of stores to get supplies as textile manufacturers concentrated on war production. The *Lowell Sun* went so far as to announce a shoe "famine" in 1943.[23] James Curran, then a buyer for several clothing stores, recalls, "You couldn't get clothing; it was awful. At that time we did a big business . . . ev-erybody did, in spite of the shortages."[24]

Phil McGowan, with his own own clothing store, enjoyed the same business surge:

We'd get clothing back in the store, we'll say on a Tuesday, and wouldn't have time to put it on the racks, cut the ropes, and sell the suits from the floor, right out of the bundle. That's how fast it was coming. . . . And the only ads I'd run in the newspaper would be three-quarters of a page and all I'd say was "Phil McGowan Has Suits." . . . I'm going to tell you this right now: when it came to men's clothing, Jordan Marsh [a major Boston department store] was not selling as much as I was.

(McGowan's memory was not totally accurate: his ads and those of his competitors did indeed offer many items, and often at sale prices.)[25]

Being in Lowell gave clothing stores some advantage in overcoming supply difficulties. McGowan:

We were put on allotments, and the allotments weren't enough to get by. We had many strings to pull in order to survive. I had a very dear friend of mine, had a mill up the street here, manufacturing taffeta. It was the Wannalancit Mill. . . . I would go to New York and I'd offer piece goods to anybody that'd get me clothing, give me finished products. And there was no less than 1,200 yards in a carton of taffeta, which acts as fabric for linings in men's coats. That's how rough things were. And I would get suits from—I don't care if they're going to Saks Fifth Avenue or going to Marshall Field or—I don't care where they were supposed to go to, I'd get the suits because I could give them material to keep their plant going. And for eighteen months, I'd spend three days a week in New York, picking up clothing.[26]

The lack of sufficient fabric in the nation for both military and civilian needs led to controls on fashion early in the war. In the summer of 1942, the War Production Board, according to its press release, "acted to assure the women and girls of America that there will be no extremes in dress styles during this war as there were during the last war, and that their present wardrobes will not be made obsolete by radical fashion changes."[27]

The WPB, using average styles as a standard, instituted measures controlling the length and sweep of skirts and outlawed double-breasted suits and cuffs on men's trousers. WPB order "L-85 banned full skirts, knife pleats and patch pockets. . . . Order M-217, conserving leather, limited shoes to six colors."[28]

These limitations seem to have been observed, although they were often violated in spirit. For example, workers at some larger Lowell and Boston stores reportedly stayed up until midnight the night before the law took effect, slitting fabric so they could say work had begun on a cuff before the deadline. On the other hand, McQuade's in Lowell gave cuff material to the Red Cross because "that was considered the thing to do."[29]

The result was a war-defined fashion standard in which manufacturers' clothing lines reflected wartime life-styles. A National Association of Cotton Manufacturers fashion show featured—in addition to items for town, country, and campus—clothing for war workers in field and factory; for heat-rationed nights; for active sports; for Southern army camps; for gala blackout nights; and for wartime brides. Lowell's Merrimack Manufacturing Company accented work clothes in its ad headlined, "Merrimack Thickset Corduroy for Women in War Work Rates A-2 Priority":

> There's a tough job ahead for the women of this country. Actual manual labor in many cases! And with women taking the place of men on the working front, they naturally turn to the type of utility clothes men prefer. Merrimack Thickset Corduroy (style 82), long a favorite for sportswear and utility, has won a priority rating for women's work clothes. Tough as nails, yet soft as velvet. . . . Merrimack Thickset will find immediate acceptance in our feminine army of production.[30]

In order to control anticipated price increases, the government in May 1942 instituted a "highest-price-line limitation." This meant that a store could introduce no new items at a higher price than during a prewar base period. Possibly because of industry-mindedness or just poor planning, the result was a concentration on more expensive lines. Manufacturers simply produced only their higher-priced lines and by 1944, according to a War Production Board study, "the disappearance of low-end items was apparent in almost every clothing category." Therefore, the government eliminated the highest-price-line limitation in 1944.[31]

Related to the regulations was a move toward established businesses closing and then reopening with higher prices. Philip McGowan:

> We couldn't put any more mark-up on the garments than we had the previous year to the war. Whatever mark-up we worked on then, we had to maintain it, but you could open up a brand new business . . . after December the Seventh and come in with your own mark-up of any kind. . . . But if you were established, you had to maintain your legal mark-up. And they'd come in and check you. They had men going around checking you, and you had to show your bill. . . . In my particular case, I only witnessed them coming once to me, but I think they found that I was 100 percent clean.[32]

Even with price controls, profits as a percentage of sales increased but stayed less than would occur in the immediate postwar years after the closing of the Office of Price Administration.[33] In either case, everything sold at the highest possible price; after the war, people purchased the items they had been unable or unwilling to buy before 1945.[34]

Through rationing, clothing businesses faced direct government intervention at the retail level just as did food businesses did. Customers needed stamps to purchase shoes, the clothing item most in demand.[35] Retailers had to keep accounts of this ration currency at a bank in order to purchase more shoes. In most cases, a discrepancy of 10 percent to 20 percent existed between the amount of stamps a store should have collected and the amount in the account. In almost every instance, the OPA accepted the retailer's explanation of the discrepancy. At one point, a store owner asked Congresswoman Rogers to intervene on his behalf when he had no ration currency to stock shoes in his store.[36]

The shoe shortage, especially of children's shoes, plagued rich and poor alike. Elizabeth Flather, mother of five children and wife of a mill manager, found shoe rationing her hardest wartime problem.[37] With one child, Lydia Howard minimized her difficulty: "I don't seem to remember terrible problems [from rationing]. There must have been problems because there was shoe rationing. And I think it was probably worst if you have a little child and shoes are rationed—but I think probably my husband and I used some of our coupons for her."[38]

Dorothy Ahearn, a worker, made do with lower quality shoes for her children: "I have three children and shoes were rationed, children's shoes were rationed, the leather ones. And the ones we could afford to buy—you know how kids go through shoes—they were made of cardboard, and of course they wore out. So in order to buy the leather ones, I had to go to work."[39]

Ahearn's husband, the labor representative on the local War Price and Rationing Board, confirmed that the worst complaints came from women who wanted shoes. He claimed that the board never refused a request for children's shoes. One woman who wanted shoes to match her wedding dress was, however, turned down because her application indicated that she already owned several pairs of shoes and her wedding dress would cover her shoes. Her anger at the refusal suggests that people did not always agree on what constituted a necessary sacrifice for the war effort.[40]

Curran has a dissenting view of how well rationing worked: "They just couldn't make it work. . . . You were shooting a sparrow with a .45." He had a friend on a rationing board in another city: "He was lucky his house wasn't bombed. . . . He tried to be honest."[41]

Despite government controls, shortages, and other wartime nuisances, most clothing retailers found that World War II definitely boosted business. As with food stores, the number of employees per store rose from 4.5 in 1939 to 7.1 in 1948.[42] To Curran, the war "gave us our real lift" into a million-dollar-a-year operation by 1950.[43] The demand for clothing was so great that McGowan remembers that if "you saw a line, you got into it."[44]

The topic of clothing had its lighter aspect. Luxury catches people's attention more easily than do necessities, and the clothing situation focused in people's minds on the stocking shortage. Because these were almost impossible to find in a store, nylons made well-received holiday presents. At the Boston Navy Yard, Doris Poisson remembers that "when nylons came in . . . at Filene's . . . the office actually gave us an hour off."[45]

Clothing and fashion reveal a great deal about society. Fernand Braudel has written: "It touches on every issue—raw materials, production processes, manufacturing costs, cultural stability, fashion and social hierarchy."[46] Clothing during World War II catered to those who had money. Price controls on consumer items instituted to ensure that everyone got basic necessities often meant instead that "popular-priced" lines disappeared, and all were forced to spend more for these necessities. Production limits reflected the priorities of a nation at war, with the requirements and demands of the armed services always taking precedence. Those who worked for a living had little choice but to obey wartime urgings to "Use it up/Wear it out/Make it do/Or do without."

The Corner Drugstore

Like food stores, Lowell's drugstores tended to be small neighborhood institutions. The average druggist had fewer than three employees (only two if the store had no soda fountain) and grossed about $23,000 per year.[47] The druggist satisfied two desires: medicine and "sundry" items, including cigarettes and candies.

Most basic drugs remained available during the war, although stocks often ran low and turnover was high. Raymond Cordeau, a pharmacist in his father's drugstore, described the situation: "As far as shortages of drugs and all, all your staples were coming through very well. Glycerin: at that time we used a lot of glycerin. Glycerin was—it's used in some of munitions. It's a by-product of soap. And that always got short during the war and could get expensive because they were using it for manufacturing munitions."[48]

More burdensome was the loss of pharmacists to the service, where their training entitled them to officers' ratings. One hundred and six

Massachusetts drugstores closed in the first year of the war because of a shortage of pharmacists or trained salespeople. The state board of registration resisted pressure to lower certification standards temporarily, although the number of pharmacists approved annually dropped by two-thirds by the end of the war, and the number of active pharmacists was down 10 percent.[49]

At the other end of the store, "young women . . . replaced the men at the soda fountain quite generally" as early as 1942.[50] Lucille Cordeau recalls that some women also took up pharmacy: "They were offering a special course to wives at the college of pharmacy, where they'd give them a crash course so that they could replace a lot of the pharmacists who had been drafted for duty. I was unable to take it because I had two small children and I wasn't able to do it. Some of the wives took that course."[51]

Those male pharmacists who stayed in Lowell encountered, as did most public figures, a great deal of disrespect from customers about dodging the draft, even if they had a legitimate excuse. Raymond Cordeau tried to enter the navy:

> The navy has always been strong on pharmacists because on smaller ships, you didn't have a doctor and they would train you, a pharmacist, to be chief pharmacist; a pharmacist's mate had quite a bit of responsibility as far as first aid, as far as doling out drugs and . . . diagnoses . . . . You automatically got a rating, which you didn't get in the army. And generally speaking you had a better set-up. You had some rank, a chance of advancement.
> But that was not open. The only thing that was open in the navy was the Sea Bees. . . . I was actually drafted and had to go to Devens. They found that I had a slightly elevated blood pressure. . . . They said, "You'll be hearing from us shortly." I never heard again.
> I resented the fact I was 4-F. And in some ways you had it thrown at you. I was dealing with the public in the drugstore and most of these people who traded with us, their sons [were in the services.][52]

The war led to several minor changes in the drugstore business. Previously, a store would stay open from at least 8:00 a.m. until 11:00 p.m. Although wartime hours stayed relatively long, some pharmacists began to close earlier because of the shortage of qualified help; the shortened hours remained after 1945 as pharmacists discovered the public capacity to adjust. Raymond Cordeau:

> This curtailed our evening business, of course, especially in the wintertime. Because around five o'clock, whenever it would get dark, we had these big shades. We had big windows. We had to put those down and keep our lights to a minimum. . . . Especially around where there'd be

stores like that, the police were cruising, they'd come in and check on you. . . . A lot of the stores decided that they'd close at eight o'clock, nine o'clock, because there was no sense staying open.

And then you had your shortage of pharmacists and some stores were stuck with one man. He would be there seven days a week and so you found yourself closing say Sunday nights or Sunday afternoons. . . . We learned that we could curtail our hours without getting hurt too badly. . . . In other words, you were serving the public by being open fifteen hours a day or something like that while you could easily have done it in ten or twelve.

One wartime law gave pharmacists extra work. Cordeau recalled that "We started collecting empty tubes of toothpaste and we waited and waited and at no time did anyone ever send us a letter to tell us what to do with the tubes. At the end of the World War, we just threw the things away. . . . After a while, you know, you didn't make an issue of it if somebody forgot to bring an empty tube to get a tube of toothpaste, because we had more—we had boxes of empty tubes out back."[53]

The real problems came with nonmedical items that, even if in extremely short supply, were not rationed because they weren't necessities. Cigarettes—with candy a close second—created the worst difficulties; 30 percent of cigarettes manufactured went to the 10 percent of Americans in the services. By late 1944, the great demand for tobacco on the home front led to a major black market.[54] Raymond Cordeau:

The shortage that affected people the most was cigarettes. . . . They would allocate according to your previous purchase, probably 30, 40 percent of what you originally had. And then their trucks used to come to the store once a week, they'd bring in the cigarettes and immediately you'd take them out back and hide them because there'd be a rush on the store. You know, we just saw the truck come and people would get actively angry. Some were your customers and it was perhaps the one shortage that caused us grief, caused loss of customers. Because you had people who probably did not [previously] buy their cigarettes from you, but they were good customers, they bought prescriptions and other things, but they [had been] buying their cigarettes elsewhere, perhaps near where they worked. . . . These people'd give you an argument. . . .

And it didn't matter what kind or brand meant nothing. They would take the so-called dogs of the cigarette business. I remember at that time there were some cheaper cigarettes like Wings, at that time were selling for something like 10 cents a package where the other cigarettes were 15 cents a package. . . . People who smoked had to have their cigarettes and there was hijacking of trucks and things like that.

Despite their inability to meet public demands, cigarette companies aggravated the situation by continuing to advertise heavily, but stressed the numbers of cigarettes being sent overseas. Cordeau:

> In fact, on radio the cigarette sponsors would say, "This week we're sending six million cigarettes to our soldiers in such and such an area. Next week we're sending them there." . . . I think this is a proven thing: even if you're selling every cigarette that you could make, if you don't keep the name in front of the people, they'll forget it. . . . They may have curtailed their advertising some, but they were still advertising in spite of the fact that they could sell every cigarette.[55]

"Sampascoopies," Charles Sampas's gossip column in the *Lowell Sun,* described the smoker's plight: "Downtown smokers have turned into overnight Sherlock Holmes, going from store to store, trying to track down their favorite brand of cigarettes—and hardly ever succeeding."[56]

From a different perspective, John Albert Notini was a cigarette wholesaler and found his work much easier:

> Naturally, the sales weren't there because the merchandise wasn't available. Cigarettes were rationed to us. We were only getting a portion of what we sold in normal times. We had no trouble selling them. There was a demand for them immediately. And no trouble collecting the money for them because everybody wanted to pay their bills so they could get cigarettes to sell. It was a different type operation altogether. . . . We had more of a selective market. . . .
>
> We tried to go by their purchase before and allocate so much in percentage, same as the companies did to us. Like if we received 10 percent of our normal supply, we tried to give each customer 10 percent of his normal supply. But they had to pay their bills on time in order to be treated that way. . . .
>
> Profit was larger because we didn't have to give any discounts. . . . During the supply and demand created by [the war] it probably went up 1 percent overall. . . . [But we] didn't have the sales we usually had because we didn't have the merchandise. So we ended up with less profit overall. The gross profit was a little larger, but the sales figure was smaller.

Notini's cigarette business was important enough to exempt him from the draft: "Out of four brothers that were in the business, three of them enlisted. . . . I was the only one left. . . . I was given a deferment because of the fact that I was essential to private business. I received a deferment for six months. And when that was up, I went back again. In all I received—I think I received eight six-month deferments. . . . They put me in a class called 4-D: essential to private business."

Having a ready supply of cigarettes gave Notini certain privileges:

Cigarettes was an excellent medium of barter. You could get a good piece of meat with a carton of cigarettes. . . . There wasn't anything you couldn't get with cigarettes. . . . We never suffered from [rationing] at all. . . .

I remember I was in the club one night, and a waitress says she hadn't had a good piece of meat for two or three weeks. I says, "Come with me." So I put her in the car, and we went someplace and I was having a nice pot roast.[57]

The Doctor Is Out

Just as stores provided Lowell with necessary material supplies, so the professions supplied the community with necessary services. Here, too, shortages set the war years apart from peacetime.

Doctors were among the first people Selective Service called, and those who remained in Lowell had to be certified that their services were needed on the home front. Even dentists had to register, and those who didn't volunteer were threatened strongly with the draft. More than 30 percent of Lowell's physicians and surgeons entered the armed forces, and the city faced an acute shortage of dentists.[58]

Nurses also went overseas and even semi-skilled assistants were hard to find, as many who had worked or might have worked in medical offices instead chose to earn more money in war industries. Claire Contardo decided working in a medical office was financially unrewarding:

I had been out of high school briefly, and I had worked two different jobs in Lowell. One I had worked for a dentist a short time, and then I went to work at a businessmen's credit bureau where they used to try to collect the unpaid bills. . . . But I wasn't at these jobs too, too long. I really was waiting to hear from civil service. . . .

When I first started working for the dentist I was working fifty-four hours a week for $11 a week. Sounds ridiculous, doesn't it? And then I went to the businessmen's credit union and there I got $17 and boy, that was really something. . . . And then I went to the Navy Yard and now what did we start—what were [the wages like]? $1,800 a year to start with?[59]

Medical professionals who remained in Lowell found their practices greatly expanded due not only to assuming the work of colleagues in the services, but also due to a general expansion in the number of people who could afford professional care. No figures are available for Lowell, but for the nation, physicians increased their income 147 percent between 1940 and 1945; dentists increased their income 109 percent.[60]

The number of people getting care for mental illness also rose. First admissions to U.S. hospitals for permanent care of psychiatric illness increased from 93,000 in 1939 to 111,000 in 1944. In Lowell, admissions rose more than 50 percent for men but dropped considerably for women, perhaps reflecting men's anxiety about the draft.[61] On the other hand, an apparently impressionistic report in the *Lowell Sun* noted, "the number of depressives . . . increased notably because of the war." These were, said the *Sun,* mostly women with sons in the service or women with no immediate relatives in the service but extreme interest in war news.[62] One national insurance company reported that the suicide rate dropped each year between 1938 and 1945. After the war, this rate sharply increased.[63]

A new type of business for doctors and dentists was examining draftees, which often brought them in contact with people who had never before had a professional medical examination. Brendan Leahey, a local dentist, was surprised at the poor condition of draftees' teeth: in his opinion, the average draftee needed about twenty fillings, and a third had no previous dental care. The draft initially turned down some men because their teeth were in such poor condition, but easing regulations and standards throughout the war eventually led to the drafting of all but the most severe cases. More rigid standards continued for officers.[64]

Medical services connected with the military benefited both clients and physicians. Many of those examined learned the advantages of professional medical care. This, in turn, gave a tremendous financial boost to the medical professionals who had a whole new group of customers educated to seek their services in the future.

The benefits of professional care also came to home-front workers. For example, Remington provided free annual physical examinations for its employees.[65] The net effect of increased medical care through both the services and through employers was that health in Lowell improved.[66]

However, the war years also presented difficulties to most Lowell people who needed professional medical care. Cases of death or serious illness because of the lack of essential medicine did not occur. However, reliance on inferior quality medicine, shortages of critical items, inadequately trained staff, and longer hours and speed-ups for industrial workers undoubtedly contributed to long-term health damage. Such damage is often unattributable to a particular cause, or even undetectable until years later.

In a more obvious example of medical problems, many families complained that they were unable to find or keep a doctor. Lucille Cordeau was especially unlucky both for herself and for the doctors she consulted when she was pregnant with her first child: "I started with one doctor and then I switched to another and he was drafted and I wound up with a third doctor to deliver my baby for the first one, because they were taking young doctors. . . . I was twenty-six when I was married. I wanted a family, and I think we just accepted the fact that we were going to raise a family, war or no war."[67]

One recourse during the doctor shortage would have been to emphasize more self-reliant and traditional forms of health care. Such an approach would certainly have had long-term benefits. This did not occur, except for some first-aid training oriented toward the unlikely possibility of an attack on the city. Indeed, the capacity of people for medical self-help tended to be ignored. As recourse to doctors increased, inexpensive and often equally effective informal treatment declined.

Modern Law

The legal professional was one of the few that did not find war immediately profitable. Before and during World War II, the law business in Lowell retained the air of "a slow casual small town practice," as Arthur Eno, Jr., a prominent local attorney (and historian), described his practice. He said, "things are done on a personal basis and law [was] after all within the comprehension of one human being."[68] Lawyers' income nationally increased only 52 percent, compared to 76 percent for manufacturing workers.[69]

Many factors contributed to the slowness of lawyers' lives during the war. More jobs meant fewer people committing economically motivated crimes. Fewer cars in the city meant fewer accident cases. For example, Labor Day auto deaths declined from 423 in 1941 to 169 in 1942.[70] Many personal matters usually settled by a town lawyer—especially real estate matters—were postponed, and younger lawyers—like Allan Gerson, who had handled wills and estates—discovered clients did not want an executor who "was in an unsettled state" regarding the draft.[71]

Even those cases that did come to court faced the problem of witnesses who might be thousands of miles from Lowell, affecting the progress of both civil and criminal cases. Courts had to establish a separate section for cases delayed until witnesses returned from the services. It was a rarity for both parties to a civil suit actually to appear in court. Criminal prosecutions and convictions in Lowell District Court initially rose in 1941 and 1942 then dropped drastically until after the war.[72]

The lawyer's wartime task further declined in the case of young male defendants. If the charge were minor, the man might be given the "choice" of enlisting rather than taking a chance of getting a criminal record.[73] Probation at conviction rose by a third in 1944. One hundred seventy prisoners in state houses of correction obtained "special war release" under an act of the state legislature between 1943 and 1945. (However, a man convicted of a felony and sent to prison was ineligible for the services.)[74]

The war did bring some compensation to Lowell's legal professionals as lawyers added draft consultations to their business, a luxury service that was not taken advantage of widely. Allan Gerson recalled that "every now and then we were consulted by people . . . about to go into the service. Most of the time, [they wanted to know] was there some way we could get out of it." In general, Gerson gave advice but did not appear at appeals.[75] The Lowell Bar Association also designated a group of lawyers to represent "the interests of the men in the service."[76]

More important than a rise or decline in traditional legal business, World War II hastened the development of a new body of law, drastically changing the scope of the profession. Regulations demanded that almost all businesses, large and small, submit regular reports to the government. Many businessmen and corporations consulted lawyers from big city firms to help in this process. For example, the Merrimack Manufacturing Company hired the prestigious Boston law firm of Ropes, Gray, Best, Coolidge and Rugg to represent the company. In many instances, legal advice was useful or necessary in preparing appeals to various agencies for raising prices, raising wages, getting increased allocations, or getting good employees classified as exempt.[77]

Local lawyers found new work as consultants in preparing income tax forms. A side effect of the new income taxes for working people was the opening of a branch of American Tax Service in Lowell, providing assistance in filling in forms for $2 each. The Lowell Bar Association, recognizing this as an intrusion into a potentially lucrative field for lawyers, sued, saying the staff of the company provided a legal service without a law degree. The court decided for the tax service.[78]

Although new laws and agencies—such as OPA, rent control, and the draft—affected the entire population as never before, it was the corporate side of the law that was most stimulated. James W. Hurst's history of the law in the United States noted the war as the culmination of a trend begun by the first corporate income taxes in the 1920s and the New Deal. "These [levies] gave more and more relevance in business decision making to what the laws allowed as deductions."[79] This trend in government toward touching peoples' lives directly while increasing the manipulative ability of more established and wealthy institutions (including both corporations and unions) had begun during the New Deal. However, it accelerated greatly during World War II, further embedding these precedents into the patterns of American life.

Middle-class Crime

On the other side of compliance with new government regulations, a new type of law-breaker emerged: white-collar criminals. Perhaps one reason rationing worked as well as it did without creating more than minor hardships for poorer people or ostentatious favoritism for the rich was the neighborhood nature of Lowell's food business. Uniform rules could be bent on a personal basis. Supplementing the regular food supplies, therefore, was an extensive but petty black market, especially in meat.

Surprisingly, little social stigma attached to black-market dealings as long as they stayed within certain bounds. Roger Kane, a ward councilor, described such arrangements as "an honest effort in a dishonest way":

> By that I mean there were some people who would have extra stamps and they wouldn't be used or something. The stamps were allocated according to the number in your family, things like that. And the stamps were distributed in such a way that some people got more than they needed and some didn't have enough. Depending on the way of life also. Because some people, instead of going for meat and things like that, they went for vegetables and they'd perhaps sometimes swap their red stamps for the blue stamps. They'd swap meat stamps for canned goods and things like that.[80]

It appeared that rather than obstructing rationing, the black market helped it work by relieving the worst potentials for inhuman bureaucracy. Nationally, the Office of Price Administration estimated that 3 to 5 percent of the nation's total retail food budget was spent on the black market, while the Department of Agriculture in 1943 estimated that 20 percent of the meat supply went into the black market.[81]

Most stores violated regulations in some way, although usually overcharges involved only a few cents. Periodically, however, the local OPA turned a case over to the the Enforcement Division, as occurred with Brockelmann's Market, then Lowell's largest store. Another petty case went to enforcement—for charging 4 cents extra on beans and 2 cents extra on tea—when the grocer refused to appear to explain the violation. Wrote the local OPA, "He seems to have no regard for rulings and does exactly as he pleases. It seems a waste of time to explain rules and regulations to him." Almost all grocers went unpunished after apologizing; in almost every instance the grocer blamed the violation on employees.[82] One store selling black-market meat, recalled Lucille Cordeau, "even had a policeman to keep the line in order. . . . Everybody knew what [the grocer] was up to, selling meat without stamps. We didn't know where he was buying so much meat, but it was good meat. Tasted good anyway. A couple of places—a few places, in fact, one of the best known restaurants in Lawrence was arrested for—or closed down for selling horsemeat."[83]

Even among local wholesalers, evasion of rationing amounted to a personal exchange of small favors. For example, the owner of A. H. Notini and Sons, tobacco wholesalers, would trade a carton of cigarettes for three pounds of butter from Ned Brox's dairy.[84]

The same lure of higher profits to be made evading official regulations affected the clothing business. One person remembered buying a shirt in Boston's North End for $7 when the legitimate price would have been $2.50—had shirts been available legitimately.[85] Curran remembers a local man who made a great deal of money by overcharging, but he indicated that "every legitimate store stayed right with the price." He didn't know how many were really legitimate.[86] McGowan agreed: "You don't fool around with Uncle Sam. You have too much at stake. If it was put in the newspaper that I was overpricing I might as well turn the key in the door."[87]

More surprising than the existence of petty offenses is the extent of black marketeering.[88] In January 1945, Chester Bowles, then administrator of OPA, said, "We have relied on the assumption that 95 percent of businessmen will comply voluntarily; that enforcement is necessary against only a reluctant 5 percent. This has proven too optimistic. We know now that, in major industry, considerably larger proportions of hitherto reputable businessmen are in substantial violation."[89]

Bowles understood the situation. During the war, the local Office of Price Administration staff surveyed Lowell food stores biweekly to determine the extent of violations. The results ranged from 28 out of 175 stores with violations to 132 stores out of 233 with violations. Most, but not all, violations were minor infringements corrected on the spot and with no legal action taken.[90] Twenty percent of United States companies received warnings from the OPA without being prosecuted. In 1944, almost half of the businesses investigated without prior complaints were found to violate wartime regulatory laws. In the five years of its existence—1942 to 1947—the "OPA instituted a total of 280,724 sanctions against violators of the price, rent and rationing regulations." This averages to more than 55,000 cases per year, but the actual numbers were much higher after 1943 when initial enthusiasm for war aims wore off, as government regulations began to seem burdensome, and as businesses figured out how to evade the law. And offenders were usually well-to-do; in a Detroit study of black-market violators, four-fifths lived in the two most desirable parts of the city.[91] The offenders were not Ma and Pa running the neighborhood grocery store.

White-collar crime pervaded wartime Lowell life. In the winter of 1943, as New England faced a severe fuel-oil shortage, one Lowell dealer announced through the newspaper that he would provide anyone with enough oil to keep a room warm. He refused to divulge where he got the oil, saying to do so would ruin his source; no mention was made of prosecution. The owner of a gasoline station on Bridge Street admitted selling five hundred gallons weekly without receiving ration coupons.[92] Allan Gerson recalled handling at least two black-market cases, one involving sugar (a syrup manufacturer needed it as raw material) and another regarding a restaurant that paid higher prices on the black market to get chicken. As white-collar crimes, both cases were settled out of court when the clients cooperated with the OPA in finding the sources.[93] An employee of Lowell's most reputable bank, Union National, was indicted for selling ration stamps obtained at the bank in a local bar.[94] One of the few rationing violations of consequence involved not a local company, but branches of the national meat-packer, Armour and Company, in Lowell and other area cities. In 1943, Armour was fined $500 for forcing retailers to buy eggs in order to get butter.[95]

The extent of white-collar crime, far more than expressions of wartime dissent, indicates a widespread lack of personal commitment to the official patriotic ideology of the nation at war. Conversely, it also reflects the feeling that black marketing did not affect the war effort and suggests the existence of opposition to the necessity of government regulation. Respected members of the community engaged in and benefited from crimes against national war measures without jeopardizing their social or economic position. In contrast, national security and the war effort were invoked to control workers. Even the punishment for those convicted suggests that middle- and upper-class crimes—crimes against society rather than crimes against property or individuals—were judged less important in Lowell than crimes traditionally associated with the less affluent. Conviction for OPA crimes carried a maximum allowed sentence of one year in jail and a $5,000 fine.[96]

A Triumph for Respectability

The impact of World War II on the middle class parallels its effect on the rich: in their commitment to business's aims and elite approach to controlling society, both groups faced potential threats during the depression through decreased profits and through increasingly organized challenges. As long as the economy stagnated, businessmen could lay little claim to knowing what was best for the community. World War II brought prosperity: Lowell bank transactions increased from $165,000,000 in 1939 to $312,000,000 in 1945.[97]

With depression behind, proponents of "the American way" found in war an excellent opportunity to improve their public image. As in the 1920s, prosperity reflected well on those who benefited most. The economically secure used the war as evidence of the necessity of their leadership in the fight against fascism, just as they would soon claim leadership in the cold war against communism. Homer Bourgeois, the president of the Union National Bank, asserted that "the bank stood out as the number one citizen in Lowell at the end of the war."[98]

War created the possibility of submerging dissent in calls for national unity. Mayor Ashe's 1942 inaugural address suggests that appeals to patriotism could and were made:

> We are involved in a time of national emergency, a time of war. It is no time for partisan politics or indifference to the obligations which we have assumed this morning. . . . We are face to face with an emergency the magnitude of which is beyond understanding. When we say that America is on trial we mean that every city, town and hamlet in America is on trial. Let it not be said that Lowell failed in its full duty but rather let it be said, with calmness and courage and an abiding faith in Almighty God, that we will emerge triumphant over our present-day fears, that our people in Lowell will carry on, however dark the days may be, and emerge into the sunlight of national freedom and security which have ever been the standards of our American way of life.[99]

Significantly, Mayor Ashe's appeal to unity and national purpose did not save him from being indicted four months later on corruption charges, as middle-class reformers and textile mill owners joined to capitalize on this opportunity to institute Plan E.

The very government agencies that ostensibly meant to avoid unfairly distributed wartime sacrifices proved to be avenues for solidifying an imbalanced status quo. Local regulatory boards were usually staffed by members of the conservative middle class as the public representatives. Lawyers, especially, were tapped for civic jobs on the draft board, OPA, and other agencies. Lowell's business and public representatives differed little in their ideology, while labor leaders believed that they, too, now had a stake in accepting the established patterns. Prosperity decreased anti-establishment protest as unemployment and severe economic hardship declined: a slice of the pie now seemed to mean something.

While people may have resented that it took a major war to end the depression, their immediate desire to share in the economic rebirth overcame their desire to protest continuing inequities. Organized labor often appeared to forget the class rhetoric and actions that characterized the CIO in the 1930s. Instead, it found itself striving to accept a middle-class ideology as prosperity and a new political alignment gave it the opportunity to join the middle class.

The tendency of Americans to emulate the middle class as the ideal of comfortable and respectable had been severely damaged in the 1930s, along with democratic responsibility. During World War II, the middle class regained its dominance, but the irony is that while wage-earners were striving to join the middle class, the middle class was itself being transformed. Some professionals—especially doctors and lawyers—moved upward, taking an ever-increasing share of the wealth and power of society. As national chains took over from corner stores, the operators of most of groceries and drugstores discovered themselves joining the newly respectable, and even conservative, working class—as consumers rather than providers. Prosperity might have meant survival for both established and new small businesses, but there were 30 percent fewer proprietors of Lowell retail stores in 1948 than there had been in 1939, despite higher profits and more workers per store.[100] The skilled and responsible tasks of once-owners rapidly devolved into, as Barbara and John Ehrenreich describe them in their study of the modern professional-managerial class, "routinized functions requiring little training."[101] The triumph of respectability—the very broadening of the middle class—was only the triumph of the few who rose into the elite.

NOTES

1. United States Department of Commerce, Bureau of the Census, *Sixteenth Census of the United States, 1940, Census of Business,* vol. 1: *Retail Trade, 1939,* pt. 3, *Kinds of Business, by Areas, States, Counties, and Cities* (Washington: GPO, 1941), 666.

2. Interview with Everett Harris, 9 September 1976.

3. United States Bureau of the Budget, Committee on Records of War Administration, War Records Section, *United States at War* (1946; repr., New York: Da Capo Press, 1972), 323.

4. United States Civilian Production Administration, Bureau of Demobilization, *Industrial Mobilization for War: History of the War Production Board and Predecessor Agencies 1940–1945* (Washington: GPO, 1947), 332.

5. Interview with Charles Fairbank, 12 December 1974.

6. Interview with Alice Swanton, 4 June 1975.

7. Interview with Constance Case, 14 December 1974.

8. Interview with Thomas Ahearn, 8 March 1976.

9. Interview with Lucille Cordeau, 2 April 1975.

10. *Lowell Daily Sun*, 14 November 1944, 5.

11. Interview with Yvonne Hoar, 6 May 1975.

12. *Polk's Lowell City Directory* (Boston: R.L. Polk, 1941 and 1945).

13. Interview with Leo McCue, Sr., Helen McCue, and John McCue, 7 January 1975.

14. *Polk's Lowell City Directory.*

15. *Lowell Daily Sun*, 19 February 1943, 1.

16. Margie Harrison, "The Supermarket: Higher Profits and a Way of Life," *In These Times*, 3 May 1977, 7.

17. United States Department of Commerce, Bureau of the Census, *Census of Business, 1948*, vol. 3: *Retail Trade, Area Statistics* (Washington: GPO, 1951), 20.28; United States Department of Commerce, Bureau of the Census, *Census of Population, 1950*, vol. 2: *Characteristics of the Population*, pt. 21, *Massachusetts* (Washington: GPO, 1952), 176.

18. Interview with Lydia Howard.

19. Bureau of the Census, *Census of Business, 1940*, 666.

20. Women's Bureau, *Employment of Women in the Early Postwar Period*, 12; Bureau of the Census, *Census of Population, 1950*, 176.

21. United States Department of Labor, Women's Bureau, *Employment of Women in the Early Postwar Period with Backgrounds of Prewar and War Data*, Bulletin no. 211 (Washington: GPO, 1946), 12; Bureau of the Census, *Census of Population, 1950*, 176; interview with James Curran, 4 February 1975.

22. Interview with William Doherty and Philip McGowan, 22 April 1975.

23. *Lowell Daily Sun*, 16 June 1943, 1.

24. Interview with James Curran.

25. Interview with Philip McGowan and William Doherty; *Lowell Daily Sun*, 2 November 1944, 2, 3, 5, 19.

26. Interview with Philip McGowan and William Doherty.

27. War Production Board Press Release, 17 August 1942, National Association of Wool Manufacturers Papers, Museum of American Textile History, North Andover, Mass.

28. Harvey C. Mansfield and Associates, Office of Temporary Controls, Office of Price Administration, *A Short History of OPA* (n.p., n.d.), 76; Richard R. Lingeman, *Don't You Know There's a War On: The American Home Front, 1941–1945* (New York: G. P. Putnam's Sons, 1970), 120.

29. Interview with Philip McGowan and William Doherty; interview with James Curran.

30. National Association of Cotton Manufacturers, *Transactions, 1930–1942* (n.p.: NACM, 1943), 721–24; *American Wool and Cotton Reporter* 56, no. 53 (1942):3.

31. WPB, *Production Wartime Achievements,* 81; Harvey C. Mansfield et al. *A Short History of OPA* (Washington: Office of Temporary Controls, Office of Price Administration, n.d.), 77–78.

32. Interview with Philip McGowan and William Doherty.

33. Mansfield, *Short History of OPA,* 75.

34. National Archives, Record Group 188, "OPA Price Records."

35. Interview with Philip McGowan and William Doherty.

36. Mansfield, *Short History of OPA,* 156; Record Group 188, "OPA, Rationing Records."

37. Interview with John Flather, 9 December 1974.

38. Interview with Lydia Howard.

39. Interview with Dorothy Ahearn, 3 August 1976.

40. Interview with Thomas Ahearn.

41. Interview with James Curran.

42. Bureau of the Census, *Census of Business, 1940,* 666; *Census of Business, 1948,* 20.28–29.

43. Interview with James Curran.

44. Interview with Philip McGowan and William Doherty.

45. Interview with Doris Poisson, 15 May 1975.

46. Fernand Braudel, *Capitalism and Material Life 1400–1800* (New York: Harper and Row, 1973), 226.

47. Bureau of the Census, *Census of Business, 1940,* 666.

48. Interview with Raymond Cordeau, 2 April 1975.

49. Commonwealth of Massachusetts, Department of Civil Service and Registration, "Annual Report of the Board of Registration in Pharmacy," typescript, passim.

50. *Lowell Daily Sun,* 25 March 1943, 1.

51. Interview with Lucille Cordeau.

52. Interview with Raymond Cordeau

53. Ibid.

54. *Lowell Daily Sun,* 25 March 1943, 1; Massachusetts, "Annual Report, Pharmacy," 1942; Lingeman, *Don't You Know There's a War On,* 253; Marshall B. Clinard, *Black Market: A Study of White Collar Crime* (New York: Rinehart, 1952), 43.

55. Interview with Raymond Cordeau.

56. *Lowell Daily Sun,* 17 November 1944, 6.

57. Interview with John Albert Notini, 12 April 1975.

58. *Lowell Daily Sun,* 16 March 1943, 9.

59. Interview with Claire Contardo, 16 September 1975.

60. United States Department of Commerce, Bureau of the Census, *Historical Statistics of the United States from Colonial Times to 1970,* pt.1 (Washington: GPO, 1975), 166.

61. Francis E. Merrill, *Social Problems on the Home Front: A Study of Wartime Influences* (New York: Harper and Brothers, 1948), 205; Commonwealth of Massachusetts, Department of Mental Health, *Annual Report of the Commissioner of Mental Health,* Public Health Document no. 117 (Massachusetts, passim).

62. *Lowell Daily Sun,* 16 March 1943, 9.

63. Merrill, *Social Problems on the Home Front,* 227–28.

64. Interview with Brendan Leahey, 27 January 1975.

65. Interview with William Pepin, 24 February 1975.

66. *Lowell Daily Sun,* 1 April 1943, 1.

67. Interview with Lucille Cordeau.

68. Interview with Arthur Eno, Jr., 13 November 1974.

69. Bureau of the Census, *Historical Statistics,* 166, 175.

70. David Hinshaw, *The Home Front* (New York: G. P. Putnam's Sons, 1943), 35.

71. Interview with Allan Gerson, 17 September 1975.

72. *Lowell Daily Sun,* 8 March 1943, 1–2; 5 March 1944, 1, 4; Commonwealth of Massachusetts, *Annual Report of the Commissioner of Corrections,* Public Document no. 115, passim.

73. Interview with Allan Gerson.

74. Massachusetts, *Annual Report,* passim.

75. Interview with Allan Gerson.

76. *Lowell Daily Sun,* 8 March 1943, 1.

77. Merrimack Papers, Baker Library, Harvard Business School, Cambridge, Mass..

78. *Lowell Daily Sun,* 8 March 1943, 1; *Massachusetts Reports* 315 (1943–44):176–99.

79. James Willard Hurst, *Law and Social Order in the United States* (Ithaca, N.Y.: Cornell University Press, 1977), 170.

80. Interview with Roger Kane, 16 September 1975.

81. Clinard, *Black Market,* 29.

82. National Archives, Record Group 188, "OPA Records."

83. Interview with Lucille Cordeau.

84. Interview with Andrew Notini and Barbara Notini, 17 January 1975.

85. Interview with Philip McGowan and William Doherty.

86. Interview with James Curran.

87. Interview with Philip McGowan and William Doherty.

88. Clinard, *Black Market,* 37, 297; Mansfield, *Short History of OPA,* 272.

89. Lingeman, *Don't You Know There's a War On,* 267.

90. Record Group 188, "Records of the OPA, Price Department."

91. Clinard, *Black Market,* 37, 297; Mansfield, *Short History of OPA,* 272.

92. *Lowell Daily Sun,* 26 January 1943, 1; 8 May 1943, 1.

93. Interview with Allan Gerson.

94. Interview with Homer Bourgeois, 5 December 1974.

95. Record Group 188, "Records of the OPA, Enforcement Division."

96. Mansfield, *Short History of OPA,* 262.

97. *Lowell Daily Sun*, 2 January 1946, 1.

98. Interview with Homer Bourgeois.

99. Lowell, "City Council Journal," 5 January 1942.

100. Bureau of the Census, *Census of Business,* 1944, 666; *Census of Business, 1948,* 20, 28–29.

101. Barbara Ehrenreich and John Ehrenreich, "The Professional-Managerial Class," *Radical America* 11, no. 2 (1977):15.

7

Children and Education

They [the children] knew that there was a war going on because we had blackouts and meat was rationed and butter
was rationed, and they knew that I had to take the book to
the store when I bought meat or butter. And they'd take
out so many stamps. And I used to tell them, "Now if we
use up all these stamps this week, you'll have to go skimpy
next week."[1]

Children could not help but realize that something drastic was happening after 1941. The disappearance of bubblegum could not be mis-
taken for an innocent event. In apparent imitation of their mothers'
search for supplies, children would race from school to stand in line
at the corner store when a shipment of gum was rumored to have
arrived. More seriously, parades from Fort Devens educated as well
as amused: one woman recalled that a laughing black tank driver fright-
ened her because he was the first black she had ever seen.[2]

That child's first view of a black person illustrates the problem very
young people had in understanding the novel and complex event called
war. In most cases, they had only a vague or distorted picture of World
War II. Young children were encouraged, just as were adults, to accept
fantasies as reality. Rationing and blackouts were serious adult problems; the more adaptable children easily transformed them into a game.
Absent fathers, severely missed in most cases, could also be forgotten
or never known in others. People did not die; they just disappeared.
Gas masks and uniforms were fun to wear and objects of pride, but
they conveyed little of war's horror.

One woman remembered that she and her brothers and sisters took
turns crushing tin cans to be recycled for the war effort. They would
jump on a can and eagerly yell, "Kill a Jap!" Their mother told them
every crushed can was equivalent to killing a Jap who must, they
concluded, be someone bad.[3] They had no idea what a "Jap" was, nor
did these children know what war was. After hearing a great deal about

the war, this woman decided that it was a battle across the Merrimack River with the United States on one side and the enemy on the other. When the ammunition ran out, the war would be over and the men would return home. She could never understand why neither side ever ran out.

The impression of World War II could be far more dramatic if a child was old enough to comprehend the scale of events. Constance Case recalled that "It just seemed terrible for a nine year old. . . . It seemed there wasn't any solution. . . . The warring nations would over-run the world."[4]

Many people who were growing up in Lowell during World War II retain a vivid memory of those years, often more so than do their parents. Joseph McAvinnue, principal of a Lowell junior high school, remembered "no great change of any sort" until his daughter, about ten years old in the early 1940s, reminded him in detail of wartime developments in both the school and their home.[5]

Their memories give an insight into the methods by which a society socializes its young people, and thereby illuminate the values and goals of that society. Education prepares children for their future roles; it also is a mirror of self-definition for society, one that can rapidly reflect ideological changes. Moreover, the process of education, the games children play, and the roles expected of children are peripheral to war's economic or military needs. As a result, these institutions can respond dramatically to less tangible wartime transformations.

The Disruption of Family Life

The most predictable changes in the lives of Lowell children resulted from their fathers' absences. To many children, war meant "father is not home." The burden fell on the mother who had to deal with a child's nervous refusal to eat because father was away; who had to get a child to write letters; who had to explain "war." Thomas Ahearn had three children: "I think it was rough on my wife. I know it was rough on my oldest daughter at the time. She was only about five or six years. That kid'd go three, four, five days, and wouldn't eat anything because I wasn't home. She was very, very close to me, and she'd be all right for awhile. She missed me more than the others. The two boys, of course, they're out playing and everything else. They missed me, but I mean, not as close, not like she did."[6]

Some assistance came from social organizations. James Conway, Sr., a high school chemistry teacher, "was connected somewhat with the . . . veterans of World War I . . . so I can remember several meetings

I went to where there was a lot of discussion, trying to help people who had troubles with their children in the war."[7] For the most part, however, tensions created by absent fathers had no institutionalized solution; to the contrary, wartime propaganda made it difficult even for parents to understand war's complexity themselves, let alone explain it to a younger generation.

Aggravating the absence of fathers was the large number of mothers who worked. Children might see neither parent for most of each day; and adults, after working all day, would be less able to cope with raising children. Again, only patchy remedies were available: extended families cared for children; older children took care of younger ones; women simply worked much harder and "made do."

Public fears that mothers and/or fathers would be unable to supervise children sufficiently, coupled with the "emotional excitement of wartime," led to predictions of a wave of juvenile delinquency. The Lowell School Committee encouraged such cases to be submitted to the School Department in private before resorting to the court. The committee also recommended that "closer supervision be made in places of amusement, taverns, and theaters, etc., regarding public health, morals, and safety of Children of school age."[8] The *Lowell Sun* proposed the Boy Scouts as a solution, but lamented that, like many organizations, it, too, had problems because of the war. "It has been conclusively proved that the scout troops definitely lower the rate of juvenile delinquency in the neighborhoods in which they operate, to such an extent that if enough units could be formed delinquency could be completely controlled. However, troops cannot be formed until a scoutmaster can be found, and the greatest difficulty in finding them is occurring at the very time when the causes and opportunities for delinquency are on the upgrade."[9] The expected rise in juvenile delinquency never materialized, however. The local court heard remarkably few cases, and schools reported no special disciplinary problems.[10]

Some delinquency did exist, of course. According to the *Lowell Sun* in 1943 and 1944, lawyers found they had a new class of criminals to defend: juvenile purse-snatchers. In 1944, a headline reported "Six Boys, Five to Nine Years of Age, Admit Setting Fires in Mill." Stealing and joy-riding by youths also received public attention, but the *Sun* believed the money to be made legitimately at war plants or in the service held these crimes in check.[11] Fear of the draft as punishment also helped keep youth in line.

As in many other areas, war offered partial solutions to the problems it created. For children who were old enough, war work either occupied after-school hours or even replaced school. Nationwide, 1,350,000 children aged fourteen to seventeen worked full-time in 1944, with another 1,400,000 combining work and school. Margaret Mead observed in 1946 that "a million girls between 14 and 18 who would ordinarily have been in school have been working part or full-time."[12]

Nor did they perform only symbolic tasks: students worked an average of twenty hours per week, temporarily reversing a long-term trend toward reducing child labor. The number of employed boys fourteen to eighteen increased 169 percent from 1940 to 1944; the number of girls employed increased 243 percent.[13]

Relaxed government standards regulating child labor encouraged employers to hire children. Soon after the war, sociologist Francis Merrill wrote, "All along the line efforts to increase the labor supply by lowering standards for adolescent and child labor were intensified."[14] Modifications came in compulsory school attendance laws, parts of the Fair Labor Standards Act, and in restrictions on hazardous and night work. At the outset of the war, the National Association of Cotton Manufacturers, anticipating the labor shortage, asked the government to allow sixteen- and seventeen-year-old females to work. The result was an increase not only in less demanding forms of child labor, but also an increase in youth employment in manufacturing, especially in clothing factories and textile mills, the mainstays of Lowell's employment market.[15]

The movement toward child labor was not universally welcomed. As early as 1943, a Lowell School Committee member urged parents to "permit and persuade their children of school age now working in defense plants to return to school."[16] The wording of this plea suggests two reasons why young people got war jobs: first, their parents encouraged them to work and, second, children preferred work to school. In fact, apparently money, not patriotism, led Lowell's young people to work, as the Red Cross discovered. A local official of this organization wrote to the regional office: "Already the girls [who are nurse's aides] have started to ask questions which I am unable to answer. The question of salary seems to be uppermost in their minds."[17]

The role teen-agers played in the work force makes the term *child labor* inappropriate. While younger children—under sixteen—filled peripheral jobs such as grocery clerk or newsboy, many of high school age held adult jobs in war plants. Joseph Normandy spent one summer working the 3:00-11:00 p.m. shift at Remington making rocket-launching tubes. He was treated as an adult with adult responsibilities, including not being able to discuss his work. Ann Welcome left school early each day to spend four hours sewing suits for the navy at Textron and worked full-time at the same job each summer.[18] In their own eyes and in the eyes of the community, independent income made teenagers full-fledged adults, analogous to "boys" old enough to die in the services.

The extent of illegally employed minors cannot be determined accurately, but its existence and expansion over the war years is certain. Investigations by the United States Children's Bureau showed a constantly rising number of children illegally employed nationally under the Fair Labor Standards Act, reaching over five times the 1940 level in 1944. According to a wartime report, "They were found in virtually every industry in which inspections were made."[19]

New England especially received warnings on violations of the Walsh-Healey Public Contracts Act regarding working conditions for women less than eighteen years old. Numerous violations, especially failing to provide the legal lunch period, were reported each day; fines were $10 per day per employee. In Massachusetts, the number of reported violations of state laws on illegal employment of minors and illegal overtime of women and minors shot up quickly and stayed well over the 1940 level throughout the war.[20]

Recreation

As a popular war and one that demanded universal participation, the influence of World War II invaded children's games. Unfortunately, such pastimes rarely were documented. Moreover, when asked thirty-five years later for information from the war, Parker Brothers refused: "We are unable to give sales figures for any product as this is proprietary information and we are not authorized to do so."[21] The only extensive source for games during World War II is people's memories.

Rationing and conservation of resources for fighting the war provided the structure for countless activities. The children in one family collected scrap paper for which they got stripes to wear on their arms for "helping to win the war." The arm band was apparently a stronger motivation than what it symbolized: winning the war.[22] Edward Larter, whose family ran both a farm and a small textile mill, recalled how he participated in and viewed the war as a teen-ager:

> We used to see the maneuvers from Devens. They used to come and have maneuvers out near us, and that was quite a display of strength. . . . We'd watch them. It was kind of exciting.
> We used to collect the newspapers in a horse and wagon because I wasn't old enough to have a license at the time. The only mode of travel for us legally was in a horse and buggy. So we'd go up with the horse and

pick up a load of papers. I remember I went off early in the morning before I fed my horse. There were three of us, and we got us a load of papers, started to head home. The horse started to run away . . . and we had quite a hairy ride coming home. As a matter of fact, it tipped the wagon over and [I was] bit banged up a little bit. Newspapers all over the place. A hell of a mess. . . .

It was exciting. It was. It made you feel good because you didn't want the war and you would do whatever you had to do to help the war effort, whatever it was. You would find metal, scrap metal, you'd take it down to the center of town where they had a chicken wire area where you'd throw pots and pans or any darn thing you could find. Especially aluminum because aluminum would build an airplane. We had to build a lot of airplanes. We knew that it would go into an airplane. Now, I don't know where it went; at least we thought it was them.[23]

Lard collecting—supposedly for munitions—was another common family effort. And many people recall the huge bins Larter described on the lawn in front of Lowell's city hall, where children and adults would leave metals to be recycled. A member of the Lowell War Price and Rationing Board congratulated school children on these contributions in his 1945 Memorial Day talk: "He congratulated the children in their wonderful work of salvaging paper and tin and told them of the need of conserving shoes. He explained the drastic sugar situation and said that he was sure they wouldn't mind a little less candy this summer."[24]

While shortages activated children's creative juices, they had a more trying effect on toy manufacturers. According to Parker Brothers' company history, "The 1940's, with the clouds of war once again looming on the horizon, saw a drastic cutback in the number of Parker games produced. From the start of the fighting, priorities for labor and material were established by the government . . . and the labor force lost all of its young and able men. . . . Hours of work were curtailed and more than half of the games in the line were cut. All except the really successful games were discontinued."[25]

Milton Bradley Company's official history similarly reported that "the outbreak of war posed serious problems in obtaining materials and in competition for labor against high-paying war industries and the personnel demands of the armed forces."[26]

Milton Bradley's 1943 catalog shows what toy manufacturers' problems meant to consumers—to children:

Not only are our efforts turned to the manufacture of war materials but we are also correlating our normal offerings to the necessities of the War Effort.

The descriptive notes in this catalog represent the games as they are produced at the time we go to press. Because of wartime priorities in some of our game materials, it is probable that some details will necessarily be changed after our present stocks are exhausted. . . .

Descriptions of many of the games in this catalog state that moves are controlled by spinning a dial. Due to wartime priorities, no more metal parts are available for use in game manufacture. Therefore, when the present stock of these items is sold, future orders for these numbers will be packed with ONE DIE in place of the dial.[27]

War, of course, stimulated children to create their own games. Dorothy Ahearn remembers a widespread practice: "Even Dotty played [war games]. They had machine guns and half the neighborhood were the Japs and half were the Americans."[28] Constance Case found a sailor's cap on a beach and fantasized about a torpedoed freighter.[29] Children started collecting money from all over the world sent home by relatives in the services. Some games, such as ship and plane models, had been held over from World War I and, used as history lessons, rekindled anti-German feeling. War-related pastimes also took place under the aegis of youth groups, especially scouts, which organized various activities to benefit the war effort.

Other new war games came, not from children's imagination, but from toy manufacturers. According to George Chartier, assistant to the director of operations for Milton Bradley Company of Springfield, Massachusetts, "games with war themes have always been more or less popular in the United States."[30] Although most stores continued to stress traditional toys, many war items were added to the selection. The *Lowell Sun* observed that "Many American parents are 'fed up with the war' and would rather not be reminded of it, particularly at Christmas-time. But their children don't share their sentiments—and war toys continue this year to get first call as Christmas gifts for the small fry."[31]

One Lowell toy store featured Parker Brothers' "new COMMAN-DOS" in its ads. The Giant Store included in its Christmas sale an equal balance of war and non-war toys. A discount store, however, advertised the "Bomb a Jap" dart game, the Young Patriot Invasion Set, the Young Patriot Construction Set, and Sailor Jack's Victory Bomber.[32] Chartier summarized Milton Bradley's war offerings for children: " 'Blackout' first appears in our 1940–41 catalog; 'Battle of the Tanks' in 1942; 'Battle Winks' and 'Broadsides' first appeared in our 1943 catalog. . . . Also note that 'Chutes and Ladders,' 'Chinese Checkers,' and 'India'—all versions of generic games from Europe or Asia—were popular before, during, and after World War II, and were not affected by the war."[33]

Toy manufacturers, however, do not necessarily limit their business to toys for children—or even to toys. Parker Brothers produced "a game of airplane recognition . . . for the Navy for training purposes and other games were devised for the Army as well. In addition to its regular 1942 catalog, Parker issued a separate catalog showing games " 'Specially selected for use by the armed forces of the United States."[34] Similarly, Milton Bradley produced a game kit for the armed services, including extra dice in each one. Much of the world-wide distribution of this kit was accomplished through Coca Cola Company, already experienced at getting their product "to every swamp, beachhead and stretch of rolling sea where a member of the armed forces found himself. . . . In time the Milton Bradley Company sold $1,600,000 worth of games to the Coca Cola Company."[35]

Milton Bradley Company also benefited from two government contracts unrelated to toys. First, in April 1942 the company won a $272,000 contract to produce gunstocks for the Thompson Machine Gun Company, thus reactivating its almost idle woodworking shop. Second, Milton Bradley president James J. Shea designed a universal joint for landing gear on certain types of planes, and the company late in 1942 received a $300,000 contract for this item.[36] But another factor was perhaps even more important for the company's profits. "Although Shea feels that these three big sales marked the turning point in the Company's fortunes, a director believes that it came about as a result of something quite different. What saved the Company, says this director, was Shea's decision to raise all prices soon after Pearl Harbor."[37]

In fact, the war *was* a turning point for the Milton Bradley Company. According to Chartier, "when the United States became involved in World War II, the Milton Bradley Company had had a new president less than two weeks. The company had not entirely recovered from the stock market crash or from a series of presidents who had not succeeded in pulling the company out of financial difficulties. James J. Shea was elected president and this was the beginning of better times for Milton Bradley."[38] In the words of its official history, Milton Bradley Company "came back from the grave under James Shea."[39]

Many comic strips contributed to the education of children in war aims. "Superman," running daily in the *Lowell Sun,* was blatant propaganda. In December 1942, Superman aided the anti-Nazi underground in Germany to rescue Santa Claus from the Nazis. Superman arrives in the nick of time to save Santa Claus from being "taught a lesson" for talking back to Hitler. Having saved Santa, Superman returns to the United States to get evidence on a German spy released by the court. The villain says to himself, "What idiots those democratic fools are! Letting me go scott free! In an Axis country they would put a suspected enemy to death first and ask questions later!" Meanwhile, Superman, flying overhead, answers this dilemma: "The humanitarian way may not be ruthless, but it gets results without stepping on peoples' souls!"[40] At least a third of the comic strips and movies available to Lowell's youth were war-related.[41]

Although play often ignored class lines, the children of the rich could engage in more ambitious projects. The five children in one mill owner's family provide an excellent example. In order to run errands without using gas coupons, the Flather family kept a horse, and it was the job of the sons to take care of it. A popular boys' game in the neighborhood, digging backyard trenches, took its toll on the Flather lawn. The oldest daughter and youngest son organized a circus to benefit British war relief. Soon all the children in the family joined in the effort and sold tickets to neighborhood women, raising perhaps $20. The boys, through scouting, acted as messengers during air raids, while the daughters contributed by rolling bandages and helping in relief work through the Girl Scouts. Mothers also played an active role in the Girl Scouts by running the Girl Scout Drum and Bugle Corps. The Flather children even dug a swimming pool in a back yard because gas rationing hindered trips to the beach, and they got to vote on which of several British children to take into the family for the duration. On July Fourth, fireworks money went instead to war relief.[42]

World War II added new components to the relationship between high school girls and boys. Joseph Normandy recalls the "connotation of manliness for someone in the service . . . a status symbol. . . . It was the patriotic duty" of women to continue relationships with boy friends who entered the services. This patriotic obligation, he added, did not extend to relations with servicemen from Fort Devens: girls who dated outsiders were thought to have suspect morals. The exceptions to this informal disfavor were meetings at USO or church dances, an accepted and social way to serve the war effort. Girls also met Devens soldiers at high school games, to which the boys in uniform were admitted free. Whether meetings came about in socially accepted or socially suspect manners, clearly young women in Lowell did meet many servicemen.[43]

War and Formal Education

The most intensive institution for socializing children is the school system. Through schools, children can be molded to fit society's needs. Schools can also act as a stabilizing safety valve, adapting quickly to compensate for sudden changes in economic institutions. For example, during the depression, school attendance rose; Lowell High School added a fifth year—equivalent to a first year of college—for more than two hundred students. This kept a number of young people from competing in the tight labor market, while giving potentially unemployed and disruptive teen-agers a place to be each day. During the war, not only did the fifth year get eliminated after enrollment dropped to less than fifty, but enrollment at all high school levels dropped significantly. The eleventh and twelfth grades showed the biggest drop.[44]

Nationally, school attendance peaked in 1940–41 at 6,713,913, then fell steadily to 5,761,000 by 1943–44. Sixty-two percent of youths fourteen to nineteen attended school in 1940, but only 56 percent in 1944.[45] In Lowell, only nine thousand pupils were enrolled in school in 1944 compared to fourteen thousand ten years earlier. Clearly, many people over fourteen considered school optional—and expendable when economic opportunities improved.[46]

The draft hit Lowell Technological Institute especially hard. As a men's technical college, its students were quickly called into the service. Of 280 students enrolled at Lowell Tech in 1941, 42 had entered the armed services by April 1942. By fall 1943, only 73 regular students remained. Their presence in the school had been replaced by hundreds of navy men receiving two weeks of special training.[47]

Great concern was shown nationally to modify school curricula to meet the material and emotional needs of the war—to make education "more relevant." The United States Office of Education called for " 'more positive teaching' of democracy and the nation's history," according to education historian Richard M. Ugland, and "announced that 'the first and abiding task of the school is to train youth for war.' "[48] The office's Wartime Commission suggested relating all programs to war needs. Math problems, the commission said, should be drawn from the war; history teachers should instruct students on the significance of and necessity for global war; vocational education should be related to military needs; and schools should institute armed forces courses.[49]

The state teachers' associations and chief school officers drew up a model wartime curriculum that was representative of standard curricula from 1942 to 1945. It included math courses "where many of the problems will be drawn from the fields of aviation, navigation, mechanized warfare and industry; . . . courses in industrial arts related to war needs; . . . revised social studies courses to give a knowledge of war aims; . . . one or more units of study dealing with an understanding of the armed forces; . . . unit preflight courses as outlined by the armed forces. . . ."[50]

In 1943, Walter F. Downey, Massachusetts Commissioner of Education, summarized the many curriculum proposals: "Our schools have new objectives; they are new high schools. We are all vocational schools now."[51]

One year into the war the National Education Association surveyed city schools to see how their curricula had responded to these admonitions: 80.1 percent reported an increased emphasis on science, followed by 79.8 increasing the emphasis on math and 75.3 percent increasing physical education programs. More than half, 54.4 percent, had augmented their vocational education programs. Social studies programs, which might study war's causes, received an increased emphasis in only 39.6 percent of the schools, and a mere 11.2 percent increased the emphasis on foreign languages.[52]

The Lowell High School curriculum, although not as consistently or conscientiously militaristic as was suggested, underwent a number of modifications to support the war effort and to carry males through the waiting period to enter the services. The school department invested $200, a relatively large sum, in an airplane for the high school. Introductory aerodynamics courses began for many boys who foresaw a military career. Such "preflight" courses attracted more than 75 percent of American boys.[53]

Lowell High instituted the aeronautics course for all junior and senior boys at the instigation of a teacher who wanted to make the city aware of the need for flyers, as Elizabeth Irish, a high school mathematics teacher, remembers:

> There were some of the men in the faculty in the high school, some of the men who were really interested in a military career. There was one man in particular who had been a flyer during World War I. And he graduated from, I guess, a military academy. And there were quite a number of men that were firmly with him. . . . And there was all this advertising from the military so that every young man should be made air-minded. And these members of the faculty really were very, very intense in their belief in their help.

Irish taught the aeronautics course:

> In World War I, I had done serving things that I didn't know how to do, and you learned something from your experience. So when it came to World War II, I knew the thing to do was something I knew how to do.
>
> So somebody sent me a young man to be tutored in math who had been accepted for flying. But he hadn't any math at all really. They rec-

ommended him to a refresher course, but when he came to me, he said he couldn't take it because there was nothing to refresh because he hadn't had anything. And he brought me a little textbook that was recommended, something about aeronautics and the navy and flying or something of that sort. And I had never been anywhere near a plane. I didn't know how to drive an automobile. [But] I opened this book, and it opened to a trig example. So I said, "Oh yes, I can do that." And when I went back, I called this man that I'm telling you about who was so enthusiastic about flying. . . . So before I knew it, I was teaching aeronautics because everybody was teaching aeronautics.

It really was a wonderful thing, because there was a lot of waiting. . . . Some of them had been accepted and they were waiting to be called, waiting to get into flying . . . And it was really very relevant because the book that I taught from was wonderful. . . . It was one that was written quick to meet the demand for high schools [to teach] aeronautics. . . . The math was introduced in such a way that just took the students as they come. A lot of them had had nothing except a little arithmetic. And yet they were to begin aeronautics class with some college prep people and so it would be a very mixed class, you can see. . . . It really was amazing what they learned because it was all attached to the plane and the plane was so important and [they had] the stimulus of thinking they were going into the armed forces so soon.[54]

The school department paid several other teachers to take courses to prepare them to teach either radio communications or aeronautics. These courses became part of the regular curriculum and as well as offerings in night school.[55]

Schools were one focus for the campaign to keep antagonism for the Axis high, resurrecting the xenophobic nationalism of World War I. The city council in 1942 directed the school committee to discontinue the teaching of Italian and German because of the alleged violations by these nations of international and human law.[56] And school children learned to count by reciting this poem:

> Major Bong is a very fine man;
> He shoots down all the japs he can;
> How many zeros did he get today?
> Let's Count them up. What do you say?
> One, two, three, four. . . .[57]

Schools and the Draft

As in the rest of Lowell, the most visible change in high schools came when large numbers of students enlisted or were drafted. Posters in schools encouraged students to join the services, as did many other social pressures inside and outside schools. In 1942, draft boards went into high schools to register boys.[58]

Young men had little choice: enlist or be drafted. Joseph Normandy, who enlisted after completing high school, recalled the mixture of emotions young men felt: "Most males had ambivalent feelings . . . especially if you had a direction. . . . At the same time you were torn by your patriotic feeling. . . . Between the two you knew you had to go. . . . [There were] no second thoughts about it. . . . In a way, it was romantic. . . . Everybody else went. . . . If you didn't go into the service, it [was] because there was something wrong with you."[59]

Despite overwhelming enthusiasm, there was some resistance to joining up. Reverend Arthur Hiley recalls that "mothers came to me, parents came to me. Even young people, young men, came to me to be counselled and some even came to see if I could get them off the draft—out of the draft—but I didn't make any attempt to do that."[60]

Being in the services did give an immediate advantage to high-school-age men. Many returned after basic training to parade around school in uniform. The respect and attention they received encouraged others to enlist, and the city continually heard stories of underage boys lying to get in the services or waiting impatiently until they, too, became old enough to sign up. Yvonne Hoar's son was an impatient one:

> I think he joined every branch of the service. My son was very patriotic, and I had to get him out of every one of them because he was only fourteen. He was big and husky for his age, and he'd forge his age. And he went into the navy, and he went into the marines, and he went into the army. . . . I had got him out of the navy because a friend was recruiting officer. . . . He knew me well, we were brought up together, and he knew the boy wasn't old enough so he talked him out of it. And of course he cried, he was mad because he couldn't get in. . . .
>
> So finally when he was fifteen he got into the marines. Well, that done it. I says, "If he wants to join that bad," I says, "let him go." So he went into the marines and after his boot training he said that he was coming home, and strut the uniform I suppose and all. But they put him right on a ship and shipped them over to China right off the bat. So he didn't come home until after he was in that marines for three years. . . .
>
> I didn't like it at all. I felt very bad about it. I didn't like the idea. He was too young. I realized he was very patriotic and it was foolish, but there was a hassle between the three of us, in fact. His father was every time going and getting him out. . . . I told his father if he wants to go that bad, let him go. He was very much against it, but we let him go.[61]

Edward Larter didn't join up, but, "I wanted to in the worst way. I wanted that in the worst way. I was about fourteen years old and I dreamed of being in the air force."[62]

Social pressure, combined with fifteen years of economic depression, emptied Lowell High School of male seniors. Even before the most drastic effects of the draft could be felt, the 1943 graduation class was depleted: one-third of the males had entered the services; more than a hundred graduates received their diploma in abstentia. In many cases, parents accepted the diploma for their sons.[63]

By 1945, it was "more common than uncommon" for seniors to be in the service, and a special listing in the school yearbook honored those who were in the armed forces. The school committee even encouraged boys to enlist by voting to give full diplomas to senior men who enlisted, but the commissioner of education never gave the necessary approval. Lowell Tech's graduating class in 1945 included only six students of the hundred who had entered in 1941.[64] Victor Luz recalls his high-school days: "Some of the older kids, they volunteered so quite a few of my friends never graduated or they would leave probably a month or two or something like that before graduation. And quite a few kids in my graduating class received their diplomas—they just read their name off, they mailed it home or something like that. And a lot of kids just never did [finish high school]."[65]

School Activities

Because extracurricular activities are informal, they changed rapidly under the pressure of war. Military-oriented groups received new attention but suffered even more because of the draft. Demolay, a high school group similar to ROTC in college, kept losing its members.[66] St. Rita's Cadets, a marching club of high-school-age women to which Ann Welcome belonged, declined for two reasons: it couldn't get gas for trips, and its members worked at war plants.[67]

Most school activities that lacked either material or emotional wartime significance found it almost impossible to function. Drama Club, for instance, was unable to put on plays either because of students' taking after-school jobs or leaving school altogether. Sports, however, were far more important than drama clubs in peoples' minds. The lack of people, equipment, and transportation all cut into team sports drastically, at levels ranging from the schools to the major leagues. Individual sports, especially those available in Lowell such as bowling, experienced a compensatory surge. Spectator sports often played to sell-out crowds simply because there were fewer teams and fewer events to watch. Especially in the schools, team members commonly failed to finish a season. Normandy recalled that often a game would be played in honor of a person about to enter the services.[68]

Students' patriotism and the school administration's desire to involve students in war efforts led to new activities. Within two weeks of Pearl Harbor, schools adopted air-raid regulations. By 1943, school activities included war-bond and stamp drives, salvage drives, victory gardens, ration programs, and the Junior Red Cross. The stamp sales were held every week, with teachers and administrators volunteering their labor. An estimated 80 percent of Lowell students bought these stamps, which were used to purchase war bonds. Contests were held on which class could buy the most stamps, thus interweaving nationalism, school spirit, and competitiveness. High School Field Day exercises in 1944 "were held near an Army tank purchased through the sale of war bonds at the school." Awards honored the biggest collections of scrap metals both in Lowell and in the region: the winners at one junior high school got to ride to school in an army amphibious craft from Fort Devens. Schools organized programs to encourage students to write letters to relatives in the service, and parochial-school students mended rosaries to send to servicemen.[69] Every school, of course, held "a lot of assemblies and a lot of the assemblies were patriotic."[70]

The most extensive war-directed activity nationally was the High School Victory Corps. Organized in the middle of 1942, the Victory Corps was intended to focus all school activities concerned with the war effort. Principally, it aimed to train students for later war service and to encourage active student participation in community war efforts.[71]

The Victory Corps had five divisions: land, sea, air, production, and community services. Because women were encouraged to join only the last two, it is notable that membership in the Corps by mid-1943 was about equal for boys and girls. At that point, 70 percent of the nation's high schools had tried the program, but only 22 percent of eligible students had signed up. After that year, interest fell, partly because the federal government provided no funds.[72]

In Lowell, the Victory Corps had its counterpart in "Boy Officers" and "Girl Officers." Boy Officers and Girl Officers were the preeminent high school organizations, especially for girls. As an organization, Girl Officers had more members and carried more prestige than any other activity. Originally members had been chosen strictly by scholarship, but by World War II, personality and leadership became prime qualifications. The girls voted most popular in 1945 also had the top position in Girl Officers. The purpose of Boy Officers, in the words of Joseph Nawrocki, its faculty advisor, was "to train the underclassmen in military discipline and close-order drill so that they may be prepared to serve their country." Boy Officers became such an imitation of the army that uniforms had to be modified during the war to stop Devens soldiers from saluting high schoolers.[73]

School as Community Centers

As with churches, decentralized locations made schools ideal sites for community activities. During World War II, schools educated, indoctrinated, and involved Lowell adults as well as children. The situation in Lowell matched that described for the rest of the country by Geoffrey Perrett: "The school became the center of community war work."[74]

Rationing was the major community business carried out through the schools. Although the War Price and Rationing Board office was in city hall, almost all coupon distribution occurred in neighborhood schools, with principals in charge and other school officials handling all the labor without pay.[75] In the United States, more than one hundred thousand volunteers, almost all teachers and school parents, assisted in distributing the first ration book.[76] And schools were one of several sites for recycling: for example, every Tuesday about twenty-five tons of paper were collected at Lowell schools.[77]

Schools also housed special wartime adult-education classes in the evenings. James Conway, Sr., a high school chemistry teacher, together with representatives of the police and fire departments, held classes a few days before Pearl Harbor to explain the significance of the war between England and Germany. Being convinced that the United States would and should enter the war, he wanted to prepare the community. "The [positive] response was the talk of the city." More than fifty women enrolled in the Women's Defense School, attending courses three nights each week for seven weeks. And the school board acted to resume an "Americanization" program for adults.[78]

The school buildings were open to many other local organizations. The evening classes inaugurated by the Boott Mill to train supervisors in labor relations and to teach potential textile workers basic mill skills were held in Lowell High School. The Red Cross held courses in home nursing in both the high school and a junior high school.[79] The International Institute used the high school auditorium for a Sunday observance of "I Am an American Day." The headquarters of Harbor Defense of Portsmouth presented their show, "Direct Hit," in the same hall. For thirteen Wednesday evenings, the Lowell "Sons of the American Legion" trained its members in the high school annex.[80]

For mobilizing a community to fight a war and unifying a community around common goals, the conversion of schools to the war effort was important, but the process carried dangers. Directing curricular and extracurricular activities to military needs distorted the ability of the educational system to teach freely. Although a school system should prepare young people for society, schools can teach critical participation. Instead, World War II accentuated the simplicities of internal propaganda and reduced the element of choice. Focusing home-front activities in the same building as educational activities further identified education with the practicalities of winning the war, inhibiting alternative or non-war activities and thinking. Combining school spirit with nationalism and patriotism encouraged students to have the same positive and unquestioning attitude toward militarism and the United States as combining economic prosperity with global war did for adults.

Teachers and the War

Teaching not only serves children; it is also how many people earn a living. The biggest change for this profession was its numerical decline: by 1945, 350,000 teachers—one-third of the total in the United States—had left the field. The turnover rate for teachers doubled and "nearly all schools faced a shortage of qualified teachers" that was met by lowering standards and issuing emergency certificates.[81] Edward Larter, then a junior high school student, recalls: "We had a problem with teachers. We went through several teachers during the war. Teachers were joining the women's portion of the military service and we'd end up with another one."[82]

Unlike the case in many other occupations, the shortage of teachers did not result from the draft because the overwhelming majority were women; in Lowell, 85 percent of teachers in 1940 were female. Pawtucket Junior High School had only two male teachers, the principal—too old to be drafted—and the manual training teacher—who was drafted. Only eight high school teachers took military leaves.[83]

Despite Larter's impression that teachers joined the services, better money elsewhere was the real reason people moved away from teaching, just as it drew workers from the mills. While income for industrial workers rose at least 40 percent, teachers' salaries rose only 20 percent from 1941 to 1945 in cities the size of Lowell.[84] In Lowell, the situation for teachers was worse: pay for experienced male teachers rose 7 percent and for women, 9 percent.[85]

Insult was added to injury. In January 1943, prosperity and high prices led to a city council proposal to increase the salaries of city employees along a sliding scale, with those in the income bracket comparable to teachers' salaries getting a 12.5 percent raise. When 10 percent across-the-board increases were finally approved in June, teachers were the only city workers excluded. Nor did teachers receive generous salaries before this. In 1942, experienced male teachers in the high school received $2,700 and women received $2,232, comparable to many jobs at Remington.[86]

As a result, Lowell teachers, like Lowell mill workers, believed it made sense to get a war job to either supplement or replace their regular salaries. When hiring a temporary military educator for the high school, the city had to offer maximum instead of entry-level pay after "the superintendent cautioned that neither [candidate for the position] would work for less." One enterprising woman took a military leave to work in the OPA regional office. After two years, the school committee noticed her case and decided that a woman working for the war effort was not the same as a man in the services. Her leave was canceled. In all, the roster of teachers fell about 10 percent during the war years, less than the drop in students.[87] This development was, however, temporary: by 1950 the number of teachers employed in Lowell matched the 1940 figures: approximately 765 women and 150 men.[88] Victor Luz recalls that "For the most part, a lot of the teachers were working part-time in the munitions factory over there, Remington Arms. . . . I know that gradually some of the teachers started coming back and in my senior year a couple of teachers that had been in the service were discharged, I guess, or separated, I'm not sure which. Then my first year up to Tech [Lowell Technological Institute], there were quite a few that were starting to come back."[89]

Teachers began a fight for and eventually won a second method to increase the income of most in the profession: equal pay for women. In this fight Lowell's women were supported by labor organizations in Lowell and elsewhere. The fight was further aided, although victory was not yet won, by the wartime enactment of equal-pay legislation in Massachusetts that made illegal the $500 pay differential between men and women teaching at the high school.

The city council moved early in 1943 to investigate the pay of women teachers after receiving letters from the American Federation of Hosiery Workers (AFL) and the Textile Workers Union of America (CIO). Similar letters went to the school committee, which ignored them in its 1943 budget requests. Three months later, in March 1943, Lowell's Central Labor Union demanded that pay be equalized.[90] As a teacher recalls, "The union helped us. There had been a teachers' union, but it had disappeared. In the Central Labor Council, it was in their constitution that they as a principle would work for equal pay for men and women doing the same job. So the union people helped us very, very much. And they didn't make any bargains with us or suggest that they would like to have us back, bring the union back to life, or anything. They just said it was a cause they believed in, and that they were for it."[91]

The motivation for women to fight for equal pay is obvious; men had more complex interests. Most important, low pay for women kept wage scales down for men. A successful organized fight to raise pay for any workers helped strengthen organized labor as a whole. Moreover, as long as women could be paid less than men, some city governments preferred hiring women. In fact, one male teacher supported his female colleagues, although his male colleagues didn't:

> The men, of course, were opposed to it. Except for one man. And I said, "Why is it, when practically all the men are against it, why are you so sympathetic?" And he said he was looking for a job during the depression, and the superintendent of schools in one of the suburbs said there's a vacancy and it has to be filled by a woman because that's all the money that's budgeted. "And if you want to take it at a woman's pay we'd be glad to have you take it, but we can't offer you any more than that amount of money." And he said, "Since then I've been very sympathetic to the cause of equal pay for the same work."[92]

Resistance to equal pay for women was high. In 1944 some members of the school committee unsuccessfully fought the appropriation of $101 to equalize the pay of male and female attendance officers, terming the appropriation "a wedge." In 1943, it took no action on a motion to set aside $31,000 to equalize teachers' salaries. At the same time, it transferred a $10,000 surplus in the salary account—from not replacing teachers who left the schools—to other accounts. When the fight for equal pay succeeded in 1946, the total cost of equalization turned out to be only $9,600 annually.[93]

The final drive for equal pay began in 1945. A member of the school committee approached a woman teaching in the high school: "The high school teachers were a kind of mild group. And one of the school committee members asked to meet us after school. . . . He said that it was a good time for the women to work to get the same pay as the men. And that's just what we needed."[94]

For the next year, the women worked hard, with the steady assistance of the Central Labor Union: "The union gave us some good lessons. They said, '*Always* give everybody the full agreement. Because even if they're not going to vote for you, they'll be mad at you if you slight them. And so always give [it to] everybody on the school committee—

if you think they're going to vote for you or not. Don't show any partiality. Use all your persuasive powers.' "

The school-committee member was another story. "The school committeeman met with one of the teachers at her home. She thought that her family was going to be there, but they went out. He'd had too much to drink. They went out, and he made it quite clear that what he wanted was a handout, that he wasn't in it for the cause at all. He was in it for a handout. And the next day she came to school and had hysterics. . . . We were so young and so—not young, I wasn't young—but I mean so immature."[95]

At about this time, the teachers enlisted the help of a lawyer. "We were little innocents! We finally had to get a lawyer because we were so innocent. We had to have protection. And he looked at me and said, 'You've lived to be 50 years old and . . . this is the first time that you encountered it—the idea that politicians don't always keep their word?' So that's how innocent we were."[95]

At last, the teachers won: "And you know what? We got a vote. We got it four to three." The school committee member who had started the women on the struggle first voted against them, then changed his vote when he saw it would pass anyway, making the final vote five to two.[96]

This move for equal pay succeeded for several reasons. First, women were willing to fight for more than a year. Second, war had provided "our big argument" in that during a struggle for democracy abroad, Lowell should have democracy at home. War brought state equal-pay legislation, exemption from pay freezes to equalize pay, and commitments from both the AFL and CIO to push for equal pay.

Significantly, the drive led to the resurgence of a teachers' union in Lowell that became the teachers' recognized bargaining agent. Thereafter, teachers actively took part in Lowell's union life, and a woman school teacher became secretary of the CLU. Women learned they could master local politics and overcome sex barriers in order to achieve their goals. The payroll of 1947–48 showed men's pay up $300 and women's up $800; both were $3,200 per year.[97]

Lowell's teachers were not the exception; rather they were part of a national women's movement, as historian the Susan Hartmann writes, "The greatest effect of the war [regarding women under the law], however, was the attention it focused on two more dramatic issues, equal pay and the proposed equal rights amendment. Women's employment in male jobs promoted efforts for equal pay legislation by groups committed to female equality as well as by those concerned with protecting the jobs and wages of men."[98]

Despite wage advances, female teachers continued to suffer from another form of discrimination. Women had long been legally obligated to stop teaching if they married. If she married a serviceman during World War II, a woman could continue as a teacher, but only until he returned.[99]

Children's Crusade

Lowell children may have played a supporting part in World War II, but the war played a leading role in their lives. Caricatures of the nation's emotions were imposed on play and education, regardless of age or class background. In fact, to a large degree war blurred childhood class differences until a person became old enough to work or fight, continuing to obscure inequalities and imbalances in Lowell and American life. Ironically, the contributions children actually made to the war effort were almost all symbolic.

The most obvious anamoly of children's view of the world lay in the widespread use of Japan—always referred to as the "Japs"—as the enemy, with little attention paid to Germany or Italy. Even the *Lowell Sun,* when reporting that school children were extremely belligerent, noted that hostility was directed mostly toward "the Japs, not the Nazis."[100] This preference does not lie in the presence of any one group in Lowell upon which to focus: the city had no significant German-American population, only three hundred Italian-Americans, and seven Japanese-Americans.[101]

The attack on Pearl Harbor is an obvious explanation, but race was also a factor: the war was the first time many children became old enough to perceive the existence of different races in the world. Just as ethnic antagonisms had always been used in Lowell to divide people, so racism could be manipulated to mobilize enthusiasm for a long war. Even before children knew what Japanese were, they were taught it was fun and good to "kill a Jap." While building support for the war, the foundation was strengthened not only for future prejudice against a supposedly treacherous, non-white race, but also for racism in general. This attitude may not have been purposely encouraged and it certainly existed before World War II, but in the postwar years nevertheless racism replaced ethnic battles as a factor dividing Lowell's working people. As the proponents of a 1942 March on Washington for jobs for black people realized, racism existed even during a war that supposedly proved democracy's superiority.

A second negative side effect of war on children was militarism. A great deal of the conditioning of children in war values was accomplished through the heavily militaristic environment. People in uniform dominated the city, ranging from soldiers to the volunteer Red Cross to the girl and boy officers of the High School Victory Corps. A soldier became a hero; games centered around the war; military parades from Fort Devens replaced circuses; and schools developed into officially recognized centers of the war effort. Football players and cheerleaders may not be ideal high school heroes and heroines, but they serve in that role at least as well as girl officers and boy officers. The universality of the militaristic atmosphere is shown by the almost complete lack of expressed resistance to the draft. The stories of fourteen-year-old boys lying to join the armed forces were greeted then as admirable, albeit misguided, patriotism.

Militarism, however, was only one segment of the overwhelming pervasiveness of wartime values in children's lives. School spirit and competition have often been intensified by identification with nationalism. Two months after Pearl Harbor, the Educational Policies Commission of the National Education Association for Elementary and Secondary Education issued "A War Policy for American Schools:" "When the schools opened on Monday, December 8, they had one dominant purpose—complete, intelligent, and enthusiastic cooperation in the war effort."[102] Although the association exaggerated, children learned primarily the necessity and the positive value of war and the absolute good of their own nation.

At no point could a child escape the impact of war, and yet few could be prepared intellectually to deal critically with the many aspects of international or racial rivalries; even adults were limited in this respect. Children's socialization reflected the most extreme prejudices of wartime propaganda. Wartime goals and ideals were reduced to their most blatant and superficial terms. The question arises why in the midst of an extremely popular war, this nation went to such lengths to indoctrinate its own children.

NOTES

1. Interview with Dorothy Ahearn, 8 March 1976.
2. Interview with Joseph McAvinnue, 30 January 1975.
3. Interview with Joseph McAvinnue.
4. Interview with Constance Case, 14 December 1974.
5. Interview with Joseph McAvinnue.
6. Interview with Thomas Ahearn, 8 March 1976.
7. Interview with James Conway, Sr., 3 February 1975.
8. City of Lowell, "Minutes of the School Committee," typescript (Lowell: School Department), 15 April 1944; 3 February 1944.

9. *Lowell Daily Sun*, 4 November 1944, p. 8.

10. Commonwealth of Massachusetts, *Annual Report of the Commissioner of Correction*, Public Document no. 115, passim.

11. *Lowell Daily Sun*, 5 March 1944, 1; 14 November 1944, 7; 8 March 1943, 1–2.

12. Francis E. Merrill, *Social Problems on the Home Front: A Study of Wartime Influences* (New York: Harper and Brothers, 1948), 79, 84, 92; Jack Goodman, ed., *While You Were Gone: A Report on Wartime Life in the United States* (New York: Simon and Schuster, 1946), 280.

13. Richard Polenberg, ed., *America at War: The Home Front, 1941–1945* (Englewood Cliffs, N.J.: Prentice-Hall, 1968), 139.

14. Merrill, *Social Problems on the Home Front*, 95.

15. Annals of the American Academy of Political and Social Science, *Adolescents in Wartime* (n.p.: AAPSS, November 1944), 103; National Association of Cotton Manufacturers, *Transactions, 1933–1942* (n.p.: NACM, 1943), 674.

16. *Lowell Daily Sun*, 3 September 1943, 1.

17. Lucy Church to Mrs. William B. Parsons, Jr., 8 September 1944, Lowell Red Cross Papers, Lowell, Mass.

18. Interview with Joseph Normandy, 16 January 1975; interview with Ann Welcome, 13 November 1974.

19. AAPSS, *Adolescents in Wartime*, 105.

20. United States Department of Labor Press Release, IR-R86, January 1945, *Boston Herald Traveller* morgue, Boston University; Commonwealth of Massachusetts, Department of Labor and Industries, *Annual Report* (Boston: 1940–44 and 1945–49).

21. Lorraine Fleming to author, 15 May 1981.

22. Interview with Joseph McAvinnue.

23. Interview with Edward Larter, 22 March 1975.

24. Minutes of the Community Service Panel, 31 May 1945, National Archives Record Group 188, "OPA Records."

25. Fleming to author, 15 May 1981.

26. James J. Shea, as told to Charles Mercer, *It's All in the Game* (New York: G.P. Putnam's Sons, 1960), 236.

27. Milton Bradley, *Catalog* (Springfield, Mass: Milton Bradley Company, 1943), preface.

28. Interview with Dorothy Ahearn.

29. Interview with Constance Case.

30. George Chartier to author, 5 May 1981.

31. *Lowell Daily Sun*, 24 May 1942, 2.

32. *Lowell Daily Sun*, 8 December 1942, 17; 22 December 1942, 9; 20 December 1943, 11.

33. Chartier to author, 5 May 1981.

34. Fleming to author, 15 May 1981.

35. Shea, *It's All in the Game*, 239–40.

36. Ibid., 236–38.

37. Ibid., 240.

38. Chartier to author, 5 May 1981.

39. Shea, *It's All in the Game,* 241.

40. *Lowell Daily Sun,* 8 December 1942, 19; 12 December 1942, 11; 21 December 1942, 22; 22 December 1942, 22.

41. *Lowell Daily Sun,* 2 November 1944, 26–27, passim.

42. *Boston Herald Traveller,* 11 October 1941; interview with Elizabeth Flather and John Flather, 13 January 1975.

43. Interview with Ann Welcome; interview with Joseph Normandy; Lowell, "School Committee Minutes," 18 September 1942.

44. City of Lowell, "Enrollment: Lowell Public Schools," ledger (Lowell: School Department, passim).

45. AAPSS, *Adolescents in Wartime,* 103; I. L. Kandel, *The Impact of War Upon American Education* (Chapel Hill: University of North Carolina Press, 1948), 88; Merrill, *Social Problems on the Home Front,* 83.

46. Merrill, *Social Problems on the Home Front,* 96; Lowell, "School Committee Minutes," 2 September 1944.

47. Lowell Technological Institute, Senior Class, *Pickout* (1947), 21–22.

48. Richard M. Ugland, "Education for Victory: The High School Victory Corps and Curricular Adaptation During World War II," *History of Education Quarterly* 19 (Winter 1979): 436, 447.

49. Kandel, *The Impact of War,* 35–36.

50. Geoffrey Perrett, *Days of Sadness, Years of Triumph: The American People 1939–1945* (New York: Coward, McCann and Geoghegan, 1973), 368–69.

51. Ugland, "Education for Victory," 443.

52. Ibid., 444.

53. Interview with Joseph Normandy; Perrett, *Days of Sadness,* 369.

54. Interview with Elizabeth Irish, 26 March 1975.

55. Lowell, "School Committee Minutes," 5 August 1942; 18 September 1942; interview with Elizabeth Irish.

56. Lowell, "City Council Journal," 17 April 1942.

57. Paul J. Heffernan, "Lowell, Mass.: A City at War, January 1, 1943–May 13, 1944," typescript (Lowell: University of Lowell Special Collections, 1974); *Lowell Daily Sun,* 18 March 1943, 10.

58. Lowell, "School Committee Minutes," 7 April 1942.

59. Interview with Joseph Normandy.

60. Interview with Arthur Hiley, 20 March 1975.

61. Interview with Yvonne Hoar, 6 May 1975.

62. Interview with Edward Larter.

63. *Lowell Daily Sun,* 17 June 1943, 1.

64. Interview with Joseph Normandy; Lowell, "School Committee Minutes," 11 June 1943; *American Wool and Cotton Reporter* 49, no. 25 (1945):43.

65. Interview with Victor Luz, 23 April 1975.

66. Interview with Hazel Fiske and Frank Fiske, 3 December 1974.

67. Interview with Ann Welcome.

68. Heffernan, "Lowell: A City at War," 5; interview with Joseph Normandy.

69. *Lowell Daily Sun*, 20 December 1941, 1; 18 January 1943, 10; interview with Joseph McAvinnue; interview with Ann Welcome; Lowell, "School Committee Minutes," 8 April 1943; *Boston Herald Traveller*, 26 May 1944.

70. Interview with Victor Luz.

71. Kandel, *The Impact of War*, 90–91.

72. Ugland, "Education for Victory," 436, 439, 441.

73. Interview with Joseph Normandy; Lowell High School, *The Spindle* (1946), 102–5.

74. Perrett, *Days of Sadness*, 370.

75. *Lowell Daily Sun*, 23 February 1943, 1; Lowell, "School Committee Minutes," 7 April 1942.

76. Harvey C. Mansfield et al., *A Short History of OPA* (Washington: Office of Temporary Controls, Office of Price Administration, n.d.), 245.

77. *Lowell Daily Sun*, 18 November 1944, 19.

78. *Boston Herald Traveller*, 30 September 1944; *Lowell Daily Sun*, 4 November 1944, 2.

79. Interview with James Conway, Sr.; *Boston Herald Traveller*, 10 December 1941; Lowell, "School Committee Minutes," 16 April 1943.

80. Lowell, "School Committee Minutes," 15 November 1942; 25 January 1944; 2 March 1944.

81. Kandel, *The Impact of War*, 61–66; Polenberg, *War and Society*, 148.

82. Interview with Edward Larter.

83. United States Department of Commerce, Bureau of the Census, *Sixteenth Census of the United States, 1940, Population, Third Series, The Labor Force: Occupation, Industry, Employment, and Income: Massachusetts* (Washington: GPO, 1943), 31; interview with Joseph McAvinnue; Lowell, "School Committee Minutes," 2 September 1944.

84. United States Department of Labor, Bureau of Labor Statistics, *Handbook of Labor Statistics Bulletin*, no. 1016 (Washington: GPO, 1950), 88.

85. City of Lowell, School Department, "Payroll" ledger, 15 June–30 June 1945 and 1 September 1942–15 September 1942.

86. Lowell, "City Council Journal," 5 January 1943; 4 June 1943.

87. Lowell, "School Committee Minutes," 18 September 1942; 2 September 1944.

88. Bureau of the Census, *Population, 1940, Third Series, Massachusetts*, 31; United States Department of Commerce, Bureau of the Census *Census of Population: 1950*, vol. 2: *Characteristics of the Population*, pt. 21, *Massachusetts* (Washington: GPO, 1952), 199, 201.

89. Interview with Victor Luz.

90. Lowell, "City Council Journal," 19 January 1943; *Lowell Daily Sun*, 20 January 1943, 1, 11; 2 March 1943, 9.

91. This entire account was related with the understanding that no names would be used; Lowell, "School Committee Minutes," 20 November 1945; 9 October 1946; 27 November 1946.

92. Confidential interview.

93. Lowell, "School Committee Minutes," 10 October 1943; 30 November 1943; 25 January 1944; *Boston Herald Traveller,* 1 December 1946.

94. Confidential interview.

95. Ibid.

96. Ibid.

97. Lowell School Department, "Payroll," 1947–48.

98. Hartmann, *The Home Front,* 137–38.

99. Lowell, "School Committee Minutes," 15 April 1944.

100. *Lowell Daily Sun,* 18 March 1943, 10.

101. Bureau of the Census, *Population, Second Series, Massachusetts,* 114; *Population: Characteristics of the Non-White Population,* 6.

102. Kandel, *The Impact of War,* 18.

8

Who Won the War?

For every class of people, in every occupation, World War II brought a new way of seeing and dealing with economic, political, and social affairs. World War II altered the structure of life in Lowell and in every American community. Out of the war, as out of every major upheaval in history, new patterns developed in the ways people participated in their society. The patterns of life were determined not only by the conditions of world war; they were also defined by two conditions preceding 1941: the American political economy that grew up before 1929 and, specifically, the Great Depression.

It is one of the ironies of World War II that until recently, its significance as an agent of change received at best superficial treatment. In the first postwar decade, several sociologists examined American communities that underwent dramatic changes. These studies focused on exceptional rather than "ordinary" communities. One of the best known, James Stermer and Lowell Carr's *Willow Run: A Study of Industrialization and Cultural Inadequacy,* examined a town that for all practical purposes owed its existence to the war.[1] Willow Run was the location for World War II's most famous war factory, the Ford bomber plant. Despite this focus on the atypical, such sociological examinations served as partial models for this study of Lowell and as points of comparison for evaluating developments there.

More useful models for this book are two studies of relatively stable Midwestern communities. Art Gallaher's *Plainville, Fifteen Years Later* and W. Lloyd Warner's *Democracy in Jonesville: A Study in Equality and Inequality* both contain small but thoughtful sections on the war years, and both provide valuable points of reference for events in Lowell. *Middletown* by Robert Lynd and Helen Lynd has nothing to do with World War II, having been written more than a decade earlier. However, its in-depth, cross-class approach was the single greatest model for this study.[2]

Only in 1979 did a work appear in which a historian attempted to look at an entire state as a tool for analyzing the impact of war. Alan

Clive's *State of War: Michigan in World War II* clearly demonstrates the role war played in putting the federal government into the center of people's lives as the apparent guarantor of prosperity. But even before Clive's study appeared, the Vietnam War had awakened historians to the impact of war on domestic life, and they had begun to direct their attention back to World War II. Richard Polenberg did the first—and most analytical—national study. His collection of documents, *America at War,* focused on several broad areas of national life: morale, national politics, economic policy, civil liberties, and the social impact of war. These same subjects formed the structure for his later analysis in *War and Society: The United States 1941-1945.* That book portrayed the war years as the turning point for American society in the relationship between civilians and government.[3]

A more recent historical survey is John Blum's *V Was for Victory: Politics and American Culture during World War II.* Like Polenberg, Blum concentrates on a few aspects of wartime life through the eyes of a critical historian who happens to have been alive during the event being examined. Both historians appear personally ambivalent regarding the ultimate influence of the period, abhorring wartime curtailments of civil liberties yet unable to convincingly intertwine social, political, and economic events before, during, and after World War II. In this regard, Gerald D. Nash has been more successful. In *The Great Depression and World War II: Organizing Modern America, 1933-1945,* he explicitly recognizes that the war years crowned the 1930s rather than departed from their general movement.[4]

A third point of reference for this book is the government, which in 1946 published its own history of the home front. *The United States at War* elaborately details the activities of the various wartime agencies that had jurisdiction over domestic life. As would be expected, *The United States at War* richly surveys statistics and day-to-day events in Washington but is weak in terms of analysis and useful insights.[5]

In the following pages, the source materials of the historians—both written and oral—are interwoven in the discussion with the fine-tooth community focus of the sociologists. Lowell is the test for theories growing out of both disciplines. But reversing the focus of writers such as Blum and Polenberg, the history of the home front begins here at home, in people's individual lives and in discrete communities. Upon this base can be built more solid and usable conclusions about the meaning of change and continuity in life and work in the United States as a whole.

A Sense of Security

One leg of the stability of a community is its members' feeling that they belong, that they have a positive role to play. Until war came, the depression inevitably implied that millions of Americans were excess baggage, a drain on their towns, their families, their nation. Although New Deal programs attempted to combat this feeling, political battles continually raged over whether the government ought to be the agency to provide work for the unemployed and whether government-created work was itself useful.

World War II ended those battles. The need for men and women to serve community and country appeared obvious. Work ceased to mean a modern version of the dole; it became socially valuable labor, whether performed in private industry or government services. Although few people went to work solely out of patriotism, morale among workers was high because one rationale for war work was to protect the country and what it symbolized from a real threat. American society had been condemned in the 1930s, but protecting it was almost unquestioned in comparison to fascist Germany and Japan. In 1948, sociologist Francis Merrill noted that war created a "high morale resulting from the clear and present danger to national symbols."[6]

Work was the most effective method for drafting individuals into home-front society, but it was not the only one. Schools enlisted the cooperation of both children and parents, social clubs ran dinners as fund-raising events, churches sponsored dances to entertain visiting soldiers, and the Red Cross and other social-welfare agencies turned their focus to raising civilian voluntary contributions to the fight. The most extensive noneconomic path for individuals on the home front to enter the war, the civil-defense program, registered more than twelve million Americans in the first enthusiasm for the war.[7] Less consequentially, *Wartime Racketeers* (1945) was a book-length primer for children and adults on how to recognize and deal with black marketeers. It strove to make every citizen an agent carrying out the police tasks of the FBI, the Justice Department, the Treasury Department, the Federal Trade Commission, and the Office of Price Administration.[8]

Individual moral, and hence social, stability was heightened, even considering activities that served no direct role in the war effort: war made people's lives more exciting. Work filled up more hours, and most Americans had more income than previously to help in occupying leisure time. Even if other diversions waned, people could focus attention on the war's progress, a diversion made more enjoyable because of the almost complete physical security Americans felt and the universal confidence that our side would win. W. Lloyd Warner observed this phenomena in Jonesville and stated it bluntly: "In simple terms, most of [the people of Jonesville] had more fun in the second World War, just as they did in the first, than they had at any other period of their lives. . . . The strong belief that everyone must sacrifice to win the war greatly strengthened people's sense of their significance."[9]

One Lowell woman confided how the wartime spirit influenced her and others:

> Do you know, it was more lively during the war! It seemed like there was life, and it was a mixture of the emotional thing about fighting and the boys were gone. And some who had no one—like brothers and sisters—that was fighting, were having a good time. . . .
>
> There was a lot of war spirit, oh yes. Everybody was displaying flags in their windows if they had someone fighting. And I remember Dad had bought little pins with a flag and if you had one star, that meant you had one son fighting. If you had two—the mothers were wearing them and the sisters and—we were proving that our boys were doing their share. Oh yeah, there was more flag waving in the homes. . . . I wore one and two and three and finally I went to four [stars].[10]

With more exciting lives and a sense of self-worth, people could release any doubts about the value of American political and economic institutions. Instead of the insecurity and stress that doubt creates, people found it simpler to separate the world into good (the "democracies") and evil (fascism), with the United States and its allies clearly morally superior. Schools played their role, responding to the U.S. Office of Education's call for "more positive teaching" of American history.[11] In Lowell, a sense of fighting together replaced conflict. Claire Contardo said, "It seems as though everybody in the section of town we came from—there were a lot of Canadian people married there—had a son or cousin or somebody else close to them [in the services], so there was always a lot of talk about it."[12]

With the encouragement of government and the media's active collaboration, criticism of the United States was minimal. The cooperation between media and government proceeded smoothly and naturally, especially because the Office of War Information was staffed, as Nash observed, with "a sizable number of advertising executives . . . who showed great skill in cultivating patriotism at home through radio broadcasts, pamphlets, and posters."[13] The Madison Avenue simplification of good and evil, tempered in the 1930s, resumed with fresh strength during World War II and helped pave the way for cold war, liberal ideology in the late 1940s and since.

Nevertheless, most people could not afford to respond solely to patriotic motivations; the initial outpouring of national feeling could not by itself survive a protracted and sacrificial war. The psychological security resulting from patriotism continued to be effective because it paralleled economic benefits. The two processes reinforced each other. After ten years of depression, Americans now felt a degree of financial security. Unemployment declined to the point most officials and public perception considered negligible, although one of Lowell's few vocal dissenters claimed twelve thousand people were unemployed in that city in 1944 and the government listed almost one million Americans still unemployed.[14] Similarly, although pay did not rise as rapidly as profits or as high as it might have without restraints on organized labor activity, most families gained a "sense of being solid."[15] Symptomatic of the financial boons was the rise of home ownership in Lowell: with wartime savings to invest, one-third more people owned their homes in 1950 than had in 1940.[16]

Unions, although they tended to blend into the wartime establishment, did, by virtue of their newly found solidity contribute to immediate economic security for their members. Nash concluded, "The American worker, not unlike the businessman and the farmer, found that large organizations had become vital instruments for achieving the twin goals of security and employment."[17] In Lowell, the war, its heightened demand for workers, government pressures, and war contracts broke its decades-long pattern as a non-union city. New Deal legislation and CIO organizing had previously failed to accomplish this feat.

The release from depression financial anxieties was even more extreme in some communities than it was in Lowell, where the boom was, after all, relatively limited. In the farming village of Plainville, "The community was caught up in a postwar 'revolution of expectations' from which it has never recovered. The people of Plainville . . . daily sense the productive might of a war-fattened industry, hungry for peacetime consumer markets."[18]

Industrialized Michigan exhibited the revitalized hopes that Gallaher found in Plainville, coupled with the sobering depression recollections evident in Lowell. Clive found that Detroit families doubled their bank deposits between 1937 and 1944, a fact he attributed to "the pall of the 1930s [which] hovered too close in the memories of too many to encourage a careless attitude toward suddenly plentiful money." But Clive also concluded that, unlike the continuing pessimism clearly evident in Lowell, "The pre-1929 faith in endless vistas of economic growth and material happiness had returned."[19] Decades later, it is clear that Detroit, the symbol of postwar affluence, would not be immune forever from the forces that made Lowell a dying city in 1945.

Nevertheless, national and local leaders freely manipulated war and patriotism to further identify their class ideology with that of the nation. David Hinshaw, using his book on *The Homefront* in 1943 to attack New Deal social programs, called for experienced businessmen to take over from government reformers. Thirty-six years later, Nash concluded that Hinshaw's call had been answered: "In the Depression, the public image of business and businessmen had been distinctly unfavorable, but in the heat of war businessmen occupied vital positions of power in the mobilization process, and their prestige grew enormously."[20]

This process was both national—as with the dollar-a-year men—and local. In Lowell, Remington's "Information for Employees" brochure warned that "your failure to report means idle machines, a condition detrimental to the war effort." Many companies used war in advertisements combining calls for patriotic sacrifice with a traditional sales pitch, as did this ad for a Lowell automobile parts dealer: "*Save a Life*/Your pint of blood may save a life/*Save Your Car*/You should install a Willard for better performance." The Lowell city council, in a move of untested legality, extended its power by declaring a special emergency in the first month of the war. This authorized purchases for civil defense without compliance with the city charter. That no one challenged the edict signifies that government could act securely and with the support of people. The office of U.S Representative Edith Nourse Rogers concluded its announcement of Remington's arrival with a long list of exaggerations, including "it is a magnificent achievement of Congressman Rogers." This same deference to the values and power of social leaders reached into rural Plainville, as "the acceptance of new living standards focused on material comfort and increased efficiency."[21]

By providing both emotional and financial security for individuals, World War II solidified and secured the American political economy after the threat that extended depression had posed. The viability and value of the U.S. system were questioned widely in the 1930s, but after 1941 social pressure combined with media and government and corporate efforts to control dissent. Conflict appeared in Plainville in the 1930s, with the loudest criticisms coming from conservatives who opposed the New Deal. When Gallaher observed Plainville fifteen years after a 1939 study by Carl Withers, the protest voices were "fewer and more muted."[22] In Lowell, 1930s' doubts about capitalism were reflected mostly in omnipresent pessimism, the same pessimism Margaret Parker expressed in her 1939 study of Lowell. War-induced prosperity at home and the spectre of fascism abroad gave the majority of Americans a stake in protecting the status quo and less reason to rock the boat.

The New Deal, Continued

Remember that Roosevelt had said that his objective was to save capitalism. He was a politician, but he was a little different. Roosevelt had established the limits. He said, "If you want to preserve capitalism, limit your appetite. . . . And if we do that, if we don't grab too much up here and if we give them a little more down here, we can prolong this [system] for a while."[23]

Individual emotional and economic security and the stability that prosperity brought to American society were part of a maturation the U.S. political economy underwent during World War II. To the extent that industrial capitalism modernized, the war years continued and strengthened developments begun during the crisis years of the depression, further solidifying 1930s' innovations. Before 1941, the New Deal often had seemed self-contradictory, appearing pro-capitalist and anti-business at the same time. During the war, the two tendencies separated: the conservative drive prevailed with the active cooperation of government and business to further American capitalism.

The most obvious facet of modernization—ironically, one most business organizations opposed and most middle- and working-class Americans welcomed—was increasing federal intervention in economic affairs. This growing government role, and the extent to which business controlled that role, was obvious after Pearl Harbor. Writing in 1943 that "our economy is rapidly becoming a completely planned economy," the political scientist Edwin Witte stressed, "it is not, however, a socialistic economy in the Marxian sense. Private property remains dominant. . . . The Government has largely relied upon industrialists." Concentrated authority was also observed in Plainville: "The people not only accept but are dependent on central authority, particularly the federal government, as a directive source of change." Nash summed it up: "What was revealed to the American people was that the federal government, if necessary, could effectively manage the economy. . . . That role, many Americans felt, should be continued after the war, lest the nation once again sink into depression and mass unemployment."[24] A Lowell politician put it succinctly: "The federal government was calling all the shots."[25]

Continuing New Deal precedent, government stimulated the creation of work for millions, work now regarded universally as vital. It created work primarily through its role as the major investor in new and expanded plants. In 1942 alone, the government directly financed more than $12 billion of war construction. Of the 6.8 million more people who worked in 1943 than in 1939, almost half—three million—worked in federally financed war plants, about equal to the number of new employees in privately financed war and non-war plants.[26]

Private industry could not have adequately handled the investments modern industrially based war called for, just as private finance could not prevent the Great Depression. At least half of the new plants cost more than $25 million each. "General Motors, for example," notes Clive, "built nearly nine-hundred-million-dollars worth of new plant [116.5 percent of GM's 1939 gross capital assets] between 1940 and 1944, almost all of which was paid for by the government."[27]

Just as government stimulated employment and became the major investor, so too did its consumer role mushroom. In 1939, civilians consumed 72 percent of the national output; by 1942, the civilian share had dropped to 56 percent as government war purchases dominated the marketplace.[28]

Although many business representatives argued against government controls, government intervention and reforms most often alleviated pressure for more drastic leftward or decentralizing shifts of power, again repeating the effect of government interventions in the 1930s. Government-as-rationalizer showed up especially clearly in the cotton industry, where a hundred years of stasis had created substantial resistance to any change. Throughout the war, the textile industry did not—perhaps could not—adapt to wartime necessities. When both civilian and government supply requirements could not be met, the government imposed minimal controls to ensure its own needs and to forestall consumer rebellion against the inequities being created by the industry's inability keep its own affairs in smooth working order.

Labor laws, similarly anathema to businessmen, increased worker protection, but also made workers more reliant on the federal government rather than their heightened collective power. Extending federal protection to more workers, as in the "guarantee" of equal pay for women, hindered more radical challenges to corporate/political control by removing the grossest inequities. But such reforms preserved the essentials of the status quo, especially the fundamental balance of power between workers and management. Establishing legal guidelines for

management-labor relations took disputes out of the potentially ex-
plosive realm of moral or class-based judgments of right or wrong,
such as the responsibility for capitalists to provide living wages and
good working conditions.

Samuel Gompers had long ago warned that what government granted,
government could take away. Most states with protective restrictions
on workers' hours adopted wartime measures allowing state administrators to exempt individual employers or industries.[29] Moreover,
putting the force of government behind equal pay for women did not
bring equal pay; only continued agitation could bring this success, and
government edicts did not stir this agitation.

With the heightened demand for employees, businessmen welcomed
government and union control that kept wages and protest down. Such
control would have been impossible without parallel government limits on profits. Left to themselves, corporations resisted any profit limitations while attempting to keep wages low, thus threatening their
own public acceptability. While average weekly pay for manufacturing
workers increased from $28.12 in 1941 to an adjusted peak of $36.72
in 1944, before-tax profits rose from $9.3 billion to $24.3 billion, an
increase that could have stimulated extensive protest about unequal
sacrifices. Taxes, especially the excess profits tax under the Revenue
Act of 1942, kept corporate profits to a more reasonable rise: from
$6.3 billion in 1940 to $10.8 billion in 1944.[30]

Limits on business were imposed only when absolutely necessary.
In the War Manpower Commission, director Paul McNutt was an
especially severe critic of corporate obstinence. Yet McNutt, writes
George Flynn, "when faced with a stubborn employer . . . had limited
leverage to enforce obedience."[31]

Not all modernization had to be forced by government; some occurred as part of the continuing development of the private sector of
the economy, albeit accelerated by war and government policies. In
Lowell, for example, the influx of national companies, including General Electric, Raytheon, and Remington Arms (a subsidiary of Du
Pont) challenged the local control that textile corporations had exercised. Although Lowell corporations had long been owned primarily
by investors in Boston and elsewhere, Lowell had been a center of
those corporations' operations. In the case of war industries, local
plants were a rather minor part of immense national corporations, and
the city seemed to retreat from metropolitan to provincial status.

Lowell's established industries also found it necessary finally to revise labor policies in response to a changing working class, labor organizing, and contemporary economic conditions. Following patterns

begun during Lowell's first economic crisis of the 1840s, the mills discovered a "new" group of workers to fill the lowest paying positions. Most employees hired for these basic jobs were women, a trend reflected by the inability of pay increases for employed women to match those of men in Lowell's principal industries.

War also led to the first employment in Lowell of non-white workers, a trend that accelerated after the war. This move, however, was far more limited between 1941 and 1945 than in other industrial centers. Significantly, white workers who were aware that ethnic prejudice had hindered prewar organizing reported that such bigotry declined in Lowell during World War II. The same people appear less sensitive to the effect of racial prejudice against today's lowest-paid workers: black, Asian, and Hispanic Americans. Thus prejudice continues to divide Lowell's working class.

An increasingly organized working class forced employers to introduce "enlightened" labor policies. Increased benefits accompanied expanded personnel offices, music in the factories, and extensive fringe benefits. Company housing had evoked particular hostility among textile workers, but textile magnates up until the war continued to believe it necessary to control workers; however, Northern mill owners found that company-owned housing had become unprofitable to maintain and difficult to actually wield as a method of control. Just before the war, the Merrimack sold its Lowell tenements—valued at $2,000 per building. Most tenants bought the houses they had rented for years.[32] The sale of company housing epitomized the move from traditional and blatant means of stabilizing and controlling labor—company towns, virulent anti-unionism, racism—and toward more sophisticated methods—fringe benefits, higher pay, cooperation with some unions, and the temptations of perhaps joining the "respectable" middle class.

Indeed, a major facet of the modernized postwar political economy was the addition of organized labor to the establishment, as symbolized nationally in the 1945 peace treaty signed by the AFL, the CIO, and the U.S. Chamber of Commerce. Despite continuing labor militance in the postwar years and continuing employer-organized resistance to unions, the role played by institutionalized labor groups in protecting the status quo was crucial to the ability of corporations to refrain from more obnoxious, nineteenth-century forms of control such as company towns. Even in Jonesville, "the strongest pressure [was] placed against the social classes to compose their differences." Joshua Freeman suggests the role the war played in the national trend within the CIO towards decreasing militance: "In a sense, the CIO moved back in time during the war. As the country mobilized, an ever greater percentage of the CIO membership resembled more the industrial workers of 1930 then the workers of 1939." That is, they were workers unexperienced in the spirit and skills of forming unions.[33]

In Lowell—even while cotton manufacturers exchanged telegrams coordinating resistance to union demands—decisions to add labor representatives to local regulatory and postwar planning boards reflected federal precedents; the stability of Lowell's labor organizations; and unions' reliability as representatives of a perceived harmony of labor and management interests. But even labor's gains on these fronts resulted from organized pressure. Those who did not present a solid front did not achieve benefits. "Women workers in Michigan," writes Clive, "were not well organized to take advantage of the opportunities for progress war afforded." Thus, their advances in the workplace and in society as a whole were more subject to postwar retrogression.[34]

Neither concessions to labor nor federal intervention lessened business control over society. On the contrary, as Nash observed, "the experience strengthened the faith of millions of Americans in big business as an institution. They came to perceive, rightly or wrongly, that full employment and maximum production somehow were closely related to the increased governmental activity in an economy in which large corporations played a major role."[35]

In fact, that new faith in business's ability to manage society for the benefit of all was not proven. Government boards, which *appeared* to be acting as impartial representatives of the community, actually represented the views of business with far more freedom and effectiveness than could private organizations. Most government agencies were staffed overwhelmingly by men identified with corporate ideology and who saw no conflict between the public interest and pursuing that ideology. Such industry-mindedness on the part of textile executives serving on the WPB—in this case, resistance to materials allocation—led to the controversial resignation of Robert Guthrie, the chief of the Textile, Leather and Clothing Branch in 1942, but not to a change in WPB policy.

Law also limited the institution of dollar-a-year men in government war work to people with substantial independent income. To serve in such a position, a person had to have a minimum of $5,600 in nongovernmental income.[36] This requirement was intended to prevent temptation for personal gain, but the level was three times that of the Lowell average annual wage. Thus workers were effectively excluded from these positions of influence, while the war effort suffered as dollar-a-year men strove to maintain their conception of the textile industry and their interests at the expense of production.

Business inefficiency, clearly evident in Lowell and its mainstay industry, was even more striking at the biggest government-corporate cooperative ventures. At the giant Willow Run bomber plant, "mistakes in design and planning . . . cluttered production" and the plant didn't receive an army-navy E-Pennant for production until April 1945.[37] This government-business tie was observed throughout the nation, and Nash tied it effectively to trends begun years earlier: "The crises of depression and war stimulated the expansion of both government and corporate bureaucracy and paved the way for the dominance in American society of giant public and private industry."[38] But neither Clive nor Nash put the two halves together. The alliance was necessarily not in the interests of efficiency, or of most people.

Just as national power was increasingly vested in the federal government—and especially the executive branch—so too did local political institutions rest with increasing safety in the hands of the respectable members of each community.[39] Lowell's municipal reform movement introduced a new government charter oriented toward professional management of city affairs. By eliminating the corrupt ward system of city government, Lowell could have been more able to develop. Instead, as Elzear J. Dionne, a city councilor under the old plan asserted, with citywide elections the new government was able to abandon even the pretense of direct responsibility to neighborhood constituencies.[40] Political campaigns, now run citywide, became increasingly dependent on larger donations. The direction of city politics did not undergo any radical changes and continued to present primarily the corporate point of view. Even had city officials wished to change economic power relationships in favor of textile workers, they would have found the locus of political power located not in Lowell, but in Washington. And no institution, local or national, was prepared to resist the major corporate attack on Lowell: closing the mills and moving them south and out of the country.

Nongovernmental institutions developed in a parallel manner, further strengthening the sophistication of elite social control. For example, government regulations transformed the legal profession. The increasing complexity of government and corporate bureaucracies encouraged lawyers, like politicians, to serve those who could pay. Those who could not afford professional assistance—the unorganized, whether they were consumers, business people, or workers—had less chance to fight their employers, the government, or competitors. In other words, the unorganized lost power.

While government became more sophisticated, the relation between rich and poor often became simpler. Although the rich had always held the real power in Lowell, they had shared social position and influence with significant segments of the local middle class. Lines between the upper and middle classes were often vague, resting partly on personal identification. The case of lawyers is that of one group that, under the pressure of new political institutions, tied itself to the interests of the controlling class. Lawyers joined the new professional-managerial middle class that helped maintain class relations without themselves exerting social control.[41]

On the other hand, many members of the traditional middle class lost power over their own lives as they lost their unique position outside the exchange of labor and capital between workers and employers. In this respect, their self-interest merged with that of the working class. A very few shopkeepers expanded their businesses; many muddled along increasingly at the mercy of corporate suppliers; many were forced out of business when they were unable to compete with chain stores. Teachers, although their pay had always been atrociously low, had also previously been respected and influential members of the Lowell community. By World War II, they recognized that, just like factory workers, they were part of the controlled rather than the controllers. Hence they resorted to collective action to resolve grievances, sacrificing social position for economic gain. In other words, never fully developed as a three-class society, Lowell during the war and after moved toward a simpler two-class society: those who held power and those who held little.

In recalling World War II, many Lowellians claim that the war modernized their city in the sense that it finally integrated itself into the United States and escaped its isolated, provincial status. For instance, Ralph Runels, a city official sent to jail on corruption charges during the war, noted that "Lowell immediately became an integral part . . . of the United States. The war tied our country together."[42] The war is also credited with extending the horizon of Lowell workers in general beyond the city borders, and of women workers specifically to new occupations. In these cases, however, change was more in perceptions than in reality and was far from fundamental.

Lowell could not become integrated into the United States after 1941. From its origin as a company town financed by Boston investors purchasing cotton from the South and selling cloth nationally, Lowell has always been a full participant in the American political economy. National and regional economic factors historically influenced the political and social life of Lowell. Major decisions affecting Lowell mills were always made outside the city. The details rather than the essential nature of Lowell's relationship to the nation changed.

Although many people did experience life and work outside the city because of the war, great resistance remained to working outside Lowell and to moving elsewhere for better job opportunities.[43] On the other hand, breaking up a community is clearly not a definition of progress. For thousands, experience outside Lowell meant rejecting entirely the city and its ethnic identifications rather than merging Lowell with the rest of the country. For women who left Lowell to seek new varieties of work, progress in redressing power relationships between employers and employees did not occur. On the contrary, mature forms of exercising social control blurred the distinction between blue- and white-collar workers; an increasingly organized corporate structure controlled the skills of both.

The Irony of Victory

Well, I'll tell you, the war didn't help Lowell. I think Lowell stayed at—really stayed at what you call the status quo, as it were. Of course, we did lose some employment when it started to level off.[44]

A common criticism of capitalism, on the one had, or of New Deal legislation, on the other, is that only World War II ended the Great Depression. Although few people would argue for war solely to maintain prosperity, individuals cannot escape concluding that economic benefits derive from massive military spending and that political harmony derives from a recognized common enemy. In fact, war—or at least a war economy—seems to be ideal for capitalism's stability. The economic pie becomes temporarily large enough so that each group is satisfied by its own piece. Doris Poisson came in contact with the different feelings war prosperity induced: "In my own family, conditions were better, you know, financial conditions. I'm not saying I liked the war because of that, although I heard that said during the war. I remember a couple of men saying, 'Let the young ones go to war, we're going to make the money,' which I thought was crude, very crude to be saying."[45]

While the necessity for war or its equivalent for prosperity under capitalism may be a valid criticism of this system, the history of Lowell during World War II suggests that war actually hinders fundamental social, political, and economic progress. Thus, war hurts all but the few who control the American political economy. Consensus politics was at a maximum and tolerance of dissent was at a minimum during World War II. Both qualities can be compared and connected to reactionary internal politics and interventionist international policies in the cold war. Many progressive social programs of the New Deal dis-

appeared, while regulative protection of corporate America from organized challenges intensified. Although a war was necessary to stim-
ulate the economy, war and prosperity did occur. With them came a
decline in those movements of the 1930s—many of which were large
enough to be a threat—that aimed to radically humanize capitalism or
replace it by changing the relations of power, rather than just to reform
the status quo mildly. The war indeed strengthened—perhaps even
saved—capitalism and elite control, with decision-making resting in
ever-decreasing numbers of hands, and with those decisions made with
little regard for the needs of individual communities.

Even more important than political or social conservatism brought
on by the wartime atmosphere were changes in economic structures.
Nationally these changes represented a maturing of capitalism in terms
such as the increasing rationalization of the relationships between management and labor. But the Lowell experience indicates a move backward toward unbalancing an already shaky economy. A 1945 report
by the United States Civilian Production Administration warned that
the nation could face this problem: "*Most of the expansion occurred
in a limited number of industries. . . .* Most of the industries can probably do little with the expansion for peace-time purposes and excessive
production plant authorized for them may result in serious damage,
or delay their healthy development."[46]

In other words, the economy was structurally underdeveloped. World
War II artificially stimulated Lowell's economy, orienting it toward
military rather than civilian and human needs. Continued growth depended in large part upon continuing war production. In the meantime,
the ability to produce for civilian needs declined; production of local
jobs also declined. Although Remington and other war companies
hired many former textile workers, offering better wages for a few years,
most of these plants closed by 1946, and workers were forced to return
to mill jobs.[47] James Curran, a Lowell store owner, phrased it, "the
Remington factory and all those businesses were doing a good business.
Without the war, they had no business being in business."[48]

Nor could all workers easily return to their old jobs, again because
of the damage war did to Lowell's economic balance. Yvonne Hoar
recalls, "it seemed that things started going down hill after the war.
Places started to close up, people moved away and things never
seemed—it seemed to be depreciating gradually."[49] For example, despite war contracts, the Boott Mill did nothing to open new civilian
markets or to replace worn-out machinery, leaving no choice but to
close down after the war. Indeed, even if the mill owners had wanted
to invest in Lowell's future, war measures made such "progressive"

moves impossible. But even the will was lacking. The Ames Worsted Company early in 1945 announced plans to expand capacity by building a modern mill, not in Lowell, but in Canada.[50] Thomas Ahearn recalls that "nobody was making progress as far as improving the city itself because of the war effort. They weren't building schools or anything like that at that time. Building materials were scarce and you just couldn't do it."[51]

One potential federal action might have combated the primary expressed reason for closing Lowell's mills but was never even seriously considered: eliminating the wage differential between Southern and Northern mills. The government, on the contrary, accepted the differentials and did not put its influence behind labor organizing in Southern mills. Local industries that could not convert readily to war production, such as the women's shoe industry, also suffered from both the lack of supplies and, after the war, from an organized Northern working class that pushed for decent wages.

Just as war production was temporary, so too was prosperity. Good times continued for several years after 1945 as production for civilian consumption caught up with the five-year backlog, but depression returned to Lowell in full force after the Korean War. By the 1970s, the city had one of the nation's highest unemployment rates.[52] Those improvements that occurred in living conditions, such as less crowded housing and low rents, derived from a steady decline in population in the decades following World War II rather than from a renewal of the city.

Despite the recognized temporary nature of the war economy and despite a common awareness of a possible return to depression conditions, little effective preparation was made for the future. Even in Michigan, the heart of the war boom, "the shape, if not the size, of [the] economy emerged from the war relatively unchanged."[53] Attempts to diversify Lowell's economy were haphazard and consisted mostly of seeking a piece of cold-war-induced production in the aerospace and electronics industries. National corporations had the power to invest in Lowell, but they, like Boston financiers, evinced little interest in saving a city that was a less profitable site for business than other areas of the nation and the world.

The labor-intensive textile industry was replaced by other labor-intensive industries. Lowell and the individuals who lived there remained embedded in the pessimism of the depression years, and many people were resigned to the depression's resuming after the end of the war. People failed to plan for the future because they saw little hope for improvement within their own power.

The manufacturing mix in Lowell two decades after the war reflected both the expansion of peacetime government-supported war industries and the failure to diversify. The textile industry remained Lowell's major employer, with almost four thousand workers in 1974, down from ten thousand in 1940.[54] The aerospace and electronics industries took over second place with three thousand workers, based on large Raytheon and Honeywell plants. Printing had become a major industry, not because of the efforts of city officials or a development commission, but because one employer, the Courier-Citizen Publishing Company, printing telephone directories instead of newspapers, had expanded to employ two thousand people. Despite a decline in population by one-fifth in twenty years, Lowell's unemployment rate remained high: 10.1 percent in March 1976, compared to 8.1 percent nationally.[55]

A city geared to nineteenth-century needs, industries, and wages, Lowell could not compete in the twentieth century. Even while experiencing a degree of prosperity during World War II, the City of Lowell declined relative to the United States as a whole. Between 1939 and 1944—the peak years of war production—Lowell's share of United States manufacturing employment dropped by one-third. In Massachusetts, Lowell's share dropped from 11 percent to 8 percent, and wages in 1950 were among the state's lowest at only $1,915 per person.[56] These figures, incidentally, suggest why Lowell, unlike many major Northern industrial centers, did not attract a large black population during World War II: economic opportunities were so limited that even those on the bottom of the economic ladder chose other locations.

Lowell's tenure near the center of U.S. affairs had ended in the 1920s. World War II to a greater degree, and the non-war years between 1925 and 1980 to a lesser degree, saw the city drained of its ability to produce goods for citizens and profits for investors. An old-fashioned city with a nineteenth-century economic base and decision-making power located elsewhere, Lowell was unable to take advantage of war prosperity in the manner in which newly rising and more adaptable regions of the United States could. Jean Bellefeuille, now living in New Hampshire, understood as well as any professional historian the forces that shape and limit his hometown:

> The struggle of the city of Lowell trying to find a solution to their problem is not only nationwide, but it's a worldwide struggle. It's a struggle of competition, using competition of one community against another as a means of being able to hold down the wage structure, capitalizing on the poverty of the people and the insecurity of the people. And this is an

established pattern, communities offering all kinds of inducements to industries to set up shop in their communities. . . .

It's an indication of the type of economy we live under, an economy whose prime concern is to invest where the highest return is. The industries that don't have the high return don't get the financing to remain in business, and they are wiped out precisely because of the fact that the return is not sufficiently attractive. . . . And since war industry is the industry that pays the highest return, then war industry is the focus of the investment process.[57]

Lowell's nineteenth-century mills had exploited New England as a source of cheap labor, and the United States has used other nations as sources of both labor and raw materials. In a very real sense, Lowell's people and economy were in turn exploited during World War II with every expectation that the city would be discarded afterward. War, a recognized accelerator of social change, accelerated the creation of used-up industries, used-up communities, used-up people.

Economic trends are impersonal, but in their effects on people's lives they acquire a vivid personal meaning. The impact, meaning, and message of victory in World War II to Lowell and its citizens was one of expendability and defeat. Every American knew the watchword of war: "Use it up, wear it out, make it do, or do without." That phrase could also have read, "Use it up, wear it out, throw it out."

NOTES

1. Lowell J. Carr and James E. Stermer, *Willow Run: A Study of Industrialization and Cultural Inadequacy* (New York: Harper and Brothers, 1952).

2. Art Gallaher, Jr., *Plainville, Fifteen Years Later* (New York: Columbia University Press, 1961); W. Lloyd, et al., *Democracy in Jonesville: A Study in Quality and Inequality* (New York: Harper and Brothers, 1949); Robert S. Lynd and Helen Merrell Lynd, *Middletown: A Study in American Culture* (1929; repr., New York: Harcourt, Brace and World, 1956).

3. Alan Clive, *State of War: Michigan in World War II* (Ann Arbor: University of Michigan Press, 1979); Richard Polenberg, ed., *America at War: The Home Front, 1941–1945* (Englewood Cliffs, N.J.: Prentice-Hall, 1968); Richard Polenberg, *War and Society: The United States 1941–1945* (Philadelphia: J.B. Lippincott, 1972).

4. John Blum, *V Was for Victory: Politics and American Culture During World War II* (New York: Harcourt, Brace, Jovanovich, 1976); Gerald D. Nash, *The Great Depression and World War II: Organizing America, 1933–1945* (New York: St. Martin's Press, 1979).

5. United States Bureau of the Budget, Committee on Records of War Administration, War Records Section, *United States at War* (1946; repr., New York: Da Capo Press, 1972).

6. Francis E. Merrill, *Social Problems on the Home Front: A Study of Wartime Influences* (New York: Harper and Brothers, 1948), 231.

7. Richard R. Lingeman, *Don't You Know There's a War On: The American Home Front, 1941–1945* (New York: G. P. Putnam's Sons, 1970), 39.

8. Harry Lever and Joseph Young, *Wartime Racketeers* (New York: G. P. Putnam's Sons, 1945), vii.

9. Warner, *Democracy in Jonesville*, 287–88.

10. Confidential interview, 9 June 1975.

11. Richard M. Ugland, "Education for Victory: The High School Victory Crops and Curricular Adaptation During World War II," *History of Education Quarterly* 19 (Winter 1979):447.

12. Interview with Claire Contardo, 16 September 1975.

13. Nash, *The Great Depression*, 132.

14. Lowell, "City Council Journal," 7 February 1944; Merrill, *Social Problems on the Home Front*, 31.

15. Interview with David Connors, 22 November 1974.

16. United States Department of Commerce, Bureau of the Census, *Sixteenth Census of the United States, 1940, Housing, Third Series, Characteristics by Monthly Rent or Value, Massachusetts* (Washington: GPO, 1943), 45; United States Department of Commerce, Bureau of the Census, *1950 United States Census of Housing, Lowell, Mass., Block Statistics* (Washington: GPO, 1951), 3.

17. Gerald D. Nash, *The Great Depression and World War II: Organizing America, 1933–1945* (New York: St. Martin's Press, 1979), 138.

18. Gallaher, *Plainville*, 233.

19. Clive, *State of War*, 51, 235.

20. David Hinshaw, *The Home Front* (New York: G. P. Putnam's Sons, 1943), 51; Nash, *The Great Depression*, 141–42.

21. Remington Arms Co., Lowell Ordnance Plant, *Information for Employees*, 13; Red Cross Scrapbook, 1941–45, Lowell Red Cross Papers; Lowell, "City Council Journal," 6 January 1942; Rogers Papers, Schlesinger Library, Radcliffe College, Cambridge, Mass.; Gallaher, *Plainville*, 226.

22. Gallaher, *Plainville*, vii.

23. Interview with Jean Bellefeuille, 15 July 1975.

24. Polenberg, *America at War*, 24–25; Gallaher, *Plainville*, 255; Nash, *The Great Depression*, 138.

25. Confidential interview, 27 February 1975.

26. United States Civilian Production Administration, Independent Statistics Division, *War-Created Manufacturing Plant Federally Financed 1940–44* (n.p., 15 November 1945), 21.

27. Clive, *State of War*, 29.

28. Lingeman, *Don't You Know There's a War On*, 63; CPA, *War-Created Manufacturing Plant*, 3; United States Civilian Production Administration, Bureau of Demobilization, *Industrial Mobilization for War: History of the War Production Board and Predecessor Agencies 1940–1945* (Washington: GPO, 1947), 332.

29. United States Department of Labor, Women's Bureau, *State Labor Laws for Women with Wartime Modifications, December 15, 1944,* Bulletin no. 202 (Washington: GPO, 1945), V-26.

30. Joel Seidman, *American Labor from Defense to Reconversion* (Chicago: University of Chicago Press, 1953), 129, 240–41. (Wage figures are in 1935–39 dollars; profit figures are in current dollars.) Interview with Frederick Burtt, 3 November 1975.

31. Flynn, *The Mess in Washington,* 36–37.

32. Merrimack Papers, Baker Library, Harvard Business School, Cambridge, Mass.; *Textile Labor* 2, no. 9 (1941): 11.

33. Warner, *Democracy in Jonesville,* 288; Geoffrey Perrett, *Days of Sadness, Years of Triumph: The American People 1939–1945* (New York: Coward, McCann and Geoghegan), 403; Joshua Freeman, "Delivering the Goods: Industrial Unionism During World War II," *Labor History* 19 (Fall 1978):587.

34. Lowell, "City Council Journal," 27 August 1945; National Association of Cotton Manufacturers Papers, Museum of American Textile History, North Andover, Mass.; Clive, *State of War,* 241.

35. Nash, *The Great Depression,* 139.

36. United States Civilian Production Administration, Bureau of Demobilization, *Dollar-a-Year and Without Compensation Personnel Policies of the War Production Board and Predecessor Agencies,* Special Study no. 27 (Washington: War Production Board, 1947), 69.

37. Clive, *State of War,* 29–31.

38. Nash, *The Great Depression,* v.

39. James McGregor Burns, *Roosevelt: Soldier of Freedom* (New York: Harcourt, Brace, Jovanovich, 1973), 343.

40. Interview with Elzear J. Dionne, 12 January 1973, University of Lowell Special Collections, Lowell, Mass.

41. See Barbara Ehrenreich and John Ehrenreich, "The Professional-Managerial Class," *Radical America* 11 (March-April 1977).

42. Interview with Ralph E. Runels, 12 March 1973, University of Lowell Special Collections.

43. Interview with James Ellis, 16 June 1975.

44. Interview with Roger Kane, 16 September 1975.

45. Interview with Doris Poisson, 15 May 1975.

46. CPA, *War-Created Manufacturing Plant,* 3.

47. Interview with Frank Fiske and Hazel Fiske.

48. Interview with James Curran, 4 February 1975.

49. Interview with Yvonne Hoar, 6 May 1975.

50. Interview with Frank Fiske and Hazel Fiske; *American Wool and Cotton Reporter* 59, no. 3 (1945):46.

51. Interview with Thomas Ahearn.

52. *Boston Globe,* 11 January 1977, supplement 12.

53. Clive, *State of War,* 237.

54. *Directory of New England Manufacturers,* 1974 (Boston: George D. Hall, 1973), 282–85; Bureau of the Census, *Population, 1940, Third Series, Massachusetts,* 32.

55. *Directory of New England Manufacturers,* 282–85; *Boston Globe,* 11 January 1977, 12; United States Department of Labor, *Handbook of Labor Statistics, 1978* (Washington: GPO, 1979), 298.

56. WPB, *American Industry in War and Transition,* 55; United States Department of Commerce, Bureau of the Census, *Census of Population: 1950,* vol. 2: *Characteristics of the Population,* pt. 21, *Massachusetts* (Washington: GPO, 1952), 298.

57. Interview with Jean Bellefeuille.

Postscript

Lowell is an up-and-down place anyway. It'd have to be
some real dramatic thing like [World War II] that's going
to pull it out of this slump here.[1]

The Irony of Victory has sought to analyze the effects of World War
II on Lowell, and, through the Lowell experience, suggest war's place
in American life. The conclusions deny assertions of positive effects
from war and indicate the lack of possibility for fundamental improvement from within Lowell. At one extreme, James Ellis, an ex-
Lowell citizen, described his home city in 1974 as "the only cemetery
with electric lights."[2]

These conclusions leave little possibility that people in Lowell can
solve the problems of their city, but it leaves open the option that
change might come from outside. As was shown by World War II, one
city cannot progress when its problems derive from the political economy of an entire nation. Lowell's problems and a century of attempted
solutions—each of which left the city deeper in despair—occurred within
the framework of U.S. society and, more specifically, within the framework of political and monopoly capitalism. The crucial question during
World War II and in every period is, Who has power? Who makes
the decisions in society?

When she wrote her portrait of Lowell in 1940, Margaret Terrell
Parker concluded that power lay beyond the city. Barring change from
outside, Lowell was doomed. One such change, a world war Parker
could not foresee, delayed that doom. In the 1980s apparent resurrec-
tion came to Lowell, again as a fortuitous result of events beyond the
city limits. Thirty-five years after World War II, Lowell stood as a
prime example of economic redevelopment and as a centerpiece of
business self-boosterism, a leader in the latest industrial revolution.
The unemployment rate was down to 3.8 percent in August 1984,
compared to a national rate of 7.4 percent. Only one year earlier the
rate was 6 percent. Wages rose, too, but as in World War II, at a less

rapid pace; here Lowell's heritage was more obvious. August 1984 weekly earnings for manufacturing workers averaged $315.17, 85.4 percent of the national average, a slight improvement over a year earlier when wages were 84 percent of the national average. To cap the new look, there were tentative plans to introduce salmon into the once-polluted Merrimack River.[3]

There are two keys to Lowell's recent success: luck and power.

First, the luck. Many American communities seek riches through using local, state, and federal funds to attract a piece of the computer industry. Lowell entered this sweepstakes and won a jackpot. In 1976, Wang Laboratories purchased a bit of Lowell land for a production site; two years later, Wang moved its corporate headquarters to Lowell. Four years later, in 1982, Wang, a world leader in the production of microcomputers and word-processing systems, had revenues of $1.2 billion, employed fourteen thousand local residents and had attracted numerous smaller companies to settle in its wake.[4]

Even more important, Lowell was lucky to be the home town of U.S. Senator Paul Tsongas. And Tsongas had power, which he wielded where it has counted since the 1930s: in Washington, D.C. Pork is the meat of Washington, and Tsongas delivered it to the city where he used to drive a truck for his father's commercial laundry.

The first large shipment—$40 million—arrived in 1978 when a bill was signed designating parts of Lowell as a National Historic Park. The idea had been around since the 1950s, but even Tsongas, as a city councilor, had rejected the idea when Patrick Mogan, an assistant superintendent of the city's schools, first proposed it to him. "I listened to him politely, but I thought his idea was ridiculous," Tsongas told *Science Digest* in 1983. "I remember thinking that if you could fill in the canals and tear down the mills, you'd be a lot better off than restoring them."[5]

Tsongas's early attitude toward a national park and his ambivalent view of the city's past are perhaps more reflective of the attitudes of working-class Lowellians than his later support for the project. In fact, many people resisted the creation of a park, viewing it as another example of a "blow-in," a Lowell term for outsiders who come in to tell people what to do.[6] Nevertheless, Lowell's leaders had a centerpiece for redevelopment and, with Tsongas in Washington, the city eventually received more than $250 million in state and federal grants for rehabilitation and public works. The keystone was the $5 million urban development action grant that convinced Wang to locate its headquarters in Lowell.[7]

High unemployment apparently became part of Lowell's past, and low wages seemed to be slowly following it, but Lowell insists that people remember history. Few national feature stories on Lowell's boom fail to take this backward glance. *Science Digest* writer Stephen Solomon asked the question directly: "Has Lowell traded a dependency on textiles for a dependency on computers? History repeats itself, of course. The U.S. computer industry could wither in the face of foreign competition, just as the textile industry did, or other companies could someday leapfrog Wang with an advanced technology, sending the company into a steep decline."[8]

In fact, in the mid-eighties, Wang appeared to be a casualty of competition and international stagnation in the computer industry. Even before then, Lowell's high-technology economic development had critics, such as community organizer Charles Gargiulo. He told *Newsweek* in 1981 that "most areas are worse off now than they were ten years ago. . . . They're going to have happy tourists, but angry citizens.[9] *Newsweek* summarized the causes of that anger:

> There is an acute shortage of housing, and the incidence of arson is alarming. In the Acre, once a shantytown for Irish immigrants and now largely an Hispanic slum, there have been nineteen suspicious fires on a single street in the past five years. Downtown rents are rising, and many small retailers have been forced out. Some community leaders charge that Lowell tax money is being siphoned off to benefit big developers, while the needs of most citizens are being ignored.[10]

Indeed, racism has struck Lowell again, with segregated schools, race harassment, job discrimination, and a lack of adequate rental housing excluding many Lowell citizens from the economic revival. June Gonsalves, an attorney and head of a human rights commission planning committee, says "People in Lowell talk about it being an ethnic city, but they only embrace that and endorse that as long as [the ethnic groups] are white."[11]

The impact of racism has fallen on Lowell's 5–20,000 Hispanics, the city's "quiet minority" for two decades. But even more clearly it has targeted Lowell's 14–21,000 Laotians and Cambodian refugees. These Southeast Asians began arriving in large numbers after 1980, attracted by the city's boom. Together, the three ethnic groups composed about a third of Lowell's population by 1987, when a school desegregation plan dominated city elections. Because so many recent immigrants crowded into the Acre, the schools had rapidly become racially imbalanced; the desegregation plan included bussing 700 of the system's 13,000 students.[12]

The irony of the newest racism is twofold. First, the situation revives the burden that ethnic conflict places upon Lowell's working class, a burden World War II had relieved for whites. Second, An Wang, an Asian immigrant and perhaps the city's most prominent citizen, is widely considered its economic savior for locating his corporate headquarters there.

Criticisms such as these have a waiting answer: economic development must come first, and neighborhood redevelopment will follow. Said Tsongas in 1983, "The first ten years are now over. Ten years from now, it will be done. We will have the city restored. The neighborhoods will be back. We'll have a city very much like it was in its heyday."[13]

Tsongas, who resigned from the Senate for health reasons in 1984, is probably correct, at least in his concluding phrase. The people of Lowell will make do with what trickles down from the hands of the power brokers, enlightened or selfish, textile or computer, Yankee or Greek or international. In the city's heyday and in its hibernation, the people of Lowell have watched as others made the crucial decisions about their own lives. As the fortunes of Wang and the rest of the computer industry rose and fell in the eighties, so too did Lowell's.

Meanwhile, what's happening in the textile mills? A few buildings are on a National Historic Park tour; some have been turned into exhibit space, genteel shops, prime office space, or comfortable housing. When the national park opened, the Wannalancit Mill was the last of the old mills running and was the high point of park tours, a living testimonial to the history of Lowell labor. In 1980, the Wannalancit Mill closed. The National Park Service, without funds to buy the looms, made do with tape recordings of the roar of the machines. Ted Larter sold his equipment elsewhere.[14]

NOTES

1. Interview with Victor Luz, 23 April 1975.

2. Interview with James Ellis, 16 June 1975.

3. United States Department of Labor, Bureau of Labor Statistics, *Employment and Earnings* November 1984, 6, 80, 103, 112; Suzanne Spring, "From Gloom Town to Boom Town, Model City Reborn," *Palm Beach Post*, 10 February 1985, C23.

4. Spring, "From Gloom Town to Boom Town," C23; Stephen Solomon, "Computer Boom Town," *Science Digest* March 1983, 108.

5. Solomon, "Computer Boom Town," 40.

6. Mary Blewett, "Notes on the Opening of the Lowell National Historical Park," typescript, author's possession, 1979.

7. " 'High Tech' Ends a Long Slump in an Old Mill Town," *U.S. News and World Report,* 6 April 1981, 65.

8. Solomon, "Computer Boom Town," 108.

9. "Lowell: A Town Is Reborn," *Newsweek,* 28 September 1981, 38.

10. "Lowell: A Town Is Reborn."

11. *Boston Globe,* 3 November 1987, 1, 13.

12. Ibid., *New York Times,* 25 October 1987, 43.

13. Spring, "From Gloom Town to Boom Town," C23.

14. David Sylvester, "Lowell's Labors Lost," *The Progressive,* July 1981, 35.

Bibliography

Government Documents, Published and Unpublished

The most important statistical sources on Lowell are the United States Census and the records of the Massachusetts Department of Labor and Industries. Most important for this study were the 1940 and 1950 censuses of population, business, manufacturers, and housing, and the 1948 and 1954 censuses of business. The U.S. Census documents Lowell conditions just as the effects of war emerged and after war's immediate impact had ended. Comparable data for the war years is in the Massachusetts monthly *Census of Manufactures.*

Other federal documents provide a basis for fitting Lowell events into national perspective. The Civilian Production Administration published several reports on the different roles that organizations played. *Dollar-a-Year and Without Compensation Personnel Policies of the War Production Board and Predecessor Agencies* contains detailed statistics on the number, background, and remuneration of business volunteers serving in Washington. *War-Created Manufacturing Plant Federallly Financed* gives aggregate statistics on the financing of new war industrial plants, but, like most government studies, lacks data for individual plants.

Two Bureau of Labor Statistics publications, *Monthly Labor Review* and *Handbook of Labor Statistics* (Washington: GPO, 1950), are the primary statistical sources on working conditions for the nation as a whole, for working conditions in particular industries, and for particular kinds of workers (i.e. women workers, black workers, migrant workers). Again, figures are usually aggregate, although *Monthly Labor Review* often contains reports on individual but unidentified employers.

Two War Production Board documents, *American Industry in War and Transition, 1940–1950, Part II: The Effect of the War on the Industrial Economy* (n.p., 1945) and *Production Wartime Achievements and the Reconversion Outlook* (n.p., 1945), give aggregate figures for each wartime year on profits, gross national product, the share of the GNP from Lowell and Massachusetts, expansion of industrial capacity and production, and many other areas of war production. *American Industry in War and Transition* has a comprehensive section on supply and production problems in the cotton industry, focusing on the bottleneck that management intransigence created.

The publications of the Department of Labor's Women's Bureau examine national war-induced changes in women's work in far more detail than is available for men's work. The nation apparently worried a great deal more about the negative effects of women's work. Fortunately, many Women's Bureau bulletins are free from prejudice against women working. The bulletins contain not only statistics, but also critical insight relevant to the concerns of the 1980s. The most useful documents here were *Changes in Women's Employment During the War* (Washington: GPO, 1944), *Employment of Women in the Early Postwar Period with Backgrounds of Prewar and War Data* (Washington: GPO, 1946), *State Labor Laws for Women with Wartime Modifications, December 15, 1944* (Washington: GPO, 1945), and *Women's Wartime Hours of Work, the Effect of their Factory Performance and Home Life* (Washington: GPO, 1947).

The federal government also published histories of several aspects of World War II domestic developments. The Bureau of the Budget issued *The United States at War* (1946, repr.; New York: Da Capo Press, 1972). This is the only publication containing both statistical and descriptive information on all special wartime agencies with jurisdiction over life in the United States. Moreover, it chronicles how these agencies' policies and activities developed. The Office of Price Administration published *Industrial Mobilization for War: History of the War Production Board and Predecessor Agencies 1940–1945* (Washington: GPO, 1947) describing production and labor supply problems, again with a detailed section on the cotton industry. The United States Employment Service for Massachusetts published a *Monthly Labor Market Report* that contains remarkably detailed information.

The National Archives houses miles of documents relating to World War II agencies. The records of the National War Labor Board, the War Manpower Commission, and the Office of Price Administration contain a great deal of information covering specific Lowell events regarding labor-management interactions and compliance (or noncompliance) with OPA regulations.

The Massachusetts *Census of Manufactures* for Lowell is the most useful of many documents the Commonwealth of Massachusetts issued, providing detailed statistics by industry. The *Decennial Census, 1945* supplements the federal census by providing population data at the conclusion of the war. *Election Statistics,* published yearly as part of a series of public documents, lists election results for every community in the commonwealth. The Department of Banking and Insurance *Annual Report* gives the finances for all banks. The Public Health Department's *Annual Report* supplies data on diseases; the Corrections Department lists crimes and convictions. Data on municipal finances are published in the same series by the Massachusetts Department of Corporations and Taxation.

Several brief reports by the Massachusetts Department of Labor and Industries provide information on the kinds of employment that were available. These reports are "Employment of Wage-Earners on War Work in Manufacturing Establishments in Massachusetts, by Leading Industries and Municipalities, August and September, 1945," "Employment on War Work in Leading

Manufacturing Industries and Municipalities in April 1945," and "Strikes of Long Duration in Massachusetts, 1935–1946."

Finally, a great deal of documentary evidence is available in Lowell. The Board of Election Returns has a breakdown by ward of all election results, plus registration figures by party and sex. Real estate tax books, personal property tax books, and poll tax records are all available. The *Annual Report of the City Auditor* gives annual budget figures for the city as a whole and for each department. The most informative public document is the *Journal of the City Council,* containing the minutes of every city council meeting. Although the minutes are often cryptic, the *Journal* as a whole paints a picture of city politics in both its petty and its significant aspects. The *Journal* was an invaluable guide in preparing for interviews.

School committee activities are detailed in minutes of its weekly meetings. Monthly payroll records of the School Department and enrollment figures for all schools supplemented these minutes, as did the Lowell High School and Lowell Technological Institute yearbooks.

Personal Papers, Organization Records, Archives

The Lowell Historical Society and the Special Collections of the University Libraries, University of Lowell, are together the major holding of archival material on the city. Unfortunately, this collection reflects the interests of historians, and therefore concentrates on the early and mid-nineteenth century. It does contain two research papers on World War II done in the 1970s by students at Lowell State University, both based entirely on the *Lowell Sun.*

In the last several years, the Historical Society has received a number of oral history cassettes. Interviews with Ralph Runels and Elzear J. Dionne, local politicians of the 1930s and 1940s, shed light on city politics. Scrapbooks of Local Draft Board #86 give insight into the impact of the draft in Lowell, with a few rare hints on the existence of opposition to the draft. The Historical Society collection also contains the text of a 1946 speech by Frederick W. Coburn, honoring Red Cross wartime achievements. More complete, and more balanced, information on the Red Cross was found in the files of the Lowell chapter of that organization. These files include correspondence, records, scrapbooks, and memorabilia. The Lowell Red Cross is the only local organization that saved extensive files and made them available. Finally, school yearbooks and city directories in the Historical Society collection provided valuable background information.

Most corporation records are unavailable, but extensive records for the Merrimack Manufacturing Company, Lowell's largest during World War II, are part of a large Lowell collection in Harvard Business School's Baker Library. Yearly income tax forms for the company were extremely informative. The Ames Textile Corporation records were made available by the company and contain rough details on corporate finances, especially on the effect of the excess profits tax. The Museum of American Textile History in North Andover, Massachusetts, has corporate records of several defunct Lowell corporation connected with the Stevens family, but all closed before the war began. The museum also has a great many corporate records for the Lawrence Manufacturing Company up until 1950. Finally, the museum holds the papers of the two major textile industry associations, the National Association of Cotton Manufacturers and the National Association of Wool Manufacturers.

The personal papers of Lowell's congresswoman, Edith Nourse Rogers, are in the Schlesinger Library of Radcliffe College. The collection contains public correspondence, speeches, brief notebooks, and extensive scrapbooks. The letters Congresswomen Rogers received gave some alternative view to the overwhelmingly positive memories Lowell citizens now report about her. The letters also include significant detail on public reaction to specific congressional legislation, especially to the nurse's draft Rogers proposed. Unfortunately, Rogers's private correspondence and most of her notes and files are not part of the collection.

Several individuals in Lowell made personal material available for study. Robert Long, an official of the Lowell Five Cent Savings Bank, provided a "Biography of a Savings Bank, the History of the Lowell Five Cent Savings Bank," which he wrote. Lydia Howard, wife of the mayor during most of World War II, loaned a scrapbook of her husband's wartime activities. The scrapbook contains articles on the change in city government to Plan E and on related political battles in the school committee.

Until a merger several months before Pearl Harbor, Lowell had two daily, English-language newspapers, but only the *Lowell Sun* existed during the war. Although biased, the *Lowell Sun* was the single best source and perhaps the only source—for day-to-day local details. *Sun* articles in 1943 and 1944 assessing the effect of the war include extensive statistical information on changes in the local economy. These general articles eased the job of organizing a wealth of data. Throughout the war, the *Sun* devoted most of its front page to the war as it affected Lowell. Articles in the newspaper were the only reliable observer of which war plants arrived in Lowell at which time, what labor-management conflicts arose, and so on. The morgue of the defunct *Boston Herald Traveller,* now in the possession of the Boston University School of Public Communications, contains material on Lowell from many publications.

Oral Histories

The foundation of this book is interviews conducted with people who lived and/or worked in Lowell during World War II. Although the interviews are not a scientific cross-section of the population, as a group they include people in most major categories, including male and female textile workers, Remington workers and employees of other war plants, corporate executives, bankers, doctors, lawyers, teachers, students, housewives, store owners, middle-level managers, foremen, union officials, politicians.

Following is a complete list of interviews conducted by the author, a brief description of the position of each person during the war and, where relevant, what they did after the war. Several interviewees asked to remain anonymous. Selected interviews are on deposit with the Special Collections, University Libraries, University of Lowell.

The Interviews

George Abodeely: assistant personnel director at Fort Devens, 20 March 1975.

Thomas Ahearn: Lowell Central Labor Union president, International Ladies Garment Workers Union organizer, labor representative on the local War Price and Rationing Board, 8 March 1976.

Dorothy Ahearn: parts assembler at General Electric, inspector at Breslee's Tent Company, 8 March 1976.

Jean Bellefeuille: shoe worker, union organizer, carpenter, 15 July 1975.

Homer Bourgeois: Union National Bank loan officer (1940–44) and later bank president, 5 December 1974.

Fred Burtt: Abbott Worsted Company superintendent, 3 November 1974.

Father John Cantwell: St. Rita's Church priest, 6 May 1975.

Dow Case: *Lowell Sun* photographer, 12 December 1974

Constance Case: junior high and high school student, daughter of textile workers, 17 December 1974.

Verner Clark: Lawrence Manufacturing Company manager, 24 February 1975.

Jesse Clark: housewife, Lawrence Manufacturing Company office clerical worker, 24 February 1975.

Dave Connors: *Lowell Sun* managing editor, 22 November 1974.

Claire Contardo: Boston Navy Yard and civil service worker, 16 September 1975.

James Conway, Sr.: high school chemistry teacher, 3 February 1975.

Raymond Cordeau: druggist, 2 April 1975.

Lucille Cordeau: housewife, 2 April 1975.

James Curran: purchasing manager for three clothing stores; started own store in 1949, 4 February 1975.

William Doherty: foundry business owner, enlistee, 22 April 1975.

James Ellis: Merrimack Manufacturing Company union business agent, union organizer, draftee, 16 June 1975.

Arthur Eno, Jr.: college student, son of judge and draft board appointee, later a lawyer and local historian, 13 November 1974.

Charles Fairbank: Parker Bobbin Company owner, 19 December 1974.

Frank Fiske: Merrimack Manufacturing Company assistant paymaster, 3 December 1974.

Hazel Fiske: department store saleswoman, Lawrence Manufacturing Company office worker. 3 December 1974.

John Rogers Flather: Boott Mill president, 9 December 1974 and 13 January 1975.

Elizabeth Flather: housewife, 13 January 1975.

John Gardner: Du Pont Company representative on the War Production Board in Washington, Ames Textile Corporation executive since 1945, 29 November 1974.

Alice Gendreau: Ames Textile Corporation secretary, 29 November 1974.

Allan Gerson: lawyer, 17 September 1975.

Patrick Gill: in charge of Merrimack Manufacturing Company security guards, 3 February 1975.

Everett Harris: plumber, plumbers and pipe fitters' unions business agent, Lowell Building Trades Council president, representative on the area War Manpower Board, 17 September 1975.

Harold Hartwell: city councilor, 26 March 1975.

Arthur Hiley: Matthews Memorial Church pastor, 20 March 1975.

Yvonne Hoar: Merrimack Manufacturing Company and Remington employee, Merrimack rank-and-file union organizer, 16 May 1975.

Lydia Howard: housewife, wife of a mayor of Lowell, 18 March 1975.

Elizabeth Irish: high school math teacher, 26 March 1975.

Andrew Jenkins: Newmarket Manufacturing Company office manager, 31 January 1975.

Roger Kane: ward councilor, 16 September 1975.

Edward Larter: elementary school student, son of Wannalancit Mill owner and later its owner himself, 22 March 1975.

Brendan Leahey: physician, 27 January 1975.

Robert Long: Lowell Five Cent Savings Bank teller, later a bank officer, 12 December 1974.

Victor Luz: high school student, now a high school teacher, 23 April 1975.

Joseph McAvinnue: Pawtucket Junior High School principal, interviewed with his daughter, who was an elementary school student during World War II, 31 January 1975.

Leo McCue, Sr.: skilled textile worker, 7 January 1975.

Helen McCue: skilled textile worker, 7 January 1975.

John McCue: skilled textile worker, 7 January 1975.

Philip McGowan: clothing store owner, 22 April 1975.

Bertrand McKittrick: McKittrick Company president (used textile machinery), 3 February 1975.

Patrick Mogan: Lowell Model Cities head in the 1970s, 8 January 1974.

Armand Morisette: St. Jean Church priest, chaplain to the French navy in the United States during World War II, 16 June 1975.

John Mullen: woolen and worsted workers' union steward, later Lowell Central Labor Union president, 16 June 1975.

Joseph Nawrocki: Ames Textile Corporation blending and dyeing department supervisor, 31 January 1975.

Joseph Normandy: high school student, 16 January 1975.

Andrew Notini: musician and tobacco and candy wholesaler, 31 January 1975.

Barbara Notini: jewelry store worker (1941–43), housewife, 27 January 1975.

John Albert Notini: tobacco and candy wholesaler, 12 April 1975.

Fred O'Brien: draftee, General Electric machine operator, 25 February 1975.

Emma O'Brien: Merrimack Manufacturing Company office clerk, 25 February 1975.

Wilfred Pearson: YMCA staff member, later Lowell YMCA director, 2 January 1975.

William Pepin: dentist, 24 February 1975.

Doris Poisson: Boston Navy Yard stenographer and secretary, other civil service jobs, 15 May 1975.

Samuel Pollard: city councilor, 7 January 1975.

Paul Santilli: Boston Navy Yard steamfitter, union local president, 21 January 1976.

Nathan Silver: Strand movie theater manager, 24 February 1975

Edward Stevens: college student and serviceman, son of Ames Textile Corporation president, later president of Ames, 26 November 1974.

Alice Swanton: Remington grease monkey, also worked at Merrimack Manufacturing Company, U.S. Rubber, Waltham Watch Company, and Sylvania, 4 June 1975.

Louis Vergados: Merrimack Manufacturing Company union organizer, draftee, 18 September 1975.

Ann Welcome: high school student, textile company stitcher, 17 November 1974.

John Zawodny: Wannalancit Company shipping and receiving clerk, 22 March 1976.

Confidential: *Lowell Sun* reporter

Confidential: young woman working in her father's downtown Lowell store

Confidential: housewife living on her husband's monthly allotment

Confidential: textile mill personnel director

Confidential: teacher

Method

The interviews for this book followed a basic format. Unlike most social science survey interviews, however, these oral histories did not follow a strict questionnaire; rather, the format guided me in eliciting historical fact and opinions from each individual. The following outline indicates general areas covered; the wording here was not closely observed in any interview. Each interview emphasized a cooperative investigation of the past. Answers to general questions determined the detailed questions for each session. Interviews lasted about two hours; most, but not all, were tape recorded.

    I. *Background*

           How long have you lived in Lowell?

           Were you born in Lowell?

           Were you married in 1941?

           Where was your spouse born?

   II. *Work*

           Where did you work during the war?

           What did your job entail?

           How did you get this work?

           What was your spouse's work and what did it entail?

           What jobs did your parents and/or children have during the war and what did these entail?

           What aspects of your work did the war change?

           What aspects of your work related to the war?

What aspects of your company did the war relate to or affect (i.e., organization, efficiency, status, stability, future, size, labor relations, labor organizations, profits, control, speed)?

What aspects of your profession did the war change (organizations, supplies, status)?

III. *Voluntarism*

What examples of patriotism at work can you remember?

What examples of patriotism in the union can you remember?

What aspects of patriotism in your home can you remember?

How did you spend your time when not at work?

How did you spend your time when not in school?

In what civic activities did you participate?

How did they contribute to the war effort?

How did the war change them?

In what civic activities did other members of your family participate?

IV. *School*

Were many teachers absent?

What was the effect of the draft on students?

How did the war affect subjects already taught?

What additions were made to the curriculum?

How were extra-curricular activities affected?

How was discipline affected?

How extensive was delinquency?

V. *Financial*

What was your income?

What was your family's income?

How were wages affected?

What were your taxes and how did you feel about them?

On what did you spend your income?

How did rationing affect you?

VI. *The Draft*

Were you anxious to join the army? Why or why not?

How did you feel about sons or relatives entering the services?

How did you feel about being drafted?

How did you feel about relative's being drafted?

VII. *General*

Before Pearl Harbor, how aware were you of the possibility of war?

After Pearl Harbor, what were your feelings about U.S. participation in the war?

What were your feelings about the federal government?

What were your feelings about Franklin Roosevelt?

What was the atmosphere in Lowell?

What was the mood at work?

What was the atmosphere at home?

What were the effects of war on your leisure time?
What were the effects of war on your home life?
What were the effects of war on Lowell?
Did the war unify or disrupt the city?
Did the war affect the relation of Lowell to the rest of the country?
How was Lowell a different city after the war than it had been before the war?

VIII.   Is there anything else you would like to add?

Studies of Selected Aspects of Home-front Life

American historians quickly devoted a great deal of attention to World War II as an international event; occurrences within the United States at first received only minimal attention. For the most part, early histories are semi-official publications that often contain a great deal of data on the state level. However, they primarily honor a state's contribution to the war effort rather than examine the impact of war on that state. One of the best of these state histories is Karl Hertzell's *The Empire State at War: World War II* (New York: New York State, 1949).

In recent years, several broad portraits of national life during World War II have been published. In addition to those described in chapter 8, two general studies appeared in the early 1970s: Richard Lingeman's *Don't You Know There's a War On: The American Home Front, 1941–1945* (New York: G. P. Putnam's Son, 1970) and Geoffrey Perrett's *Days of Sadness, Years of Triumph: The American People, 1939–1945* (New York: Coward, McCann and Geoghegan, 1973). Both are rich in contemporary detail, drawing heavily on newspapers and journals. As opposed to Polenberg, Lingeman and Perrett give popularized views of the war years, covering many areas of general interest from fashions to work to entertainment. Perrett included an especially useful section on education. But neither work is analytical; both appeal more to nostalgia buffs than to scholars.

Studs Terkel's *The Good War: An Oral History of World War II* (New York: Pantheon, 1984) is the best of several collected recollections of the war years. Two others are Roy Hoopes's *Americans Remember the Home Front: An Oral Narrative* (New York: Hawthorn Books, 1977) and Archie Satterfield's *The Home Front: An Oral History of the War Years in America, 1941–1945* (Chicago: Playboy Press, 1981). As personal narratives, each is worth reading, but, despite—or perhaps because—the fact that each looks at the whole nation, none give much feel for how war changed American life in the long term. For the lives of individuals, these books serve well, but they are not full histories. Satterfield's book, with the most narrative, is still a popular rather than a critical study.

Historians wrote few detailed studies of wartime community life until the 1970s, but in the immediate postwar years sociologists found wartime life of great interest, and their contributions to this study have also been noted in the chapter 8. Sociologists considered these years notable because they were a crisis period in American life. Similar in approach to *Willow Run* (see chapter

8) is *Social History of a War-Boom Community* (New York: Longmans, Green, 1951) by Robert Havighurst and H. Gerthon Morgan.

A number of studies on specialized facets of wartime domestic history have appeared over the last forty years. Special studies provided a useful guide to studying Lowell, while also providing a wealth of facts on the national level to which local observations were compared.

Women's work has been the most studied aspect of World War II domestic history. The International Labour Organization's comparative examination of women's work, *The War and Women's Employment, the Experience of the United Kingdom and the United States* (Montreal: ILO, 1946), gives detailed information for all but the last year of the war on hours, wages, legislation, and the subjective aspects of work, all in the context of a broad analysis of war's impact on women's working conditions. Joan Ellen Trey's, "Women in the War Economy," in *Review of Radical Political Economics,* 4 (Summer 1972):40–51, brings the analysis up to date by using the ILO work in conjunction with extensive documents made available since then. In *Women in Defense Work During World War II, an Analysis of the Labor Problem and Women's Rights* (New York: Exposition Press, 1974), Chester Gregory supplements Trey's essay by stressing women in trade unions and legislation pertaining to women workers. Two books appeared in the 1980s that integrate women's work lives with their non-work lives: Karen Anderson, *Wartime Women: Sex Roles, Family Relations, and the Status of Women During World War II* (Westport, Conn.: Greenwood Press, 1981) is a study of three cities; Susan M. Hartmann, *The Home Front and Beyond: American Women in the 1940s* (Boston: Twayne Publishers, 1982) is probably the best overall survey of women's history in the period.

Publications of the textile unions contain a wealth of material on the industry in general, and on Lowell events in particular. The Textile Workers Union of America's, *The Nation's Most Prosperous Industry, an Accounting of the Postwar Financial Experience of America's Textile Manufacturers* (New York: TWUA, 1948) contains extensive statistical information from 1937 to 1947 on wages, corporate income, corporate profits, taxation, assets, and so on. Union periodicals—*Textile Labor, The Advance, The Textile Challenger, Labor's Monthly Survey*—detail the successes of the labor movement. The TWUA biennial *Executive Council Report* gives statistical and descriptive summary information of the union's activities.

Two excellent histories of government controls are available, both written by people with access to the federal bureaucracy. These are Harvey C. Mansfield et al., *A Short History of OPA* (Washington: OPA, 1946) and David Novick, Melvin Anshen, and W. C. Truppner, *Wartime Production Controls* (New York: Columbia University Press, 1949). Two other books follow the same approach from a more current and analytical perspective: George G. Flynn's *The Mess in Washington: Manpower Mobilization During World War II* (Westport, Conn.: Greenwood Press, 1979) and Gerald T. White's, *Billions for Defense: Government Finances by the Defense Plant Corporation During World War II* (University: University of Alabama Press, 1980).

Several special studies appeared in the 1970s, two of which combine an enlightening view of their subject with restrained analysis. In *The First Casualty* (New York: Harcourt, Brace, Jovanovich, 1975), Philip Knightly provides a journalistic account of the media's voluntary news distortions for propaganda purposes. Knightly is outraged at the willingness of journalists to cooperate, but does not examine the consequences for either American society or for journalists. More analytical is an article by Clayton Koppes and Gregory Black, "What to Show the World: The Office of War Information and Hollywood, 1942–1945," in the *Journal of American History* 64 (June 1977): 87–105. Mary Penick Motley compiled and edited oral histories in *The Invisible Soldier: The Experience of the Black Soldier During World War II* (Detroit: Wayne State University Press, 1975). This book has only short accounts of events within the United States, but a great deal on the achievements of, and obstacles facing, blacks serving overseas.

Interest in several areas of social history or sociology died out soon after the war. Written as the war was winding down, Harry Lever and Joseph Young's, *Wartime Racketeers* (New York: G. P. Putnam's Sons, 1945) gives examples of a favorite topic of discussion during the war: the varieties of illicit activity. The book is primarily a primer for citizens on how to aid law enforcement agencies in recognizing crime. *The Black Market: A Study of White Collar Crime* (New York: Rinehart and Company, 1952) by Marshall Clinard is far more scholarly. It shows that the principal black marketeers were already financially well off and indicates the pervasiveness of both petty and large-scale black-market activity. Francis Merrill, *Social Problems on the Home Front: A Study of Wartime Influences* (New York: Harper and Row, 1948) examines a wide range of topics in separate essays, including education, suicide, health, morale, racism, and children at work. The most comprehensive study of education is by I. L. Kandel, *The Impact of War Upon American Education* (Chapel Hill: University of North Carolina Press, 1948). Kandel focuses on curriculum changes as reflected in standards issued by national organizations and on nationally organized efforts to enlist schools into the war effort. The impact of war on public education is also detailed in Richard M. Ugland's "Education for Victory: The High School Victory Corps and Curricular Adaptation During World War II" in *History of Education Quarterly* 19 (Winter 1979):435–52.

During the war, the American Academy of Political and Social Science devoted each November issue of its *Annals* to a collection of essays on a selected topic of the effect of war on domestic life. All three—*Labor Relations and the War* (1942), *Transportation* (1943), and *Adolescents in Wartime* (1944)—give an interesting view of the topic, but suggest primarily the advantages hindsight gives to historians.

Index

About the Author

MARC S. MILLER is an activist, journalist, and historian. He edited *Working Lives: The Southern Exposure History of Labor in the South.* After working with *Southern Exposure* and its publisher, the Institute for Southern Studies, in Durham, N.C., for eight years, he is now a senior editor of *Technology Review* and a member of the editorial collective of *Dollars and Sense.* He received his doctorate in American history from Boston University.